W9-DFL-027

Say It Loud!

Say It Loud!

African-American Audiences, Media, and Identity

Edited by Robin R. Means Coleman

Routledge
New York and London

Published in 2002 by
Routledge
29 West 35th Street
New York, NY 10001

Published in Great Britain by
Routledge
11 New Fetter Lane
London EC4P 4EE

Routledge is an imprint of the Taylor and Francis Group.

Printed in the United States of America on acid-free paper.

10 9 8 7 6 5 4 3 2 1

Library of Congress Cataloging-in-Publication Data

Say it loud! : African-American audiences, media, and identity / edited, and with
an introduction, by Robin R. Means Coleman ; foreword by Herman Gray.
     p. cm.
  Includes bibliographical references.
  ISBN 0-8153-3761-2 (acid-free paper) — ISBN 0-8153-3762-0 (pbk. :
  acid-free paper)
  1. African Americans and mass media. 2. Mass media—United States—
  Audiences. 3. African Americans—Ethnic identity. I. Means Coleman, Robin
  R., 1969–
P94.5.A37 S28 2001
302.23'089'96073   2001019456

Printed on acid-free, 250-year-life paper.
Manufactured in the United States of America.

Contents

028781

Foreword

African-American consumers of popular culture are a much invoked and often described sector of the American media culture. In the name of Blackness, all sorts of political, social, and cultural claims are made.

Yet, as various claims are made in the name of Blackness, we know very little about the complexity (and complicity) of Black viewing habits, listening choices, reading practices, and general engagement with media. Polling and survey data offering profiles of Black media consumption patterns abound; but in the main, Black audiences are taken for granted. They continue to appear in journalistic, industrial, and scholarly accounts and reports as little more than demographic indices of consumer habits and tastes. As the pieces in this collection make clear, Black media audiences are also subjects, agents, and constellations of community and political interests whose social locations, relations, and identities are historically and culturally constituted.

There are good reasons for the persistence of simplistic and one-dimensional formulations of Black audiences and the dearth of more complex research about Blacks as social entities. It is time-consuming and costly to gain access to the habits, practices, and spaces where encounters with media and popular culture take place. Systematic studies of Black audiences are difficult because they require a sophisticated understanding of all of the constitutive elements and moments in the circuit of production, textualization, and reception of media images and representations. To be done well and thoroughly, such studies demand that theoretical, if not empirical, attention be given to the structuring forces, historical circumstances, and social relations within which meanings are made and contested by Black audience members. Finally, such studies require that scholars attend to the signifying structures and practices of different media.

By systematically approaching Black audiences and taking seriously their meaning-making activities and interpretations, the essays in this collection make a series of fundamental interventions. First, they see beyond the limitations of the positive/negative paradigm. This paradigm, most evident in journalistic practices and entertainment coverage, discusses Black representations and reception in terms of fixed and unchanging images, characters, and situations. A pervasive variation on the positive/negative model is the mantra-like call for access, as if simply getting more Blacks involved in the production of Black images in the mass media is the solution to a major impediment to the productions of more complex representations. It is true that access to the sites of production is important. This access must be accompanied by a modification of the structuring forces, interests, and conventions that guide production and organize media content.

As some of the exemplary and innovative research on audiences in general indicates, scholarship and discourse about the representation of Blackness as well as discussions of Black audiences begin by viewing Black audiences as active meaning-making agents. Blacks read, listen, view, and engage with media in the context of complexly organized social lives, circumstances, and social relationships. Thus, Black lives and circumstances must be socially located and made visible discursively by scholars as subjects of complex life ways and practices rather than reduced to a potentially attractive segment of a consumer demographic that can help media and entertainment companies gain an advantage in market share.

Black audiences are deeply embedded in the consumer culture and thus consumption patterns and market forces are of critical importance for structuring social meanings and framing cultural identities. However, the meanings and identities of Black people are not reducible to economic and demographic indicators of consuming habits and tastes alone. Indices of consumption and taste, while important, neither describe nor explain the complexity of meanings and identities produced within the media in general and within Black experience of the media in particular. In the end this means that the contradictory and paradoxical character of our social positions and cultural identities must be considered in relationship to the combined impact of social, economic, and cultural forces and circumstances.

The activities and meanings produced by Black audiences are also structured by the social location of audiences within a historical field and by the organizational structures and industrial imperatives of global technologies that are changing the signifying practices of media. The Internet and new information technologies are as important to the production and representation of news as are print and broadcast. The way in which these synergistic innovations structure and signify cultural meanings bear increasingly on what we can say about how meanings are made and where.

As representations become affected by the increasing synergy among different technologies, there is a need to account for the shifting terrains—national and international—where Blackness travels and how such circulation shapes what Blackness means, how and for whom. The conceptions of discrete and separate media technologies and media systems are no longer accurate or productive. Hence, scholars concerned about Black audiences need to think in more complex terms about the primary sites in which to study processes of interpretation, moments of encounter, and the signifying practices from which notions of Blackness are shaped.

The study of Black media reception, then, is a very large and challenging undertaking, one that requires sustained and long-term attention. Such study demands the careful accumulation of research that systematically identifies, documents, theorizes, and interprets the habits, practices, and sites of encounter and meaning making. The materials collected in *Say It Loud!* contribute to this arduous process by making visible the Black audience in a range of discourses and media that have either ignored Black media consumers or taken them for granted. This collection is a contribution toward the careful and systematic examination and inquiry of Black audiences in American media culture. *Say It Loud!* centers the production of identity and meaning through Black audience encounters with various forms of media with the aim of understanding just how this audience makes meanings and, just as importantly, what these meanings imply for Black audiences.

Making the interpretive strategies of Black audiences visible is of enormous cultural and political significance. Such visibility helps widen the conversation, and gives us new and different ways of thinking about, advocating for, and framing the issue of Black representation in the popular media. To be sure, the multiple and myriad investments in and commitments to various meanings on the part of journalists, activists, industry personnel, and everyday folk are expressions of the contested terrain of media representations. It is all too easy to speak on behalf of Black audiences and the meanings that their activities represent within industrial media systems, open markets, and political skirmishes. It is more difficult and much riskier to ask directly of people what meaning Black representations hold for them, and to observe where and how they engage with and use media images. It is more difficult yet to theorize the observed relationship, the implications of those relations, and the meanings and significance of it all for organizing a more just and equitable society.

I have always believed that Black media audiences have sophisticated media knowledge(s) that have been cultivated over years and under conditions of exclusion, exaggeration, spectacle, and contestation within dominant systems of representation. Robin R. Means Coleman and her colleagues have had the good sense to take this cultivated knowledge seriously and to ask Black people to share their notion of the order of mediated images and representations. I hope we'll have the courage and the good sense to pay attention to their responses and to see Black audiences as active makers of their social and cultural worlds.

Herman Gray

Acknowledgments

I would like to thank the New York University School of Education Challenge Fund Grant committee for awarding me the School of Education Challenge Fund Grant. This book was made possible, in great part, because of this financial support. Thank you Charles Sprague!

I would also like to thank my colleagues, friends, and family for their critique and support of this effort. They include: Neil Postman, Rick Pieto, Kiran Pervez, JoEllen Fisherkeller, Trish Anderson, and Nancy Silverman, all of New York University, Department of Culture of Communication; Damon Zucca and James Morgan of Garland/Routledge; and Randy Coleman.

I would like to give special thanks to MJ Robinson, doctoral candidate, of New York University who is the very best copy editor I have ever encountered (and she types over 80 w.p.m.!). She has made films, published on Hitchcock, and taught writing. MJ is THE Renaissance Woman. It has truly been a pleasure working with you on this project, MJ, and I hope that this is the beginning of a wonderful intellectual and professional relationship. This book could not have been completed without you.

On behalf of the authors (yes, thank you for submitting your manuscripts), I would also like to extend my deepest gratitude to the participants of the studies presented here. This effort is truly by you and for you. Thank you for sharing. Peace.

Say It Loud!

! 1

Introduction

Robin R. Means Coleman

Now we demand a chance to do things for ourself. We're tired of beatin'
our head against the wall. . . . Say it loud, I'm Black and I'm proud.
—James Brown, "Say It Loud"

The past three decades or so have been witness to a charged postmodern culturalist movement that has positioned identity-based politics at the scholarly fore. A great interest in all peoples, individuals, and subjectivities, issues and concerns from ideologies and identity politics to everyday, lived experiences, and the unique voices of people who belong to marginalized groups has been matched by a steady supply of books, journals, monographs, chapters, essays, and presentations that work to meet the tremendous demand for knowledge. Quite expectedly, the broadly defined "subcultures" that have so enamored cultural studies scholars have greatly benefited from the scholarly spotlight. If the sheer quantity and pervasiveness of the intellectual discourses mean anything, scholarly contributions such as *Migrancy, Culture, Identity* by Iain Chambers (1993), *The Black Atlantic* by Paul Gilroy (1993), *Black Popular Culture* by Gina Dent (1992), *Feminism and Youth Culture* by Angela McRobbie (1991), and *The Rites of Men* by Varda Burstyn (1999) to name a very few have assured that we know much more about the repressed/oppressed/marginalized than ever before. Infused with the theories, methodological paradigms, and methods of feminist/women's studies, queer studies, critical race theory, film theory (also known as screen theory), Marxism, psychoanalysis, media studies, (post)colonial studies, anthropology, and ethnography, cultural conversations around gender, sexual identities, race and interracial relationships, representation, the subaltern, lived experiences, and meaning making are now offered up in all their multi-culti, diverse glory in the scholarly literature. Lawrence Grossberg (1996, 161) cites Stuart Hall (1981),[1] who calls for an examination of our histories and current existence as they are shaped by emerging forms of cultural power:

> [T]he domain of cultural forms and activities as a constantly changing field . . . [to look] at the relations which constantly structure this field into dominant and subordinate formations . . . [to look] at the process by which these relations of dominance and subordination are articulated . . . [to place] at its centre the changing and uneven relations of force which define the field of culture—that is, the question of cultural struggle and its many forms . . . [to make our] main focus of attention . . . the relation between culture and questions of hegemony.

Hall's charge is an important reminder that the exploration of dominant cultural forms, their rearticulation of dominance and even oppression, and peoples' various levels of preference (what Hall called "hegemonically preferred meanings") for the purposes of uncovering the impacts these cultural forms have on identity formation, social participation, and continued cultural consumption is a necessary process as we work to better understand our social world and processes of (dis)empowerment and (un)democratization (Grossberg 1996).

Enter *Say It Loud! African-American Audiences, Media, and Identity*, a collection of qualitative, audience-centered, empirical research efforts. These essays work to reveal the manner in which African Americans, as members of a media culture, engage with dominant cultural forms, work to make sense of their own conditions, and consider the convergence of these conditions with the represented worlds of media. Framed by a postmodern, culturalist tradition and its adjoining literatures, theories, methodologies, and methods, *Say It Loud!* offers its own diversity of cultural conversations around the treatment of African Americans (and the cultural signifier Blackness) in media, as well as how such media treatments impact upon, and play a role in, African Americans' lives—social formation, the meaning making of reality, and power relations. The narrowly focused research I have compiled has two goals: first, to locate where race (African

American–ness/Blackness), akin subjectivities, and media consumption, as well as media, as a dominant cultural institution that imprints our historical, social, political, and ideological orders, merge. The second goal is to present and privilege the voices—that is, the African-American participants in this research and their discourses—that work to more fully position and shed light upon Blackness in response to media's hegemonic potential. Beyond these core requirements, the research I have compiled here offers both depth and breadth as it presents a wide variety of focal media genres and texts, a diversity of insights in response to these media offerings, and numerous ideological, political, and economic positions in which the subjected/mediated African American can be located. From *The Boondocks* comic strip, print news coverage of the Million Man March, and talk radio, to *The Cosby Show*, *The Color Purple*, *Menace II Society*, television press treatment of Blackness, rap artist DMX, and the role of media technologies and genres in a Black youth's life, a vast array of media and texts are assembled here as a context for Black folks' struggle over definitions, meaning, and power.

The theoretical tie that binds here is the presupposition I hold that African Americans and Blackness have, in part, become defined within the symbolic media culture and hence are a product of American mass media—an industry and institution that is similarly informed by this society's histories, politics, and ideologies. Fully interwoven into these myriad social structures, race, as discussed here, manifests itself as repetitor, resistor, reinscriber, reinforcer, and rebel to these influences. The studies presented in *Say It Loud!* are also guided by the following research questions: How is Blackness dealt with in media? How are media's racial discourses key to and/or hampering an understanding of African-American life, culture, and experiences? How do African Americans negotiate or make sense of media's treatment of race? What social, historical, cultural, economic, and individual identity positions are brought to bear upon this meaning making? And, of course, the "So what?": what are the implications of both the media's and the participants' racial discourses, and, more, what are the implications of the participants' racial (mis)identifications as informed by their relationship with media?

The Relevancy of Identity

Taken together, these research questions make it clear that *Say It Loud!* takes the relevancy of identity construction and the social institutions that inform that construction quite seriously. The question of identity—"Who am I?"—has become a hotbed of scholarly debate within cultural studies/ media literatures. At issue is how the widely varying and, at times, disparate conceptualizations of identity work to move us toward a moment of "knowing" or identification, that is, the ongoing process of seeking a unified sense of self—joining who we are, who we are as a result of identifying with powerful, significant forms outside of the self, who we are via our encounters with symbolic systems, and what we want to be (Woodward 1997). Developed, rigorous inquiries into identity (e.g., Chapkis 1986 on beauty; Gilroy 1997 on race; Hannerz 1996 on nationalities; Holmes 1997 on cyberidentity; Kellner 1995 on identity theories; Lamm 1995 on body image) have successfully advanced multidisciplinary approaches into queries and critiques of (1) who we are; (2) who we are in relationship to others; (3) how identity is formed and maintained; (4) how who we are is negotiated within varying contexts; and (5) how our identities can lead to struggle, resistance, or solidarity. More, such inquiries have resulted in conceptualizations of the term "identity," which are necessarily expansive to attend to the variants of identity considerations such as:

- classification (e.g., race, sex, sexuality)
- contestation/struggle/crises
- difference and the "other"
- essentialism/nature/biology
- fluidity versus fixedness
- inclusion/exclusion and opposition
- location (e.g., global, national, local)
- membership (e.g., community, religion)
- material and economic conditions
- nonessentialism/social construction
- performance/spectacle/the body
- power and politics
- subjectivity/identification
- symbolic/representation.

These variable identity topics have been, and continue to be, thoroughly questioned as Hall (1996, 1) offers in this brief genealogy:

> The critique of the self-sustaining subject at the centre of post-Cartesian western metaphysics has been comprehensively advanced in philosophy. The question of subjectivity and its unconscious process of formation has been developed within the discourse of psychoanalytically influenced

feminism and cultural criticism. The industry performative self has been advanced in celebratory variants of postmodernism. Within the anti-essentialist critique of ethnic, racial and national conceptions of cultural identity and the 'politics of location' some adventurous theoretical conceptions have been sketched in their most grounded forms.

And still, some cultural critics continue to work toward solidifying identity studies, hoping to provide a canonical answer to Hall's (1996) query, "Who needs identity?" Hall posits, in response to his own question, that, simply, we all do. As long as identity is constituted within, not outside, the symbolic, and as a result remains politicized, then identity politics—power, inclusion, and exclusion—must be interrogated. Kathryn Woodward (1997) extends Hall's thesis to maintain that the concept of identity matters because we are faced with a crisis of identity. Whether or not one looks at identity formation, the processes involved from the psychoanalytic to the symbolic, we must not lose sight of the central issue: "what is significant for our purposes here is that the site of struggle and contestation is the cultural construction of identities" (Woodward 1997, 18).

Like Janice Radway, who confessed in February of 1999 at the Advancing Cultural Studies conference that she did not feel confident enough to "provide the kind of assured diagnosis or to prescribe a specific regimen that would root out the problems and advance cultural studies to a stable condition of health" (Fornäs 1999, 23), I too am reluctant here to broach the enormous task of taming the volatile field of identity. What is to be gained by reductionism, the marking of boundaries, or solidifying the arena of identity study? I fear that to diagnose and prescribe will not bring a cure (I don't think one is needed); rather, to do so will simply anesthetize and diminish the very vibrancy of identity itself. Identity is complexity, diverse, multiple, heterogeneous, and negotiated; thus it seems necessary to engage it, similarly, from equally open theoretical and methodological vantage points. More, the upside to the "discursive explosion" around identity, as Hall (1996, 1) describes it, is the prolific, studied inquiries that work to necessarily examine and critique identity concepts and tenets for their relevance, application, strengths, weakness, gaps, and potentials. This kind of scrutiny can only serve to further our understanding of identity in all its facets.

Unlike Todd Gitlin (1995), who, in *The Twilight of Common Dreams: Why America Is Wracked by Culture Wars*, finds the pluralistic and open nature of identity a troubling concept—though identity is just as much about the shared, the common, and the whole as it is about multiplicity and differences—I propose that looking at the plurality of *peoples* does not, as Gitlin offers, prompt groups or individuals to "swerve into [their] own sense of superiority" (164). Rather, such examinations provide improved understanding into the ways in which culture establishes boundaries (e.g., What is Whiteness?), marks differences (e.g., What does it mean to be Polish, Irish, Irish Catholic, or Jewish within Whiteness?), and identifies commonalities (e.g., White Polish, White Irish, White Jews, White Catholics united under American nationalism). The study of identity and its politics does not have to be about "impasse" or "divide,"[2] but can reveal why people invest in certain identity positions, how such identifications are formed and maintained, and toward what end.

The Union of Identity and Media

About a quarter of the way into my undergraduate course Media and Identity, after I have introduced the variant identity considerations (e.g., difference, essentialism, membership, etc.), I share with the students my adaptation of Plato's "The Allegory of the Cave" from the *Republic*. My abridged story goes:

> Imagine a human being, an adult female, if you will, living in an underground cave with an entrance a long way up. The entrance is open to some light, outside noises, and shadows. Since infancy, this lost woman has been fixed in this cave with dirt, rocks, and bramble preventing her from climbing out. When daylight seeps in, the woman sees long-forgotten artifacts all around—cave paintings of people, animals, and the environment, rock and wood carvings, stone tools, and the like. In all, this woman is a strange prisoner.
>
> What does she make of the people rendered on the wall? Does she think these people are the same beings as her, especially given her limited view of her own self? Does she have a name for the people who look so remarkably different in form from the four-legged creatures also pictured? And what does she make of the shadowy movement passing in front of the cave? How can she make sense of who she is and her place in the world given her limited knowledge—light, shadows, noises, symbols, and artifacts? How is she to know what or who is important, honored, held powerful, or of consequence?
>
> Then what if someone suddenly discovers the woman and drags her from the cave into the light of day and into the busy, bustling populated

world? What sense would she make of electric light versus the sun versus shadow versus night? And of noises and voices and language versus her own still, unschooled tongue? What should she make of mammals and reptiles versus humans of all shapes, colors, sizes, and sexes? What could she infer and conclude about this real, tangible place, not just the imagistic world painted in the cave? And would it confuse her if the imagistic representations from inside the cave in some way fit the reality of the physical world? In the end, how will she move into the complex, intelligible, and knowledgeable realm where she can come to identify things in her world and understand? Especially, keeping in mind that such knowing is informed by her interactions, experiences, history, who she thinks she is, and who she is not. Just as she moved from darkness into the light, what is necessary to move her sense of self out of the dark (the unknown) and into the light (consciousness and identification)?

I use this story for several purposes. First, to impress upon the class that identity is often marked by difference, that is, we know who we are (humans) by knowing what we are not (e.g., four-legged animals). Second, I use it as an acknowledgment of the many approaches to the concept of identity, be it difference, membership, biology, location, the body, or the symbolic. I urge the students to keep at the fore of their thinking that, indeed, identity is variously constituted, that it is defined through representation—how we are represented and how we represent ourselves—and that our interest should also be with how we come to gain knowledge about our identities; that is, how we come into knowing. In sum, the theories on how identity is determined are just as multitudinous as the concepts that define it.

Sarup (1996, xv), in *Identity, Culture and the Postmodern World* writes, "there exist many theories that inform us that identity is determined. They include socialisation (role theory), ideology (the state apparatuses that Althusser describes), discourse theory (the early Foucault), discipline and the technologies of the self (the later Foucault)." A commonality among these, and many other perspectives on identity, is the notion that identity is influenced by, and constructed through, institutions: family, school, government, law, religion, language/communication, media, and so on. This brings us to another lesson from my version of Plato's allegory: identity does not just occur, that is, we as individuals do not just come into knowing. Rather, identity is a construction that is the result of interactions, relationships, and influences between individuals and institutions. I support the notion that discussions around identity such as those presented in *Say*

It Loud! must scrutinize these relationships and their impacts. Thus, an added concern and a question that drives this book is: How are identities formed and maintained as a result of experiences with cultural institutions in general and the media in particular?

The role of media in identity formation should not be taken lightly. Hall (1996, 4) advances that "actually identities are about questions of using the resources of history, language and culture in the process of becoming rather that being: not 'who we are' or 'where we come from,' so much as what we might become, how we have been represented and how that bears on how we might represent ourselves. Identities are, therefore, constituted within, not outside representation . . . we need to understand them as produced in specific historical and institutional sites within specific discursive formations and practices, and by specific enunciative strategies." Hall's declaration is useful as he places several key issues at the center: the power of cultural industries (such as media); the relationship of these apparatuses to identity, the circulation of identity through cultural industries; political and cultural concerns as a result of such circulations; identity considerations of becoming, acting, and being; and the individual. Likewise, *Say It Loud!* places similar interests at its center. Here it is the relationship media, as a powerful cultural industry, have to individual identities and the political and cultural concerns raised as identities are circulated and constructed through the symbolic. More specifically, it is the relationship individuals, in this case African Americans, have with representations in culture through media: How have they been represented? What might they become as a result of those representations? How do they represent themselves? How are their identities constructed in and/or through representations?

The Media Audience Matters

At the core of an examination of the relationship between media and identity is the individual media consumer/media audience member. With its emphasis on research that is audience-centered, *Say It Loud!* is foremost concerned with African Americans who are consumers of media. It is an effort that is informed by an audience-study legacy that has long worked to interrogate audiences' relationships with media along related structural, behavioral, economic, and cultural considerations. Given the book's postmodern, culturalist orientation, there are questions that are outside its purview (e.g., causality); however, the transferability of insights into a number of media audience interests is marked. Thus, its ability to intersect and compliment the variety of audience research traditions, be it to directly inform and extend or to offer supplementary information, should not be discounted. Nor should these rich audience research traditions be overlooked as they greatly influence the vantage point of *Say It Loud!* as a contemporary audience-study initiative.

As I reflect back upon the history of media audience research traditions, I am struck by the great vibrancy and tremendous growth of such a relatively youthful field. Although an interest in the features of the audience of popular culture, for example Greco-Roman theater, dates back several millennia (McQuail 1997), this past century has been witness to great surges in research activity and significant theoretical advances in the arena of media audience studies. It should be recognized that market concerns and akin structural questions about the media audience predate the twentieth century. However, notable behavioristic and sociocultural-oriented research movements have distinguished themselves over the last one hundred years.

The early part of the twentieth century saw the emergence of the ideation of the mass audience and its correspondent mass society theory. Here the media audience was viewed as a large, heterogeneous mass (thanks to the rise of industrial capitalism and the resulting perceived challenge to familial and social group unification) who responded to media, with their "powerful" messages, in a uniform, nondiscriminatory manner. It was during this period that Hadley Cantril (1940) offered his provocative, serendipitous *The Invasion from Mars* study, which questioned why segments of the 1938 *War of the Worlds* live radio broadcast's audience were effected so strongly, via fright and panic, by the program's content. In a similar vein, the classic Payne Fund series of thirteen studies concerned itself with the effects of motion pictures on children. Of particular interest was film's potential to harm youths' health, to erode their moral standards, and to promote misconduct (Lowery and DeFleur 1988).

Right on the heels of the mass audience/powerful effects era (as early as the 1930s–40s), the scholarly view of the audience began to shift. This time, the audience, now deemed to be individuals and members of social groups rather than a heterogeneous mass, were thought to be "selective" in their attention to media messages. It was during this period that the limited effect of media messages upon the audience was theorized. Best detailed by Joseph Klapper (1966) in his seminal piece "What We Know About the Effects of Mass Communication: The Brink of Hope," the limited-effects view works to account for changes in taste (e.g., high culture versus low culture) or responses to specific media messages (e.g., violence or voting behavior) in the short term. Klapper, informed by a metaanalysis of hundreds of effects studies conducted from the turn of the twentieth century to mid-century, concluded that audiences do not simply respond to media; rather, they are selective in their media consumption choices, with their selections informed by their own tastes, preferences, and social backgrounds. These preferences "mediate" change, not in the form of whole and full persuasion, as theorized by the early powerful-effects scholars, but through the reinforcement of preexisting ideas and attitudes. Klapper's treatise was greatly influenced by the classic, foundational empirical efforts of the 1940s and '50s of Lazarsfeld and Hovland. The results of this pair's studies concretized the supposition that media's great influence over the audience was scientifically elusive (it could not be a controlled variable) and that few people were affected directly by media. Rather, key factors such as social status, cohort, and education played an important role in whether media messages "get in" and to what degree. This viewpoint was best evidenced through Lazarsfeld's (1944 with Berelson and Gaudet, 1955 with Katz) two-step flow studies. Here, it was theorized that people played the most significant role in the attention paid to media messages. In its simplest, heavy, sophisticated consumers of media sought out as much information about an issue as possible (e.g., political views). These heavy consumers acted as a sort of gatekeeper of information for others as the heavy consumers culled and passed on information gleaned from media, as well as shared their own views. These "opinion leaders" advised people like themselves (same social status), but these advisees attended to media less, or with less savvy. In short, media became influential only if heavy, critical media users gave credence to their messages—messages that are largely correspondent to these users' thinking anyway. Hence, in the limited effects era, the social and psychological become mediating factors in the selection, perception, and retention of media messages. Each plays a significant part in the way media have limited, reinforcing effects and move audiences to interact with media in a variety of complex and diverse ways. The interest in active, selective audiences and the potential to reinforce or modify behavior, views, and tastes—the theory of limited effects—ruled as the dominant paradigm for several decades well through the 1970s. Much media audience research was based, and continues to be based, upon this tradition.

The decades of the 1950s and '60s were witness to several standout media audience research initiatives that examined the impact and the (limited) effects of media upon those who consume it. The Surgeon General's Report on Television and Social Behavior, an enormous five-volume study commissioned by Congress soon after the Kerner Commission's investigation of violence in 1960s America, focused, in part, on the role of television violence in everyday life. A complex, detailed study best known for its one-million-dollar budget, questionable composition of researchers (some with network television ties), and, at times, flawed methodology, the research was the largest of its kind at the time (1969–1971). Given the violence of the 1960s (the Vietnam War and the assassinations of the Kennedys and Martin Luther King, Jr.), there was great concern over televised violence and its impact on society (of course, with particular concern over the impacts on children and adolescents). The study, summarized in the compendium *Television and Growing Up*, resulted in the cautious, qualified statement that there may be a causal relationship between aggressive behavior in youth predisposed to aggression and the viewing of increasingly violent programming within certain contexts.

George Gerbner's long-term, longitudinal research into television and violence, which began in 1968 and continues today, has had a much greater and respected impact in the scholarly community. Gerbner similarly questioned the effects of living with media violence, and after engaging in extensive content analyses and surveying of respondents, he concluded that for most television and film viewers (as detailed in his documentary *The Killing Screens*) television content is fraught with violence that tends to "cultivate" a sense that the real world is a mean one—one that is gloomy and dangerous—making us feel insecure, mistrustful, vulnerable, and alienated. Such an outlook was especially prevalent in heavy television viewers, while light viewers held a decidedly different, optimistic view of their world.

This "transmission view" (Carey 1975) of media's relationship to the audience, defined by a focus on the transmission of information from sender to receiver, remains the dominant theoretical and research paradigm in media audience study. It is characterized by a preoccupation with the sending and imparting of media messages, disseminating them over great distances (hence the "mass" in mass media) for the purpose of some level/form of control, be it persuasion, evoking emotion, informing, and so on.

The dominant media audience research paradigm, with its interests in media effects (e.g., Cantril), media's potential to change attitudes (e.g., Lazarsfeld), and media's ability to inform (e.g., the Payne Fund studies) and enlighten as well as convolute and confuse our reality (e.g., Gerbner) failed to attend to media's function as a social activity for its audience. That is, there was an emphasis on people who used media (e.g., heavy viewers), but little was uncovered as to why media were used. Enter uses and gratifications, with particular interest generated in this approach during the mid-1970s. In this audience research tradition, the active audience selectively uses media for its own psychosocial purposes. A "laundry list" of media uses and human needs or gratifications was established. Survey research such as that conducted by Blumler and Katz (1974) yielded the findings that media consumers generally use media for entertainment—relaxation, escape, pleasure; for personal and social identity—a model for behavior, taste, or styles, for fitting in or a sense of belonging with a peer group; and for information—discovery and learning. James Lull (1980) in his study "The Social Uses of Television" mounted ethnographic research in a domestic setting, documenting the social uses of television within the context of family viewing. Lull uncovered a social-uses typology. First, he found structural uses defined by the use of television as background noise or as a behavior regulator that marks activities (e.g., when you finish your homework, you may watch TV). Second, he found relational uses of television, including communication facilitation (e.g., "television talk" or a way for an individual to enter into a conversation), affiliation/avoidance (e.g., bringing the family together by using media to lessen talk), learning and competence/dominance (e.g., displaying intelligence by correcting the information presented on television or exercising control over the family by regulating viewing).

As a sort of liminal stage beyond an understanding about the impact of the transmission of media messages and toward media's role in the lives of its audience, the uses and gratifications approach, with its focus on media's utility, was an adequate first step. Uses and gratifications broached the gap between the audience's participation with media messages and media's role in building community. The approach told us why people attend to media, but still said little about what people take away from their media encounters, specifically their interpretations and meanings.

What was needed, and what came next, was what Carey (1975) defined as the "ritual view" of mass communication. In the ritual view, audiences are not solely regarded as targets of media messages, though information acquisition does takes place. Rather, the audience enters into a participatory relationship with media whereby the construction of social meaning takes place around symbolic forms and other representations of the social world.

In essence, a particular view of the world is offered through media that prompts the concern over the manner in which the world is portrayed, how those portrayals work to structure the world (that is, what is made common through media), and how the portrayals are constructed, maintained, transformed, used, and struggled over. In the ritual view, the driving question becomes the way in which audiences live within a media-produced reality (sharing and participation). More, it asks, What does the audience bring to this media encounter as they struggle with definitions and constructions of what is real?

If the ritual view, characterized by the sharing and participation between media and audience, is the call for a deepened examination of the relationship—from information gathering to meaning making—between media and its audience, then reception study provided the theoretical and methodological answer. Reception study, an approach that gained particular prominence in the late 1970s and the 1980s, is defined by an examination of the relationship between the audience or "reader" and media message or "text" to uncover the manner in which an audience makes sense of (meaning making) a media text (the act of decoding). In this most recent audience research tradition, active audiences formulate readings, readings that Hall (1980) theorized in his encoding/decoding model as preferred, negotiated, or oppositional, given their social positions, as they work to produce meanings that make sense of the represented cultural world. In this culturalist framework, meaning construction, not media effects, is deemed central, as the process of meaning making reveals the relationship the audience has with a media text, its response to its discourse/commentary, an audience's sociocultural history, and what parts of that history are brought to the reading of a media text. Further, it is also those sociocultural experiences in everyday life (e.g., class, social position, education, even critical competencies when attending to media) that inform what is also taken away from media texts, through decoding, as meaning is created.

Reception study also supports the notion of a polysemic or open media text where messages, though encoded by the text producer in one way, may be decoded in another. Hence, interpretations are the result of constructions, not the result of inherent, fixed messages. Though media texts are not made sense of by audiences in identical ways due to their unique lived experiences, reception researchers acknowledge that common interpretations can be had by "interpretive communities" (Fish 1980) or "interpretive repertoires" (Jensen 1991). These audience groupings are not formally constituted; in fact, individual media consumers can be members of a cohort that is not so readily apparent, and thus they are contextually defined. For example, these communities may be around the more or less media savvy, be socioculturally and economically diverse, and are often identified around a specific media text. To illustrate, Ang (1985) and Liebes and Katz (1986) with their research into Israeli and Dutch viewers of *Dallas*, respectively, evidenced that Americans are not the only community of viewers of the popular prime-time drama. Radway (1984) found a band of readers around certain romance novels. Brodroghkozy (1992) discovered an interpretive community of fans (and antagonists) of the series *Julia* through their letters to the carrying network. Means Coleman (2000) with a focus on a city's African Americans, Jhally and Lewis (1992) with a focus on White middle-class viewers, and Inniss and Feagin (1995 [see chapter 8 of this volume]) with their focus on Black middle-class viewers, all identify an interpretive community situated around Black situation comedies.

David Morley (1980) is one who set the reception study standard as he sought to uncover the meanings a diverse group of British viewers created around the TV news program *Nationwide*. Drawing on twenty-nine focus group interviews, Morley sought to create a typology of decodings—how and why they vary, how interpretations are generated, and the fit between cultural factors and interpretations. He found that audiences indeed are a set of cultural groupings, not a mass of individuals nor a definite demographic category. Likewise, texts do not construct the audience. For example, Morley would oppose the notion that violent texts create violent people as is the concern with effects practitioners. Morley confirmed that a media text can be decoded and appropriated during reception in a variety of ways, be they oppositional, negotiated, or dominant. More, variations in patterns of decoding are influenced by cultural and sociological factors. Morley reminds us, however, that the manner in which texts are decoded can, to a degree, be constrained by the media text's conventions. The production's conventions can, at times, foreground readings, though not in the absolute.

Radway's (1984) exploration into women's readings of romance novels is similarly pivotal. Her individual, in-depth interviews, group interviews, and document analyses (letters) revealed that the women's relationship with the romantic fictions became one of empowering fantasy and liberation. Specifically, she found that women, often bound by patriarchally defined/relegated domestic work (e.g., child rearing and home maintenance) and the selflessness and sacrifice that comes with "women's work," used romance novel reading as a momentary block against such demands. For example, Radway discovered the book itself served as a physical barrier and a signal to family members to not interrupt women's reading time. The open book was a declaration of "me time" and also symbolically marked off uninterruptable space so that women could fulfill their rest, privacy, and entertainment needs. Independence, and, thus, resistance to traditional patriarchal roles, Radway discovered, was also exercised when the women readers engaged in romantic fantasy. The readers often gladly lost themselves in the fictional social world, as they placed themselves in the role of the beautiful, sexualized heroine who engaged men on her own terms. In the end, the novels, in part, enabled necessary selfishness and resistance, and provided a model for love relationships and role-play, as well as a fantasy outlet.

Reception study—which is the theoretical and methodological frame for *Say It Loud!*—is built upon Hall's (1980) seminal essay "Encoding/Decoding" which outlines a revolutionary theoretical model for identifying and interpreting the multiplicity of readings and generated meanings, and their sociopolitical significance, that emerge during receptions of media texts. Hall's model is defined by a useful analytical tool that classifies the variety of potential readings into three categories: dominant/preferred, negotiated, and oppositional. Hall theorizes that the social, cultural, political, and power conditions that define the individual audience member will be brought to the engagement with media and collude, resulting in meanings informed by those conditions and positions. Hence, an audience member may engage in a dominant reading where an individual will identify with, prefer, and decode a text that has the dominant institutional, political, and ideological "answer" permeating it. The decoding, or interpretive end, is a reflection of such discourses. Conversely, an oppositional reading describes resistance to a text and its messages (institutional, political, and ideological) and decodes in a manner contrary to the preferred, dominant ideological encoding. In between these two points on the interpretive spectrum comes, according to Hall, the negotiated reading. In this most frequently held reading position, an individual is neither in whole and full conformity nor in opposition to the inscribed ideologies. Rather, an audience member negotiates a media encounter by conforming in some ways, especially those ways that coincide with their own value system, but rejecting in other ways. Often, there is a general acceptance of the media messages, but it is an acceptance that is transformed to meet the audience members' needs and/or match their value systems.

It is important to acknowledge that the triumvirate of reading positions Hall proposes is not without its criticisms. Indeed, two key concerns emerge. The first has to do with the rigid, determined categories that make up the encoding/decoding model. A bit too tidy in their delineation, it can be questioned whether distinct preferred and oppositional readings exist, and if all other readings are truly negotiated, thereby making this last reading position a virtual dumping ground for all that is less distinct or in between. It may be argued that either pure readings do not exist, thereby making every reading a negotiated one, or reading moments within the different categories possess a variety of sublevels or categories that can account for the complexities found even within the (seemingly precise) preferred and oppositional positions. A second critique is of the reductive, deterministic nature of the model. In its original manifestation, class was at the fore over other sociopolitical concerns. As for the latter criticism, much of the scholarship emanating out of this cultural studies tradition that includes *Say It Loud!* has found a neo-Marxist remedy by privileging power relationships inside and outside of class. As for the former concern, the research presented here, inspired by Hall's work, capably extends discussions of meaning making by employing theoretical discussions to attend to complex reading positions that emerge from these audiences.

Another critique has been that reception has gone too far afield of the social uses question by focusing singularly on meanings. One question that is left to be answered is how people live with and integrate media into their everyday lives. Enter the latest, and so-named research tradition. The "study of media in everyday life" picks up the mantle of uses and gratifications/social uses by acknowledging that media consumption is an activity of differing significance and roles for each individual. For example, television viewing for one person after work may be an activity for shutting out the world and "vegging out" after an overwhelming day. For another person, television viewing may be purposeful viewing, for the goal of getting useful, sought-after information. Similarly, this tradition concurs with the Lull (1980) conclusion that first media consumption rarely occurs in isolation, but tends to be conducted with family or friends. Nor is media consumption an individual process, but part of a community phenomenon (e.g., the viewing of *Survivor*, the Super Bowl, or Super Bowl commercials to be able to discuss such texts with your cohort). Furthermore, media consumption can be a secondary activity, such as for background noise or zapping through channels with the remote control without fully attending to any one program. Hence, media do not always command an audience's full attention. Beyond this, the study of media in everyday life has its own theoretical basis. The first assumption is that life is bursting with media—from billboards to music videos, fliers and leaflets to film, the web to video games, and all that in between—which we all interact with in varying meaningful ways. Therefore, an examination of audiences' relationship to media should take into account the role a multiplicity of media and their discourses play, rather than a single medium/text vacuum. Toward this end, one research interest is in what manner, and to what end, media are integrated into audiences' everyday life. Second, media as social institutions, frequent daily interactions, and economic forces must be viewed as an integral part of our social world, not as isolated variables. As media fuse with other activities, from the creation of slang and catch phrases to creating peer groups (e.g., music fans), to informing and entertaining to companionship, and so on, media become inseparable from other life influences and practices.[3]

Enter again David Morley, whose body of scholarship (1986, 1994, 1990 with Silverstone) has ably united reception study with its focus on audience interpretations and the belief that media and their use play a significant role in everyday life. Specifically, Morley has devoted considerable attention to the domestic context of media use (particularly television), to include the meanings audiences make in response to certain programs, the significance of media consumption, and favored media consumption activities (from channel surfing to doing chores while attending to media), tastes (news, drama, soap operas), and styles (viewing attentively, exerting power by controlling access to a medium). Morley is not alone in this most recent research tradition. Today many scholars, including contributors to this book, combine text-audience/meaning-making concerns with the contexts in which media are consumed and media's role and importance in everyday life.

Based upon the chronology-in-brief presented here, media audience research is clearly a vibrant, ever-evolving field. While the years between the late 1980s and today have been witness to the union of reception/everyday life studies, and while behaviorists/effects researchers continue their efforts, most recently audience research has also moved beyond issues of identity, power, and resistance in relation to media texts to examine the manner in which audiences *disengage* themselves from media's storytelling conventions. This latest approach to the audience is characterized by the research of Ron Lembo (1997), which, as he describes it, moves "beyond the text" to uncover audiences' recognition of media's commercial basis, to include the recognition of formulaic programming to implausible storylines and events. An extension of cultural studies inquiries such as reception and social uses studies, this exploration into audience viewing practices continues to rely on qualitative data collection methods such as in-depth interviewing and participant observation. Lembo, focusing on television consumption, argues that there are generally two types of viewing practices. The first is the more familiar "narrative-based viewing" that reception researchers often focus on. Narrative-based viewing describes the manner in which the individual audience member embraces television texts and makes connections between the texts and the larger social world. Lembo also offers that narrative-based viewing may include a focus on the production values of programming (e.g., writing, lighting, editing, ambient music) as an audience member becomes emotionally involved in the narrative. Or, viewers may focus on the "realities" of the text, that is, aspects of the narrative that are not taken for representation but for the real. Lembo's more interesting finding is the practice of "image-based viewing," which describes a viewer's ability to disrupt the narrative by not seeing media representations as linked to any social reality and thereby to deflect meanings. Not implicated in media's discursive power, image-based viewers engage in either simultaneous viewing (doing other things while viewing), channel switching (scanning quickly through programming by zapping with a remote control), or image-play ("vegging out" during viewing with brief attention paid to visual imagery/aesthetics such as colors or movement, or to displays of wealth, poverty, strength, or sexuality without necessarily identifying with the people or events seen). Lembo concludes that image-based viewing demonstrates how indifference toward a text can be cultivated, and though this distancing takes place in response to the actions presented in the images, it does not take place outside the logic of the text. That is, viewers see the images as part of corporate culture/televisual world and, thus, the images become a less significant factor in their domestic lives.

To be sure, the contributors to *Say It Loud!* have been greatly influenced by the audience research traditions outlined here. In their own research, none of the authors has taken lightly questions about the impact media messages may have upon their audiences, the relationship audiences have with media, what audiences do with media, and what media do for audiences. More, each has taken quite seriously the proclamations from their audience research peers of the last century that there remains much we still need to know about media audiences. Though the contributors featured here present research situated within the recent reception or reception/everyday life research traditions, thereby making their method-ological and theoretical frames different from some of their audience re-search predecessors, the contributors' concerns and interests can be seen as related.

For example, the Payne Fund studies were concerned with film's po-tential harmful effects upon youth behavior. I seek to uncover the role a film played in the lives of youths accused of committing copycat crimes based on that film. George Gerbner's cultivation research revealed media's ability to prompt a particular view of our social world. In the present vol-ume, Debbie Owens's examination of responses to print coverage of the Million Man March reveals, in part, a concern by readers that media may contribute to a fear of the Black world. The social uses and media in every-day life traditions taken on by Morley and Lembo demand that researchers not overlook the role of media in our domestic settings and daily lives. JoEllen Fisherkeller heeds this bidding by chronicling the role of media in a youth's life for over one decade. And part of the *War of the Worlds* broad-cast's power over the audience had to do with the trust and confidence au-diences had in radio. Catherine Squires uncovers the power a community of listeners assign to talk radio. The strength of these culturalist/postmod-ernist approaches to audience study is that entering into a dialogue with au-diences yields deepened insights into the tastes, preferences, consumption contexts, interpretations, and political/identity understandings around an important cultural institution. It is these insights into such issues that have preoccupied researchers for over a century.

Bringing African-American Audiences, Media, and Identity Together: The Chapters of *Say It Loud!*

What additionally preoccupies the contributors of *Say It Loud!* is the open-ing that postmodernism has provided for an exploration into media as a dominant cultural institution whose ability to (re)produce and circulate cultural power and capital is marked. As media industries and culture merge, in such a moment, there is space for questioning the impact such a process has upon our society. What does it mean for cultural politics when the narratives of experience, history, language, and identity are passed through media's filters of technology, representation, formulas, stereotypes, and storytelling, and are commodified in the process? What happens to certain groups' stories as cultural dominance prevails? Such a focus is moved on here, not because it is the latest movement in a symphony of audience research trends, but because this research tradition privileges the interrogation of the dominant in relation to the subordinate or marginal. As Hall (1992, 22) elaborates, "Even if postmodernism is not a new cultural epoch, but only modernism in the streets, that, in itself, represents an important shifting of the terrain of culture toward the popular—toward popular practices, toward everyday practices, toward local narrative, toward the decentring of old hierarchies and the grand narratives."

The second chapter of *Say It Loud!* presents research that departs from conventional, mainstream media study by focusing on a nontraditional genre, the comic strip, and on a new technology, cyberspace. Through a phenomenological inquiry, Mark Orbe and Nancy Cornwell examine African-American postings to Aaron McGruder's *The Boondocks* website to uncover the interpretations of racial representations and the constructions of racial identities by *The Boondocks'* readers. Several themes emerge, to include issues of stereotyping, personal/racial identification, and the social responsibility of McGruder as an African-American artist and one who strives to make political statements, albeit couched in humor. Within these themes, however, the African-American responses to *The Boondocks* are as diverse as African Americans themselves.

Catherine Squires examines one of mass media's oldest, and today often-neglected, technologies—broadcast radio. In her chapter Squires argues that Black-owned media, specifically Chicago radio station WVON and its talk programming, has been instrumental to African-American listeners' participation in the critique and protests of mainstream media's depictions of the racial group. After contrasting past instances of African American audiences' use of Black-owned media outlets to address the shortcomings of mainstream media to commentary of present-day users, Squires concludes that although contemporary Black-owned media that encourage audience participation provide an adequate forum for discussion, these media could do more to prompt action to affect change, not just focus on stimulating critiques.

Debbie Owens continues the focus on mainstream media's treatment of Blackness by detailing African Americans' responses to newsmagazine coverage of the 1995 Million Man March. Owens offers how evaluations of the coverage reflect the reader's own identity and, ultimately, his/her sociopolitical association with issues (according to the Million Man March agenda) facing Black communities. Two additional, important themes emerge: the impact of the march and the impact of coverage of the march on race relations.

Jennifer Wood turns to television network news for a broader reception study into the treatment of race within the genre, and the impact such treatment has upon constructions of African-American identity. Specifically, she seeks to identify the ideologies of race, as perceived by participants, that are inscribed in news. She uncovers what she describes as "Afrocentric talk" that is engaged in by participants as they work to make sense of treatments that include exclusion, marginalization, and stereotype.

Chyng Sun, Leda Cooks, Corey Rinehart, and Stacy Williams take on research claims circulating in other disciplines that low-achieving African-American secondary-school students are drawn toward media texts that disparage academic achievement while implying that those who shun education are more authentically Black. The authors present focus group interview data with African-American male teens from three public high schools. They use a music video, starring rapper DMX, which includes a message of antiachievement, and a segment of *The Cosby Show*, which hails educational success, to glean responses to these very different media texts and the impact of their messages. Their research shows that in different schools and across different academic achievement levels, African-American students emphasized the importance of education, family values, self-support, and hard work, hence, disrupting the notion that low-achieving participants oppose school or career success messages. Additionally, one provocative finding the authors uncovered was that students from certain public schools articulated color blindness and perceived the United States as a meritocracy wherein people who failed only had themselves to blame.

JoEllen Fisherkeller contributes one of the true audience ethnographies in the book with her decade-long tracking of a youth's relationship with mass media. Her study focuses, longitudinally, on how an African-American male uses his favorite commercial media, particularly television, to deal with his identity dilemmas. Fisherkeller draws on interview data gathered with the youth at ages twelve, thirteen, seventeen, and twenty-one to examine his talk about his life and mass media's role in it. His talk reveals the identity and social issues he negotiates at different times of his coming into maturity, and how media play a part in this negotiation. She finds that as his life changes and he grows physically and mentally, his use of media and the meanings he finds in his preferred programs and personalities shift to reflect his coming to new terms with himself, others, and the larger so-cial world. What is beyond the obvious are the nature and contents of the new understandings he gains, and the different roles that media and actual life experiences play in his understandings. Fisherkeller argues that we can learn more comprehensively about youths' particular processes of develop-ment, cultural learning, and media experiences, which are all complex, dy-namic, and interrelated.

Leslie Inniss and Joe Feagin turn to African-American middle-class viewers of *The Cosby Show* to garner their perspectives on a series that de-picted an ever-so-solidly middle-class family in values and socioeconomic standing. In their chapter, the researchers report that the responses to the series by the viewers interviewed are a mixed bag. For example, the partici-pants both hailed the long-in-coming positive portrayal of African Americans and Blackness on network television, and were concerned with the series' overly assimilationist tone.

Through Jacqueline Bobo, concern over the representation of Blackness continues. However, here the emphasis is in more favorable read-ings of a media text, to include an identification with the characters and the depicted situations and relationships. In her chapter Bobo chronicles African-American women's responses to the film *The Color Purple*. Acknowledging that some African-American men denounced the film for its portrayals of African-American men as buffoons, pedophiles, misogy-nists, and abusers, Bobo finds that African-American women defend the film by focusing on its message of female self-empowerment. Bobo con-cludes that in supporting the film the women are articulating resistance to dominant patriarchal ideologies.

Celeste Fisher, like Sun and her colleagues, turns to the classroom. This time the classroom setting is useful to glean insights into an educative mo-ment brought on by a media encounter. In her chapter Fisher analyzes the responses of African-American students in a self-managed focus group dis-cussion after viewing the ghettocentric street film *Menace II Society* within the context of a culturally diverse classroom. The participants respond to a controversial (hyperviolent) text as it presents narratives of race, gender, and socioeconomic class in Black America. Her goal is to determine how African Americans negotiate their potential identification with film characters of the same racial background in a mixed race setting.

Finally, I offer a different perspective on the ghettocentric film *Menace II Society*. Here, I present in-depth interview data offered by an incarcerated African-American youth involved in the high-profile *Menace II Society* murder case. The case is based on confessions made by the youth (and four other adolescents who were involved) that they viewed the film and then acted out scenes of mayhem and murder. I engage one of the youths to tap into the role the film and other media play(ed) in his life. The study's impetus, though provocative, is the springboard for an examination of identification with ghettocentric narratives, of viewing practices, and of critical viewing capabilities. The findings reveal themes of hypermasculinity ("thug life"), narrative-based viewing practices, and of an emerging critical engagement with media.

The research presented here not only extends the developments emanating from audience, media, and identity study traditions, but also works to refute some old assumptions and contribute new theories. The authors have devoted considerable time and energy to recording the participants' interpretations, and what's more, the participants, all in the name of advancing scholarship, reveal their innermost thoughts about weighty matters of race—relations, representations, identity, authenticity, and the like. The authors and participants together have worked very hard for your attention. Please consider their voices carefully as they "say it loud!"

Notes

1. Hall's important call is written in its original form in the genius, ornate prose that characterizes his writing. The statement is key, and Grossberg does a fine job of synthesizing the critical elements. Hence, I cite Hall through Grossberg rather than directly.

2. As part of his critique over the troubling, fragmented nature of identity politics, Gitlin uses the "colorline" as an exemplar of the dilemma. He writes, "nothing is more responsible for the current impasse than the black-white divide, which is unlike any other" (1995, 163).

3. Ang (1990) was most useful here in formulating this discussion of the tradition of media in daily life.

References

Ang, I. (1985). *Watching "Dallas": Soap opera and the melodramatic imagination.* London: Methuen.

———. (1990). The nature of the audience. In J. Downing, A. Mohammadi, and A. Sreberny-Mohammadi, eds., *Questioning the media: A critical introduction* (pp. 155–65). Newbury Park, Calif.: Sage.

Blumler, J., and E. Katz. (1974). *The uses of mass communications.* Beverly Hills, Calif.: Sage.

Brodroghkozy, A. (1992). "Is this what you mean by color TV?" Race, gender, and contested meanings in NBC's "Julia." In L. Spigel and D. Mann, eds., *Private screenings: Television and the female consumer* (pp. 142–67). Minneapolis: University of Minnesota Press.

Burstyn, V. (1999). *The rites of men: Manhood, politics, and the culture of sport.* Toronto: University of Toronto Press.

Cantril, H. (1940). *The invasion from Mars: A study in the psychology of panic.* Princeton, N.J.: Princeton University Press.

Carey, J. (1975). A cultural approach to communication. *Communication* 2: 1–22.

———. (1989). *Communication as culture.* Boston: Unwin Hyman.

Chambers, I. (1993). *Migrancy, culture, identity.* London: Comedia/Routledge.

Chapkis, W. (1986). *Beauty secrets: Women and the politics of appearance.* Boston: South End Press.

Dent, G. (1992). *Black popular culture.* Seattle: Bay Press.

Fish, S. (1980). *Is there a text in this class? The authority of interpretive communities.* Cambridge, Mass.: Harvard University Press.

Fornäs, J. (1999). *Advancing Cultural Studies.* Stockholm, Sweden: Stockholm University, JMK.

Gamson, J. (1998). Publicity traps: Television talk shows and lesbian, gay, bisexual, and transgender visibility. *Sexualities* 1: 11–41.

Gilroy, P. (1993). *The Black Atlantic.* London: Verso.

———. (1997). Diaspora and the detours of identity. In K. Woodward, ed., *Identity and difference* (pp. 299–346). London: Sage.

Gitlin, T. (1995). *The twilight of common dreams: Why America is wracked by culture wars.* New York: Henry Holt.

Grossberg, L. (1996). History, politics, and postmodernism: Stuart Hall and cultural studies. In D. Morley and K. Chin, eds., *Stuart Hall:*

Critical dialogues in cultural studies (pp. 151–73). London: Routledge.

Hall, S. (1980). Encoding/decoding. In S. Hall, D. Hobson, A. Lowe, and P. Willis, eds., *Culture, media, language* (pp. 128–38). London: Methuen.

———. (1981). Notes on deconstructing "the popular." In R. Samuel, ed., *People's history and socialist theory*. Boston: Routledge and Kegan Paul.

———. (1992). What is this "Black" in Black popular culture? In G. Dent, ed., *Black popular culture* (pp. 21–33). Seattle: Bay Press.

———. (1996). Introduction: Who needs identity? In S. Hall and P. DuGay, eds., *Questions of cultural identity* (pp. 1–17). London: Sage.

Hannerz, U. (1996). *Transnational connections: Culture, people, places*. London: Routledge.

Holmes, D. (1997). *Virtual politics: Identity and community in cyberspace*. London: Sage.

Jensen, K. (1991). Humanistic scholarship as qualitative science: Contributions to mass communication research. In K. Jensen and N. Jankowski, eds., *Qualitative methodologies for mass communication research* (pp. 17–43). London: Routledge.

Jhally, S., and J. Lewis. (1992). *Enlightened racism: The "Cosby Show," audiences, and the myth of the American dream*. Boulder, Colo.: Westview Press.

Katz, E., and P. Lazarsfeld. (1955). *Personal influence*. Glencoe, Ill.: Free Press.

Kellner, D. (1995). *Media culture: Cultural studies, identity and politics between the modern and the postmodern*. London: Routledge.

Klapper, J. (1966). What we know about the effects of mass communication: The brink of hope. In A. Smith, ed., *Communication and culture* (pp. 535–51). New York: Holt, Rinehart, and Winston.

Lamm, N. (1995). It's a big fat revolution. In B. Findlen, ed., *Listen up: Voices from the next feminist generation* (pp. 85–94). Seattle, Wash.: Seal Press.

Lazarsfeld, P., B. Berelson, and H. Gaudet. (1944). *The people's choice*. New York: Columbia University Press.

Lembo, R. (1997). Beyond the text: The sociality of image-based viewing practices. *Cultural Studies: A Research Volume* 2: 237–64.

Lewis, J. (1991). *The ideological octopus*. New York: Routledge.

Liebes, T., and E. Katz. (1986). Patterns of involvement in television fiction: A comparative analysis. *European Journal of Communication* 1: 151–71.

———. (1990). *The export of meaning: Cross-cultural readings of "Dallas."* Oxford, U.K.: Oxford University Press.

Lowery, S., and M. DeFleur. (1988). *Milestones in mass communication research.* 2d ed. White Plains, N.Y.: Longman.

Lull, J. (1980). The social uses of television. *Human Communication Research* 6: 195–209.

McQuail, D. (1997). *Audience analysis.* Thousand Oaks, Calif.: Sage.

McRobbie, A. (1991). *Feminism and youth culture.* London: MacMillan.

Means Coleman, R. (2000). *African American viewers and the Black situation comedy: Situating racial humor.* New York: Garland.

Morley, D. (1980). *The "Nationwide" audience: Structure and decoding.* London: British Film Institute.

———. (1986). *Family television and domestic leisure.* London: Comedia.

———. (1994). *Television, audiences, and cultural studies.* New York: Routledge.

Morley, D., and R. Silverstone. (1990). Domestic communication: Technologies and meanings. *Media, Culture, Society* 1: 31–55.

Press, A. (1992). *Women watching television: Gender, class, and generation in the American television experience.* Philadelphia: University of Pennsylvania Press.

Radway, J. (1984). *Reading the romance.* Chapel Hill: University of North Carolina Press.

Sarup, M. (1996). *Identity, culture and the postmodern world.* Athens, Ga.: University of Georgia Press.

Surgeon General's Scientific Advisory Committee on Television and Social Behavior. (1971). *Television and growing up: The impact of televised violence.* Report to the Surgeon General, U.S. Public Health Service. Washington, D.C.: U.S. Government Printing Office.

Woodward, K. (1997). Introduction and concepts of identity and difference. In K. Woodward, ed., *Identity and difference* (pp. 1–50). London: Sage.

2

"Keepin' It Real" and/or "Sellin' Out to the Man"

African-American Responses

to Aaron McGruder's *The Boondocks*

Nancy C. Cornwell and Mark P. Orbe

Introduction

In April 1999 a comic strip appeared that drew immediate and tremendous media attention (Hornblower 1999; Sanford 1999). *The Boondocks*, created by African-American cartoonist Aaron McGruder, predominantly features African-American characters and provides an uninhibited critique of African-American life in the suburbs. *The Boondocks* represents various aspects of hip-hop culture and Japanese manga-style art, and candidly discusses racial issues, including tokenism, biracial identity, educational curriculum bias, stereotyping, racial profiling, U.S. census representation issues, and criticisms of various African-American politicians, entertainers, and sports heroes. McGruder's comic strip enjoyed one of the biggest launches in comics history—just two months after its national debut it appeared in newspapers in close to two hundred U.S. cities (Hornblower 1999). The attention that the strip has generated since its initial appearance has propelled it to the status of a cultural icon. Almost immediately, most newspapers received a large volume of comments from their readers regarding *The Boondocks*, prompting different responses from editors. Some

The authors would like to acknowledge the assistance of Ashley Macha, who served as an extraordinary research assistant for this project.

invited comments from readers thereby creating open discussions about the value of the strip ("Comics page is a serious matter" 1999). Others moved *The Boondocks* from the comics page to the editorial section (Sanford 1999). Some describe it as "racist," "mean-spirited," and "degrading;" others applaud its honest, direct, cutting-edge approach to racial issues as something that isn't represented in "daily, white-bread newspapers" ("Trudeau praises 'The Boondocks'" 1999). A number of newspapers, in both large and small communities, canceled the comic strip (Hornblower 1999). Some, as documented on *The Boondocks* website, have continued to feature McGruder's work but censor certain strips—most notably those that critique the images of sexuality on Black Entertainment Television (BET) by depicting African-American female "jiggling buttocks" as a parody of the music videos seen on the channel.

Interestingly, *The Boondocks* has received from its readers both praise and criticism, which do not break down neatly along the lines of race and ethnicity ("A sampling of reactions" 1999). It is important to note that African-American responses to the strip run the range of critiques and praises for its depiction of African-American life. This in-group diversity, however, is made invisible in most media coverage of *The Boondocks* controversy. Given the media's tendency to essentialize diverse African-American voices, our chapter is designed to counter this problematic approach to representation. Specifically, we utilize *The Boondocks* as a site of analysis that allows us to feature the various ways in which African-American audiences interact with mass-mediated images.

Existing research positions phenomenological inquiry as an effective means to thematize descriptions of lived experiences (Lanigan 1979; Spiegelberg 1982). Therefore, that is the methodological framework we chose for our study. However, prior to an explanation of our methodology, some background information concerning racial images in comic strips is necessary.

Racial Images in Comic Strips

Since the first comic strip appeared in 1897 (Kanfer 1994) newspaper comic strips have spanned the spectrum from entertainment to insightful critiques of society, cultural practices, norms, and prejudices. Early comic strips tended to present more derogatory images of minorities, but recent strips reflect a more representative and sophisticated look at society and its cultural/political practices (McLean 1998). Recent literature reveals a curi-

THE BOONDOCKS by AARON MCGRUDER

BOONDOCKS © 1999 by Aaron McGruder. Distributed by UNIVERSAL
PRESS SYNDICATE. Reprinted with permission. All rights reserved.

ously small amount of research that explores how people of color are represented in comic strips. Of the few studies that do explore such representations, most have focused on editorial cartoons (Stein 1997; Thibodeau
1989). Fewer have focused specifically on how racially diverse characters
appear in comic strips (McLean 1998).

Why is this? It could be that historically, racially diverse images have
only appeared marginally in comic strips (Orbe and Harris 2001, 247–49).
When they have appeared, these images reflected blatant racist thinking or
limited stereotypical roles (McLean 1998). Comic strips, like other mass
media venues, have attempted to diversify their characters in order to better reflect the general public (and, subsequently, attract a wider audience).
In most instances, however, these attempts have taken the form of a single
minority character within a predominately "White cartoon" (e.g., *Peanuts*
or *Beetle Bailey*). In more recent times, however, images of people of color
featured in comic strips have increased. A number of comic strips currently
have predominately African-American characters (e.g., *Curtis, Jump Start,
The Boondocks*). Yet, as far as we can tell, no research has focused specifically
on how people of color perceive, and interact with, these daily comic strips.
This line of inquiry, then, becomes increasingly important in light of how
some of the more politically oriented comic strips have evoked substantial
public response to their social critiques and controversial characters.

As discussed in our analysis, many African-American readers view *The
Boondocks* as a valuable source in countering existing stereotypes in comic
strips. However, according to McGruder—a twenty-six-year-old African-
American studies graduate from the University of Maryland at College
Park—that is not the central purpose behind his work. He describes his
philosophy for the comic on his website (http://www.boondocks.net) as
being "an intelligent and satirical view of Black/White relationships as well

as Black/Black relationships." Without question, the comic strip is grounded in his experiences moving from a predominately African-American neighborhood in Chicago to a predominately European-American Washington, D.C., suburb at the age of five. The strip is intended to "represent larger issues and larger facets of the Black community"—in essence to "keep it real." In light of this mission, McGruder responded to some readers' postings to the website's guest book by saying:

> I care nothing about tearing down stereotypes. If I did I would be giving the opinions of the racists and the ignorant more prominence in my life than such things deserve. I only want to represent the truth, inspire thought, and make people laugh. I don't do *The Cosby Show* and I find that over-romanticized, bourgie portrayals of Black America which spread intra-racial classism are no better than the stereotypical buffoons on UPN. I feel it is my right and responsibility to be self-critical of the Black community.

Being aware of McGruder's perspective as creator of *The Boondocks* is important in contextualizing the various ways in which African-American readers perceive the strip. However, we do not privilege his intentions as much as we do African-American readers' responses. The remainder of this paper, then, focuses on how phenomenology can reveal thematic understanding of these responses to McGruder's creations.

Methodological Framework

Through the use of a phenomenological framework (Lanigan 1979; Orbe 1994), a thematic analysis of African-American responses to *The Boondocks* was conducted as a means to reveal the complexities of how African-American identities inform perceptions of mass media images.

The first step in phenomenological inquiry is the description. Within this stage narratives are collected. In order to gauge the diversity of African-American responses to *The Boondocks*, we accessed data directly from *The Boondocks* website. Specifically, we downloaded and reviewed messages from the website's guest book for the first six months following the national introduction of the comic strip (April 20–September 15, 1999). Within this time period, a total of 1,314 messages were posted. Of these, 530 were from African Americans who identified themselves directly ("I am an African American who lives in the 'burbs' and I love the comic strip") or indirectly ("Yo Huey is smart as hell for a little kid. Both he and Caesar remind me of myself and my friends. This is gonna blow up, I can tell. Keep reppin'!").

The second step involves a reduction of narratives. Within this stage, each researcher reviewed and analyzed the 530 comments posted to the website by African Americans. This preliminary analysis resulted in the identification of over twenty possible themes. Over time, the themes identified by each researcher were merged into a collaborative analysis of African-American responses to *The Boondocks*. The result was the emergence of three central themes (plus three subthemes), which will be explicated in a subsequent section.

The third step of phenomenology—interpretation—begins during the description and reduction processes. The interpretation of themes involves a constant consideration of how they relate to one another (Spiegelberg 1982). In other words, it entails discovering one central idea from which the interpretations can be understood. Consequently, phenomenological interpretations are only feasible through a "hyper-reflection" (Merleau-Ponty 1962) whereby researchers constantly review descriptions of lived experiences, themes, and their (meta)meanings. Prior to explicating our interpretation of African-American responses to *The Boondocks*, we provide a summary of our themes.

As you will see, focusing on the comments on *The Boondocks* website allowed us to access rich data for our analysis. However, this form of data collection was not without its limitations. First, it only provided responses from African Americans who had access to the Internet *and* felt strongly enough about the comic strip to actually log on and post comments. This may have resulted in an overrepresentation of polarized comments. Additionally, we acknowledge that some of the comments that we analyzed may have been authored by non–African Americans who were "online perpetrators." Second, given the research that indicates that African Americans' use of the Internet is largely an upper-middle-class phenomenon ("Report: Online Gap Grows for Blacks" 1999), we recognize that important segments of the African-American community may be underrepresented in our analysis. These limitations notwithstanding, our analysis provides interesting insights as to how African-American audiences consume media products.

Thematization

Out of our phenomenologically informed inquiry, several themes emerged that reflect a wide range of responses by African Americans. If the responses to the strip's website are any indication, *The Boondocks* reflects a new level of cultural sophistication. They also challenge the opinion that other comic strips with minority characters simply contain mainstream characters in blackface. Yet these comments present a common thread, even within their diversity, in that they reflect multiple positions on issues related to representations of African Americans. This can be seen from reader debates about how the strip is "keepin' it real" versus how the strip reinforces negative stereotypes; or from disagreements about McGruder's role and responsibility in the representation of his characters versus applause for the success of a "brotha." Our discussion will tease out the following themes through the selected centralizing of comments by African-American readers posted on the website: (a) personal connections to *The Boondocks*; (b) breaking down and/or reinforcing stereotypes (which includes three subthemes); and (c) the role/responsibility of Aaron McGruder. These themes help illuminate the diversity of African-American responses to *The Boondocks* as well as provide insight into studying racial identity, perception, and representation in media images.

"Finally a Strip That's Relevant to Me": *Personal Connections to* The Boondocks

One of the most pervasive and prevalent themes to emerge from the postings on the website appears in comments about how *The Boondocks* reflects either an individual's personal experience as a minority or the racial experience of African Americans living in the suburban United States.

There were many postings from African-American men and women that connected the strip to their personal experience of being Black in the United States. Some of the comments reflect deeply personal satisfaction in experiencing a comic strip that, as one reader put it, is "like looking in a mirror at times." The strip was referred to as a "time travel." One comment talked about how the strip took the reader "back to my childhood as the first Black family on my street in 1964 in the midwest."

As if anticipating the range of views yet to appear on the website (as well as the media attention resulting from the comic strip's syndication), one reader posted, "Yo, on April 25, *The Boondocks* was in the paper. The first thing I noticed was Huey's hair. I was like, 'Damn. Yo Huey is smart as hell for a little kid. Both he and Caesar remind me of myself and my friends. This is gonna blow up, I can tell. Keep reppin'!" In another clear identification with the comic's characters, one reader wrote, "I love your comic. Me and Riley could be real tight if he was real. That's the way I feel. And his political ideas—that's me. This is the funniest funny in the paper."

Some readers responded to the similarities between their lives and the social conditions facing the characters in the strip. One reader wrote: "Hotep (peace), most impressive . . . truly on time and ahead of its time . . . I will always make sure my children read and educate themselves at the same time with your strip . . . it is great and so true to life . . . we have just relocated in Utah and find the strip is just what we need . . . thanks again your brother in da struggle." One young woman posted, "I'm a teenaged Blackgirl who's lived in the 'boondocks' all her life, and it's good to find someone who knows what's really goin' down out here." Similarly, a young man posted, "I can feel for these shorties, this is what I went through when I was young."

Numerous other responses reflected the readers' connection to the strip in their otherwise isolated media experience. For example, one nine-teen-year-old man wrote, "[Y]our strip is the only reason why I read the newspaper everyday. Your strip is the only thing in the paper that relates to me." Another reader stated, "Your characters reflect me and many of my friends personalities; as if you were drawing our everyday lives and attitudes."

However, postings that illuminated the readers' identification with the strip and McGruder's characters went beyond personal connections. "Just wanted to say your strip is funny and really relates to today's youth," was the posting of one reader. Another reader wrote, "What the detractors forget is that art imitates life. The characters in your strip are reflective of our society. The fact that some people are offended just means that you're doing [a] good job of showing us ourselves." Finally, there were postings that tied so-cial representation to a lack of media representation. For example, one reader stated, "I live in Los Angeles and for the first time in a long while I picked up the paper to check out the strip—Keep the flavor alive—we need more representation on the otherwise starched pages of the *Times*." These are examples of the kinds of postings that bridge the personal connections to *The Boondocks* to a sense of its role in the larger African-American expe-rience. They scratch the surface of a hotly contested issue debated on the website: the question of whether *The Boondocks* represents the African-American race.

Interestingly, we found that this plethora of comments about how *The Boondocks* "represents the race" existed in tension with other com-ments about how the strip does not reflect the African-American racial ex-perience. Additionally, a related theme emerged: the strip *cannot be expected* to reflect some type of totalized African-American experience. Many of these opposing positions ran as part of a single conversational thread between numerous readers posting to the website and/or responding to each other's comments. These are described as part of the second theme we identified.

"*Is Our Entire Culture Based around Poverty and 'Jail'?*": *Breaking Down and/or Reinforcing Stereotypes*

These concerns are raised throughout the postings. At times comparisons are drawn between *The Boondocks* and the claims of unrealistic representations of African-American life that were launched against other media products, such as *The Cosby Show* in the 1980s. Readers' comments reflect a sophisticated awareness of, and concern about, how media products are often taken to represent an essentialized image of groups. In this case readers expressed concern not only about whether the strip is "keepin' it real," but about the implications of audiences perceiving *The Boondocks* as *the* characteristic African-American experience. In other words, readers pondered whether *The Boondocks* reinforced or broke down racial stereotypes.

This is slightly different from the question of whether *The Boondocks* represents African Americans. This thread of postings reflected on the *impact* of representation. We found that the impact of *The Boondocks* representation of racial stereotyping was one of the most frequent themes appearing in the website postings during the period of study. It was also one of the most divisive among African-American respondents. The comments below were offered by a young Morehouse University law student:

> I have to admit that your strip is unnecessarily offensive. The last one I viewed (today) had a little White girl telling a bi-racial girl that she never knew she was Black, she just thought the bi-racial girl had a "really bad hair day." How is this funny or enlightening? How many little Black girls will see this and think their hair is inferior? . . . You offer no corrections, you just repeat the negative messages. . . . We can't have you hurting our community like this.

As with other postings, this quote reflects the concerns that stereotypical images presented in *The Boondocks* remain unchallenged by McGruder. But not all comments reflected this single position.

Numerous postings addressed both sides of the racial stereotype question. As a result, three subthemes further addressing the impact of representation emerged in the analysis. They are: the issue of negative stereotypes perpetuated by African Americans themselves, the impact of stereotypes on youth, and the way in which *The Boondocks* portrays "what is."

"Playa hatin'": Negative stereotypes as "Black-on-Black crime"
One of the most provocative subthemes concerned a discussion of how the negative stereotyping some readers found in the strip was damaging because the strip's creator is Black. Respondents considered how McGruder, as an African American, reinforced negative stereotypes of his own people in comments such as: "White folks must sit at home and wonder why we accept such bull from our own. I know I do and brother, I am as dark as we come," and "Haven't you noticed that we are the only group who identifies with 'ghetto life' as our right of passage. Everyone is entitled to his/her view but I say, this strip hurts us. Can't we make it without ridiculing our own as a stepping stone?"

Further postings question whether such stereotyping would be tolerated from a White comic strip writer.

> Tell me, if a White boy wrote the stuff in the strip like the fella here, would you be laughin or calling complaining. If we don't like THEM writing about us like that, why do we accept it from ourselves? . . . It's self-hate no matter how you color it.

Other African Americans saw accusations about negative stereotyping as counterproductive.

> *The Boondocks* is not about repeating stereotypes, but it is about two inner city youths that move to the 'burbs, and make observations. Through their observations, we are, or should be capable of seeing do we fit these, or are we doing something pro-actively to change these views among the masses. . . . Attacking the creator of the strip is not pro-active, it is reactive, and also repeating another Black stereotype . . . Black-on-Black crime.

"How many of our youth believe they need to be 'gangsta's'?"
The Boondocks *and young readers*
Another subtheme revolved around the strip's impact on young readers. Readers were concerned that McGruder's strip was "feeding children's heads with horrible thoughts." Readers raised concerns about the lessons being taught to children, especially as they relate to larger societal stereotypes.

> We need to see the stereotypes to know if we fit? That's silly, printing and

reprinting the stereotypes only ingrains the images in the rest of America and our kids. How many of our youth believe they need to be "gangsta's" because of the stereotypes?

Concerns were also expressed by readers in terms of the negative impacts on both Black and White children.

> I am a 17 yr. old student and I think you comic strip is a disgrace to the entire Black community. . . . You make the Black children who are poor and living in the "ghetto" think it's okay to act a certain way. Adults know you're parodizing Black stereotypes, but how are children supposed to know that. The White children that read the strip are being exposed to racism at an early age. Their parents may already be advocating racism and you're not doing anything to stop it.

Interestingly, the fact that these images were being produced in the form of a comic strip seemed to heighten the concern of readers. While many acknowledged the increased need to monitor children's exposure to several media forms, comics had been seen as "safe."

> Congratulations, you have found a clever way to get negative images and thought into the minds of youth without the parents realizing. I guess they never saw you commin'. While parents are exercising their parental discretion duties by riggin' the Internet and the cable box you come in the front door . . . literally. When it comes to comics we typically relax, but thanks to you not anymore. . . . We are dealing with children and the IMAGES they see that help form who they become.

All in all, even comments about the strip's impact on the young spread across a range of positions. African-American readers of *The Boondocks* both praised and criticized the effect of the strip on young readers, both African-American and European-American. One reader responded to concerns about the comic's images reinforcing negative stereotypes in young White children writing, "So if the little White kids read this strip and decide that this is how they want to act toward Black people, then so be it. And if there are weak-minded parents who are afraid to raise their children, and instead let a comic strip do it, then so be it."

Other fans stated positive comments such as, "My whole family, including my six year old daughter reads *The Boondocks*," and "[W]hen she [little sister] gets older, I'm going to print out all of your strips and show her every single one!" Finally, one reader commented, "You show young kids out there today that you can be anything in this world and don't be afraid to say what you feel. You show there is more to the Black community than meets the eye."

"It's about what is": The Boondocks *as cultural anthropology and political voice*

Not all readers thought the stereotypes were problematic. Another subtheme reflected the importance of *The Boondocks* in reflecting the reality of African-American life—not all African-American life, but that which exists in White suburbia. Although the pattern was subtle, comments under this subtheme reflect two different descriptions of the ways in which readers saw *The Boondocks* explicating African-American reality. For example, readers posted comments to the website that spoke of *The Boondocks* as a political voice for the African-American community, one that may be jeopardized by excessive criticism from those who see the strip negatively.

> I've heard the terms "stereotypes" and "negative" from readers who obviously see the glass as half empty. The amazing thing is that Aaron's already succeeded in waking folks up. Our brothers and sisters who cry, "Foul," either don't know that we exist, or are ashamed of us. Unfortunately, they may succeed in silencing our voice before we truly use it.

Other postings also commented on the way that *The Boondocks* reflected "what is," but from a cultural standpoint. In other words, postings spoke to the way in which *The Boondocks* reflects African-American lived cultural experiences—a cultural anthropology, so to speak. For example, one reader posted a message stating, "No matter what type of image you set for your characters, there will always be someone that will have something negative to say; remember *The Cosby Show*, the family wasn't 'real' enough for some." Readers added comments that attempted to separate out the specific reality presented by *The Boondocks* from an essentialized view of African-American cultural experience. One such reader stated, "No, the entire African American culture is not based around poverty, jail, thug faces, and talk of stealing; but this is a part of this young man's community."

In all, this subtheme suggests that *The Boondocks* reflects specific African-American cultural and political positions, best summed up by one reader's comments: "It's not a question of what's negative/positive. It's about what is. And taking the time to examine who we are, at this point in time, is important for future growth as individuals and as a people."

"Forget Those Fool Athletes, YOU McGruder Are a True
Positive Role Model for Brothers and Sisters across the Nation":
The Role/Responsibility of Aaron McGruder

Many postings debated McGruder's creative decisions with regard to representations and stereotyping of his characters. This, another related theme to the racialized role of *The Boondocks* is represented through comments targeting the strip's creator. Many were complimentary of the strip and its artistic quality and style (particularly its similarities to the Japanese *animé* style). More important for the purposes of this research were postings lauding McGruder's rise as an African-American media creator. For example, one reader posted, "It's nice to see one of your 'brothas' come up in the world." Others wrote to provide encouragement during the rash of criticism over negative stereotyping, "I love the comic, and it's good to see enterprising Black men doing well with business. Don't let these haters hold you down, do your thing son." Also, "Brother, don't allow anyone in our 'self-hating' family or 'the OTHER man' to dissuade you from what you are doing." One lengthy posting offered the following support:

> Aaron, be encouraged. Do not give in to the distractors. Your credentials
> of holding a degree in African-American studies, your experience as a
> Black man, your perseverance and dedication, and your genius make you
> more than qualified to comment of the Black American experience
> through your comic strip. I thoroughly enjoy The Boondocks. Not since
> Spike Lee started making movies, have I been so moved by and proud of
> the work of an artist. Continue to be true to yourself and say what you
> feel. No one is gonna like everything you have to say, but do not water
> down your feelings to try to please everyone's. Take some of the negative
> criticism as a compliment because it means that your strip is hitting
> home. Stay strong and continue to uplift the race through your excel-
> lence.

As is evident from earlier examples, McGruder was not immune from criticism regarding his responsibility as an African-American artist. Attacks ranged from questions about his economic motives to whether his particular representation of African Americans (one that the reader found problematic) was a disservice to his race—a sellout, so to speak:

> Most of us hate racism but instead of increasing it, you need to try to
> stop it. I suspect that your reasons for writing this awful strip has to do
> with the almighty dollar. Some Whites wanted to see Blacks degraded
> like this, and for no matter how much money you were willing to sacri-

fice your own people's hard work, such as MLK and Rosa Parks. We have worked too hard as a people to break the race barriers, and you are just conforming to the "Uncle Tom" ways. And for what, money? If my assumption is correct, then you are really sad and you should be totally ashamed.

Discussion

As demonstrated throughout our chapter, African-American responses to Aaron McGruder's *The Boondocks* are as diverse as African Americans themselves. Specifically, we utilized a phenomenological framework to gain thematic insight into hundreds of comments posted by self-identified African-American readers on the comic strip's website. The variety of these responses were captured through the identification of the three central themes. A cursory examination of these themes, as markers of interconnected African-American voices, illustrates the somewhat polarized views of the readers of the comic strip. However, a theoretically grounded analysis of these themes provides deeper insight into the significance of studying media images as they relate to racial identity, perception, and representation.

Years ago, Kobena Mercer wrote about the dialectical tension that people of color face when playing a role in the creation of media products (Mercer 1992). African-American producers/creators, for instance, must understand the larger context in which their media images are situated. Historically, images of African Americans in all media forms have been sparse—so much so that *any* presence was lauded and embraced by African-American viewers (Gates 1992). However, the stereotypical nature of these media images has resulted in a heightened awareness in terms of the role that they play in creating, reproducing, and sustaining racial ideologies (Omi 1989). Given the central role that popular culture plays within this process, characterizations of African Americans are never neutral. Instead, each image either "advances or retards the struggle" of representation (Elise and Umoja 1992, 83). Therefore, African-American creators/producers are faced with an additional responsibility that their majority counterparts do not.

Specifically, they are confronted with two ideological questions: Do I create only favorable images of African-American culture as a means to counter the abundance of negative portrayals? Or do I produce realistic images of African-American culture that include both positive and negative features? This dilemma captures the connectedness of themes reported ear-

lier. In fact, it assists in providing greater insight into the ideological differences that may fuel the polarized perceptions that African-American readers have of *The Boondocks*. Drawing from different African-American
comments helps to illustrate the connection between the expectations for
and perceptions of African-American-created media products. Without
question, some readers understood the larger responsibility faced by
McGruder.

For instance, *The Boondocks* website was full of accolades such as,
"Thanks for representin' US to tha' fullest," and, "Finally a strip that represents the peoples!" Interestingly, other readers articulated their concerns
about whether (and how) the comic strip could fully represent "the"
African-American experience in the suburban United States. This is a crucial point that further problematizes the additional responsibility placed on
African-American producers/creators. In essence, they are faced with being
called to represent all features of African-American life in a vastly limited
number of outlets. Consider the following posting:

> I am frustrated by the type of criticism I'm reading of The Boondocks
> by other Black readers who should be supporting you. It is unfortunate
> that because we produce so little media product, everything that IS
> produced, featuring Black characters, has to bear the weight of "repre-
> senting" all of us at the same time, which is a ridiculous concept. We
> are not a monolithic community. There is no single "correct" image.
> And you can't please everyone. If the portrayal is optimistic and for-
> ward looking, it will be blasted as being unrealistic. If it deals with is-
> sues head on, and confronts popular perceptions of Black culture, it's
> considered "negative."

Based on our analysis, we believe that the diverse African-American
responses to McGruder's *The Boondocks* reflect the multidimensional nature of issues surrounding the ideological questions posed by Mercer
(1992). Existing research has explored these issues with other media images
created by African Americans, such as FOX TV's *In Living Color* (Cooks and
Orbe 1993). The analysis provided within this chapter contributes to the
growing amount of scholarly literature that addresses issues of racial representation in the mass media. However, additional research is needed to further probe into the intricate complexities of these issues.

Without question, this line of research has tremendous heuristic value.
Given the large number of postings, future studies can compare and contrast perceptions of African Americans, European Americans, Asian

Americans, and Latinos/as. However, the next step in extending our research on *The Boondocks* may be of particular interest to readers of this anthology. One limitation of accessing African-American readers in the way
we did was that it did not allow us to actually interact with these persons.
In other words, we chose to refrain from entering the guest book discussions because we wanted to avoid affecting the "natural flow" of the online
discussions. This decision, while appropriate in exploratory research, limited our ability to use phenomenological inquiry to actively engage—and
become actively engaged by—those African-American readers who documented their perceptions of *The Boondocks* on the web. Given this limitation, our next step is to post several messages on the web informing readers
of our research and provide a link to a website that summarizes our findings and has a bulletin board where comments/feedback can be recorded.
We look forward to the insight that will be generated by this ongoing dialogue. We also anticipate the possibility of facilitating several traditional
focus groups to access perceptions of African Americans who may not have
Internet access. This extension of our current research project is significant
in that it allows for an extension of the phenomenological spiral where diverse racial/ethnic voices in scholarly research are not only centralized, but
included in meaningful ways as their lived experiences are interpreted by
researchers (Orbe 2000).

The intersubjective nature of phenomenological interpretations is
such that they represent "an ongoing construction, not a fixed point of de-
parture or arrival" (de Lauretis 1984, 159). In other words, phenomenological inquiry never positions itself as arriving at a definite set of conclusions.
A final set of answers is never derived. Instead, researchers are always left
asking, "What have I missed?" As is the case with the research described in
this chapter, the closer we get to the phenomenon under investigation, the
more we recognize how much more there is to know. Given the prominence
of Aaron McGruder's *The Boondocks*—which includes a series of books and
a forthcoming television show—it stands as a valuable point of analysis for
researchers interested in understanding the intricate relationship(s) between media products, culture, and identity.

References

A sampling of reactions. (1999). *Kalamazoo Gazette*, June 13, p. E5.
Comics page is a serious matter. (1999). *Kalamazoo Gazette*, June 13, p. A14.
Cooks, L. M., and M. Orbe. (1993). Beyond the satire: Selective exposure

and selective perception in 'In Living Color.' *Howard Journal of Communications* 4: 217–33.

de Lauretis, T. (1984). *Alice doesn't: Feminism, semiotics, and cinema.* Bloomington: Indiana University Press.

Elise, S., and A. Umoja. (1992). Spike Lee constructs the new Black man: Mo' better. *Western Journal of Black Studies* 6: 82–89.

Gates, H. L. (1992). TV's Black world turns—but stays unreal. In M. L. Andersen and P. H. Collins, eds., *Race, class, and gender: An anthology* (pp. 310–16). Belmont, Calif.: Wadsworth.

Hornblower, M. (1999). Comic n the hood. *Time*, July 5, p. 78.

Kanfer, S. (1994). From *The Yellow Kid* to yellow journalism. *Civilization: The Magazine of the Library of Congress* 2 (3): 32–37.

Lanigan, R. L. (1979). The phenomenology of human communication. *Philosophy Today* 23 (i): 3–15.

McLean, S. (1998). Minority representation and portrayal in modern newsprint cartoons. In Y. R. Kamalipour and T. Carilli, eds., *Cultural diversity and the U.S. media* (pp. 23–37). Albany: State University of New York Press.

Mercer, K. (1992). "1968": Periodizing postmodern politics and identity. In L. Grossberg, C. Nelson, and P. Treichler, eds., *Cultural studies* (pp. 424–49). New York: Routledge.

Merleau-Ponty, M. (1962). *The visible and the invisible.* Translated by C. Smith, translation review by F. Williams. London: Routledge and Kegan Paul. (Original work published in 1948.)

Omi, M. (1989). In living color: Race and American culture. In I. Angus and S. Jhally, eds., *Cultural politics in contemporary America* (pp. 111–22). New York: Routledge.

Orbe, M. (1994). "Remember, it's always Whites' ball": Descriptions of African American male communication. *Communication Quarterly* 42 (3): 287–300.

———. (2000). Centralizing diverse racial/ethnic voices in scholarly research: The value of phenomenological inquiry. *International Journal of Intercultural Relations* 24: 603–21.

Orbe, M., and T. M. Harris. (2001). *Interracial communication: Theory into practice.* Belmont, Calif.: Wadsworth.

Report: Online gap grows for Blacks. (1999). *Kalamazoo* (Mich.) *Gazette*, July 8, p. A14.

Sanford, J. (1999). Boondocks' battle. *Kalamazoo Gazette*, June 13, pp. E1, E4.

Spiegelberg, H. (1982). *The phenomenological movement*, 3rd ed. The Hague: Martinus Nijhoff.

Stein, M. L. (1997). Racial stereotyping and the media. In S. Biagi and M. Kern-Foxworth, eds., *Facing difference: Race, gender, and mass media* (pp. 125–28). Thousand Oaks, Calif.: Pine Forge Press.

Thibodeau, R. (1989). From racism to tokenism: The changing face of Blacks in *New Yorker* cartoons. *Public Opinion Quarterly* 53: 482–94.

Trudeau praises "The Boondocks." (1999). *Kalamazoo Gazette*, July 1, p. D2.

3

Black Audiences, Past and Present

Commonsense Media Critics and Activists

Catherine Squires

Introduction

When mainstream media producers are faced with criticism about content,[1] the pat answer is: "If people didn't like it, they wouldn't use it." High ratings and sales are equated with happy media consumers. However, consumption does not ensure enjoyment or necessarily signal acceptance or agreement with the form and content presented by mainstream media channels. Consumption without acceptance may be particularly common for groups such as African Americans, who are underrepresented in mainstream media production, editing, and gatekeeping but whose images are generated and presented by non-Black producers for profit. While African Americans still use mainstream media for information or pleasure, they often supplement mainstream fare with alternative, Black-owned media products. Furthermore, many Black audience members engage in critiques of mainstream media content, and make comparisons to alternative media treatments of the same subject or event. If these media consumers were disaggregated from the ratings numbers and listened to, what would we hear about media content?

This chapter compares how past and present Black audiences have utilized Black-owned media to respond to, critique, and protest against mainstream media depictions of Black Americans. The historical and contemporary data suggest that African Americans have long looked at both entertainment and news media texts differently than Whites, and that this pattern often results in conflict over media representations and ownership. In the first part of this chapter, examples from past media protests as reported in Black-owned newspapers are introduced to give a historical context for interactions between Black audiences and mainstream media. In the second, data from a study of a contemporary African-American talk radio station is presented, highlighting participants' discussions of mainstream media depictions of African Americans. Analysis of broadcast transcripts and interviews with listeners reveal a strong sense of mistrust toward mainstream media, as well as a sophisticated critique of news media in particular. Furthermore, the critiques of the listeners resonate both with past protests against White representations of Blacks in news and entertainment media and current media scholars' views of race and media. As these two sets of examples show, Black-owned media have been integral to the process of Black audiences' media critiques and protests, articulating and asserting alternative representations of Blackness and calling for the end of Whites' use of harmful stereotypes. In providing a venue and support for alternative visions and critiques, Black-owned media can provide important loci for critiques of mainstream media and foster Black efforts to define and redefine Black images that circulate in wider public spheres.

Black Audience Research

Traditional audience research has been concerned with "vulnerable audiences": children, women, and racial minorities. It is assumed that these groups need protection from content that is deemed harmful to their mental, political, and physical well-being (Ang 1996). This approach is problematic, Ien Ang explains, because it implies that members of these groups who choose to consume such media are acting irrationally. Using women's attraction to soap operas as an example, Ang (1996, 92) writes:

> Fictional female heroines are seen as . . . role models for female audiences. . . . [But] this approach . . . implies a rationalistic view of the relationship between image and viewer (whereby it is assumed that the image is seen by the viewer as a more or less adequate model for reality), it can only account for the popularity of soap operas as something irrational. In other words, what the role/image approach tends to overlook is the large emotional involvement which is invested in identification with characters of popular fiction. As a result, [these images] cannot be con-

ceptualized as "realistic" images of women, but must be approached as textual constructions of possible modes of femininity.

Hence, the assumption that audiences are always looking to televised representations as role models overlooks the context of viewing. Jacqueline Bobo's (1995 [see chapter 9 of this volume]) work suggests that Black female audience members are constantly integrating their own life experiences and cultural knowledge into their readings of media texts. For example, even though most critics considered Steven Spielberg's filmed version of Alice Walker's novel *The Color Purple* a disaster, many Black women who saw the film were deeply moved. Bobo found through interviews that the women were weaving their knowledge of Walker's original work and the feelings the novel gave them into their viewing experience (Bobo 1995). These women were able to transfer the *emotional involvement* of reading and talking about the book with their friends into the movie environment.

However, what happens when the text in question is a news report, documentary, or other reality-based show? How do the emotional investments described by Ang, along with the lived experiences used by Bobo's filmgoers, come together when African Americans watch or read texts that contain real, not fictional, events? There is evidence that "real" representations of Blacks in mainstream news media and reality-based programs have a negative effect on White perceptions of Blacks. Studies show that a great number of Whites are still likely to believe that Blacks are more violent, lazy, and less intelligent than other social groups (Bobo and Kluegel 1993), and scholars believe media help form or reinforce those beliefs. Textual and content analysis research has long indicated that mainstream media regularly disseminate negative stereotypes about Blacks in entertainment media (Dates and Barlow 1990) and overrepresent Blacks as criminals (Entman 1990, 1992; Dixon and Linz 2000) and welfare recipients (Gilens 1999) in news and reality-based programming. Furthermore, recent research in priming public opinion suggests that these negative racial images reinforce Whites' fears of Blacks and prompt them to exhibit anti-Black sentiments and opinions (Gilens 1999; Gilliam and Iyengar 1997; Kinder and Sanders 1996; Valentino 1999). For example, news about welfare, which disproportionately presents Blacks as lazy dependents, may lead White viewers to judge pro-welfare policies negatively because the stereotype of the undeserving welfare mother has been activated (Gilens 1999). Thus, a large body of empirical and historical research suggests that mainstream media are sources for stereotypical and racist information and images about Black

Americans (Dixon 2000), and that these images—particularly those generated in the news—exacerbate racial divides over public policy (Kinder and Sanders 1996).

If news and entertainment media contribute to a divide between White and Black opinions about racially charged issues, we should expect that Blacks are reading mainstream news media texts differently than Whites. Audience-centered studies could help us better understand these reading differences. While there have been some ethnographic investigations of Black audiences, most studies focus on entertainment media, such as MTV, movies, and prime-time TV. Interviewing Black audiences in Britain, Ross (1997) found that Black viewers felt White British media texts homogenized and marginalized Blacks. The participants in Ross's focus groups believed the mainstream images reinforced White audiences' stereotypes of Blacks. Brown and Schulze (1990) found that Black teenagers interpreted Madonna's videos much differently than White teens. Jhally and Lewis's (1992) controversial study of White and Black viewers of *The Cosby Show*—long considered a universally "positive" representation of Black life—found that Blacks and Whites read the show quite differently. Here I bring a historical perspective to this discussion, comparing Black newspaper readers' protests against White-produced entertainment *and* news media in the past to the present displeasure with White news media expressed by a Black talk radio audience.

Past Reactions of Black Media and Audiences

Of the means for the advancement of a people placed as we are, none
are more valuable than a press. We struggle against opinions.
Our warfare lies in the field of thought.
—Freedom's Journal, March 16, 1827

Blacks have long questioned and protested White news reports and other reality-based texts through Black-owned media and other means of protest. Beginning with the publication of *Freedom's Journal* in 1827, African-American periodicals have sought to refute racist and misleading mainstream news. The struggle continued into the twentieth century with the work of Ida B. Wells and others who sought to debunk the myth of the Black rapist and the sexually insatiable Black woman (Giddings 1984; Wells 1892, 1909). During the Red Summer of 1919, Black writers spoke out strongly against White coverage of the riots and lynchings that occurred at the end of World War I.

> *The Houston Chronicle* . . . charges that "the colored people themselves try to protect and shield [rapists]." . . . It is an age-worn and over-worked lie of the deepest dye. Let us deal in facts and figures for a while, so that such damnable and insidious propaganda can be shown up in its real form. (Kerlin 1920, x)

The *Houston Informer* refuted the White press' attribution of the rapes to primarily Black perpetrators:

> Of the five alleged race riots, rape was only assigned by the White press (mind you) in one case and that was the Washington affair. Yet, according to the data of Major Pullman, Washington's chief of police, there occurred in that city between June 25, 1919, and the outbreak of the riot, ONE CASE OF RAPE and three cases of attempted rape. The first case of attempt was on a COLORED SCHOOL TEACHER [by a White man]. (1919, reprinted in Kerlin 1920, 95–96)

The *Black Dispatch* also commented on biased representations in the White press:

> In the press of America, all that the Negro gets is headlines for his faults, "BIG BURLY Black BRUTE DOES THIS AND HUGE Black NEGRO FIEND DOES THAT." This is the advertisement and the only sort of introduction that the Negro daily gets to White masses. (October 10, 1919, reprinted in Kerlin 1920, 3)

One major task of the Black press has been to show more sides of the story where race was involved, hopefully reaching not only Blacks to build up their spirits but also aiming at Whites to challenge their views. As movies and radio became widespread, the contents of these new media were examined for racial bias as well. This scrutiny resulted in more critique from Black journalists and, unlike the mostly textual protest against news media racism, large-scale Black audience revolts against the producers of racist entertainment media.

Birth of a Nation, Birth of a Protesting Audience

Although Hollywood films had a history of depicting Blacks in an unflattering light, D. W. Griffith's *Birth of a Nation* added insult to injury because it was marketed as a masterpiece of both history and film. White audiences flocked to the film in droves and many critics gave it great acclaim. The script, based on *The Clansman,* grossly manipulated Civil War and Reconstruction history and portrayed Blacks as buffoons and rapists. Despite the obvious racist portrayals, President Woodrow Wilson praised the film, and his remarks were printed in its advertisements (Cripps 1969). The opposite reaction came from Blacks who saw the film. Black audiences, working with the Black press and the NAACP, led the charge to close the film down, constructing a campaign that won some small victories in the reediting of certain scenes. Still, the film received wide distribution, leading some Blacks to organize more vocal protests and to take the fight directly to the theaters.

African Americans in Boston rushed the Whites-only movie house where the film was opening to buy tickets. Eleven were arrested by the police. William Monroe Trotter, who encouraged Blacks to shut down the film through editorials and articles in his Black newspaper, the Boston *Guardian,* posted bail (Cripps 1969, 157). The next day a crowd of Blacks and some members of the United Irish League gathered at Faneuil Hall to protest the film. Orators made speeches throughout the morning on the steps of the hall as rumors of race riots filled the city. The demonstration prompted the governor and attorney general of Massachusetts to discuss how to stop the film from being shown. In the meantime, the police were ordered to stop the Sunday showing of the film and to disperse the crowds (Cripps 1969, 156). Three months after its release, the pressure from Blacks and a few White allies was strong enough that President Wilson retracted his earlier support in an open letter to the clergy and the press.[2] Meanwhile, the *Chicago Defender*, which supported Trotter's activism, argued for suppressing the film *before* it opened. As Illinois's film censorship board debated whether the film would cause similar racial unrest in Chicago, the *Chicago Defender* published multiple editorials and readers' letters against the film. Claiming the film would incite race riots, the paper's editors wrote:

> Big, broad Chicago wants nothing that is any way going to affect the pleasant relations between the two races. It is not good public policy needlessly to invite breaches of the peace. . . . The motto of the race in Chicago is "I will" strike a telling blow whenever and wherever necessary at the demon prejudice, it matters not in what form it may come. ("The Death of a Movie" 1915)

The main headline for the *Chicago Defender*'s May 22, 1915, edition was "HISTORY MAKING WEEK FOR AFRO-AMERICANS: Mayor

Thompson Puts Ban on 'Birth of a Nation.'" In the same issue, the paper printed a letter from Booker T. Washington that praised Black Chicagoans and the *Chicago Defender* for the preemptive strike:

> I wish to urge our people everywhere to take time by the forelock and adopt in advance such measures as will prevent the showing of the photoplay, "The Birth of a Nation," in any community, North or South. . . . [O]nce the play has been put on in a city, the managers encourage, and even skillfully initiate opposition, on account of the advertising the play receives when attempts are made to stop it. ("Time to Fight Bad Movies" 1915)

The ban on the movie, however, was eventually rescinded and a heavily censored version was allowed to play in Chicago theaters. The *Chicago Defender* responded with an editorial cartoon depicting Thomas Dixon, the author of *The Clansman*, as a devil stirring a cauldron labeled "Chicago" with a ladle labeled "Birth of a Nation." A review by Mrs. K. J. Bills was printed in December. Mrs. Bills claimed that she went to see the film "not because I wanted to see it, but to be able to criticize intelligently." Using her own experiences of growing up during Reconstruction as a guide, Mrs. Bills (1915) questioned the authenticity of the film.

> It is false from beginning to end. . . . Was there ever a Congress composed entirely of Negroes who passed laws to govern all the Whites in the South? Was there ever a time when Southern White people were at all submissive to the Blacks as this picture would have people believe? Does anyone believe that after the war the Negroes have no other ambition than to marry White women? . . . I wonder if Mr. Griffin [*sic*] lived during those days, and does he really remember things as they were.

Black newspapers followed the career of *Birth of a Nation* long after its release. As late as 1919 the *New York Age* argued that the film should not be distributed overseas to prejudice foreign audiences.

> D. W. Griffith, who got his real start as a motion picture producer by defaming 12,000,000 loyal Americans, is quoted as saying: "The motion picture will Americanize the world . . ." Mr. Griffith has taken his "Birth of a Nation" to Americanize the world, and a no more sinister emissary of anti-Negro propaganda could be sent across the waters. ("World to be 'Americanized'" 1919)

In the end, the campaigns against *Birth of a Nation* failed to stop the film's success with White audiences. But, the film and related controversies made Blacks hunger for their own filmmaking industry and more wary of White portrayals of Blacks in general. More importantly, the protests "demonstrated the seriousness with which films had come to be regarded both as creators and reflectors of [the] opinions and attitudes" of all audiences (Cripps 1969, 161). Although Blacks overwhelmingly saw Griffith's film as a piece of racist propaganda, other "entertainment" vehicles were not as easy to judge.

Amos 'n' Andy: Divided Perceptions of Humor and Authenticity

The minstrel show was a huge influence on vaudeville and other urban entertainment, and these arenas became wellsprings for radio shows.[3] The most successful radio minstrel show was *Amos 'n' Andy*, often posting the highest ratings in the nation (Ely 1991). Because the humor of *Amos 'n' Andy* was so familiar to some Blacks, it was hard for many to criticize the show as strongly as they had opposed *Birth of a Nation*.[4] Ely's study of audience reactions to *Amos 'n' Andy* in the Black press found that there was no class or gender split in support or protest of the show. Just as many working-class as middle-class Blacks found the show offensive as found it amusing, and both women and men equally liked and disliked the portrayals of Amos, Kingfish, Sapphire, and Mama. Despite the pleasures experienced by some Black audience members, many were willing to show their disapproval. The Chicago Bishop of the African Methodist Episcopal Church began the first organized protest against the radio show in 1929, a year after its debut on WMAQ Radio, Chicago (Ely 1991, 174). In 1931 *The Courier*'s editor, Robert L. Vann, ran a petition drive which received over 700,000 signatures in an attempt to get *Amos 'n' Andy* off the air (Ely 1991, 176). In addition to joining the petition drive, Blacks also wrote letters to *The Courier* and other Black papers expressing fears such as Theresa Kennedy did in the *Post-Dispatch*. Ms. Kennedy felt that the show taught "Black lads and the world at large . . . that the Negro in every walk of life is a failure, a dead-beat, and above all shiftless and ignorant" (Ely 1991, 161). Those who answered *The Courier*'s call for boycotts were worried about the same issues as those who protested *Birth of a Nation*: that the "history" of *Birth of a Nation* and the intimate portrayal of the "common Negroes" Amos and Andy would be taken as fact by Whites. But it wasn't until the show moved to television in 1951 that the Black public presented a more united front with the NAACP leading the charge against the show's televisual reincarnation.

The controversies over *Amos 'n' Andy* and *Birth of a Nation* are precursors to today's criticisms of Black representations in mass media. First, arguments over what make negative or positive portrayals of Black life, and whether particular characterizations should or shouldn't be utilized, accompany almost every media text involving African Americans. Valerie Smith (1997, 4) writes, "the imprecise nature of the positive/negative distinction has the potential to essentialize racial identity and deny its dynamic relation to constructs of class, gender, sexuality, religion and so on." In the above cases, Black newswriters and audience members felt that "negative" is violent, illiterate, and lower-class. But, as the fans of *Amos 'n' Andy* pointed out in their letters opposing the boycotts, these criticisms posit the "positive" as middle- or upper-class, screening out those who hadn't yet been "uplifted" by the Talented Tenth (Ely 1991).

The questions raised by these examples are: Who has the right to represent Black people in the media? Whose experiences should guide those representations? Can Whites create adequate news and/or entertainment texts concerning Blacks, or are Whites, by definition, tinged with racism? These questions continue to be asked today, as less repulsive but still troubling images of African Americans are transmitted daily.

Looking back, we can see that five major motifs arise in Black audiences' critiques of White media:

1. Mainstream media only show extremes in the Black community, not a continuum of actions and identities. Negative events and actions of Blacks (usually in lower economic classes) are emphasized.
2. Whites believe stereotypical depictions of Blacks, thus perpetuating harmful racial stereotypes.
3. Differences between Blacks and other ethnic groups are blown out of proportion to incite conflicts and controversy.
4. Media producers must be held accountable for racist texts.
5. Blacks need to create and use their own media to distribute better information and less racial bias in coverage of Black life.

These themes recur in the conversations heard on Black-owned talk radio today. In today's news environment there is more coverage of Blacks than there was in the first part of the twentieth century.[5] This provides a window on the Black world for many Whites. Unfortunately, the mainstream window most often opens to a scary, urban world of crime and joblessness. Is this picture of reality as convincing to Black audiences as it seems to be for White audiences? Below I share my analysis of a contemporary Black audience's responses to mainstream news media via a Black-owned radio station, WVON–AM. The analysis reveals not only a similarity to past audience and Black press critiques of media, but also resonates with contemporary scholarship on race and media. Unlike *The Courier's* call to action, protests voiced on the talk shows are not translated into direct actions against mainstream media firms. However, as I will discuss in closing, WVON's history and community activism make the station a potential spark for future audience activism.

A Brief History of WVON–AM Radio

Since its earliest days WVON has been a station aimed at Black Chicagoans. The Chess brothers, the White proprietors of Chess Records, a company that made "race records," bought the station in 1963 (Spann-Cooper 1996). The station played R&B and hired Black deejays known as "The Good Guys." One of these men, Wesley South, a writer and editor who had worked for the *Chicago Defender, Ebony/Jet*, and the *Pittsburgh Courier*, was also given an hour-long talk show called *Hotline*, which first aired on April 1, 1963. South hosted guests such as Jackie Robinson, Mahalia Jackson, and Martin Luther King, Jr. (Ruffin 1991, 6). In 1970 Lu Palmer, a journalist and local activist, began *Lu's Notebook*, a talk show that was aired not only on WVON, but also WGCI, WJPC, and WMPP. The show, initially sponsored by Illinois Bell, was canceled: Palmer believes his show lost its sponsorship because "it was too political for Illinois Bell" (Palmer 1995).

In 1974 competition from larger crossover stations and record companies cashing in on Black music forced the Chess brothers out of the radio and record business (Spann-Cooper 1996). However, this was not to be the end of WVON. A few of "The Good Guys," including Wesley South and Purvis Spann "the Blues Man," formed the Midway Broadcasting Corporation. In 1979 they won the rights to the spectrum at 1450 AM, then known by the call letters WXOL.[6] Midway got the WVON call letters back in 1984, after Gannett Broadcasting dropped them in order to give their 1390 AM station the same call letters as their successful FM Black-format music station, WGCI.[7] The WVON call letters stand for "Voice of the Negro," and the major shareholders of WVON, Spann and South, wanted to retain the symbolism. As Spann's daughter, Melody Spann-Cooper, explained, WVON "has always been a station that was for the African American community" (Spann-Cooper 1996).

Under the leadership of Spann and South the station hired a predominantly Black staff and all-Black on-air talent. At first the station produced a music format, blues and gospel. However, in 1983, Harold Washington ran to become the first Black mayor of Chicago, a city known for its racism and machine politics. The station began to air talk programming, tapping into the desire of Black listeners to hear information about and discuss the campaign. "The Black political movement has been alive and well right here at this station," said South. "We had a little victory here and there, but we hit it big with Harold Washington" (Ruffin 1991). When Melody Spann-Cooper took over as president and general manager of the station, she placed even more emphasis on talk, expanding the range of topics and encouraging her production staff to be innovative.[8] They called their format "Black Talk":

> And when we say "Black Talk" it's a talk station just like any other station, but it's geared towards the African American community. And when you have, um, committed yourself to following a format like this, it's got to be more about information than [it would be] for the general market talk stations. They tend to have more, "entertainment talk," more sensationalism. . . . Black talk radio in Chicago has to be the information point for African Americans. Because that's what we miss. (Spann-Cooper 1996)

What is being "missed" by Blacks is a complex, diverse portrayal of their communities, issues, and lifestyles in mainstream news and information programming. Into this gap WVON has inserted itself, providing an alternative to the unidimensional coverage of Black Americans in mainstream media. This maneuver has created a dynamic site of public talk for listeners, politicians, activists, and members of the White and Black intelligentsia; it also has consistently generated revenues for the station.[9]

In addition to providing a "Black Talk" forum, WVON sponsors many events throughout the year that give listeners a chance to meet each other and gain useful information and services. The station regularly sponsors candidates' debates in election years, issue forums, job and health fairs, and panel discussions, free of charge. WVON also sponsors jazz cruises and other entertainment events for listeners. Furthermore, not only does the staff talk about politics on the air, they are often participants in local and national political organizations and protests. Cliff Kelley is a former Chicago alderman and a member of the ACLU; Lu Palmer heads the Chicago Black United Communities (CBUC), an organization known for picketing of construction sites that do not hire Blacks. In short, the station is pro-Black. Around the station paintings and prints by Black artists are displayed; memos and photocopies that advocate "buying Black" are posted on bulletin boards, and short pieces on Black history and maps of Africa are posted on the walls. The combination of the talk show format and WVON's Black and community-oriented spirit, therefore, make it an excellent site at which to study the intersection of media, identity, and social activism.[10]

Methods

I began my interactions with WVON in 1995. In order to become a participant-observer at the station, I applied for an internship with the producer of Cliff Kelley's morning drive-time talk show, *World Objectives*. My duties included handling callers, researching materials for show topics, and contacting guests, publishing companies, and politicians for the show. In addition to assisting in the production of Kelley's show, I also attended and helped out at some community events put on by the station. I interviewed listeners at these events and handed out questionnaires in order to gather more data on the audience. I continued as a part-time volunteer intern at the station over the next three years, building my field notes and conducting a formal mail-in survey of the listeners.

The survey was conducted in order to gauge the wider Black audience's relationship to the station. Specifically, I wanted to explore whether the listeners were utilizing the information transmitted by WVON in their political decision-making processes and in interactions with their communities. I also wanted to discover whether the listeners felt that they were true members of the "WVON family." The list of audience members was generated through WVON's first subscription drive in the winter of 1995–1996. From this database (WVON's only official listing of any of its listeners at the time) I randomly selected 515 names. Fifteen were used to pretest the questionnaire and the remaining five hundred were sent surveys with return postage and mailing included.[11] The response rate was 46 percent (N=232), a high rate for a mail survey of this type. The questionnaire contained open-ended items, dichotomous choice questions, and Likert-scale styled questions that required respondents to answer whether they strongly agreed or disagreed with statements about WVON and other media.

WVON's audience has grown since I finished my research there, but the characteristics of the audience remain similar. The majority of the audience is Black, between thirty-five and sixty years old, votes Democrat, and has a yearly income of $25,000–$45,000. Most have had at least two years of postsecondary education, and some have advanced degrees (Squires 1999). WVON listeners reported that they read and watch multiple news sources, local and national, Black-owned and mainstream. Thus, they are well versed in both Black and White media portrayals of Black life. The excerpts related here come from three sources: responses to open-ended questions on the survey, personal interviews with listeners I contacted at station-sponsored events and through a survey, and the collection of tapes of Cliff Kelley's show I recorded while I was a volunteer production assistant at the station.[12] These comments echo the criticisms voiced by past Black audiences: that only extremes in Black life are shown by the mainstream media, that differences between Blacks and other groups are exaggerated, that media elites should take more responsibility for their representations of Blacks, and that Blacks need Black-owned media to remedy these problems.

Confronting Extremes in Coverage

The idea that media treatment of Blacks tends to show only polar opposites is well-entrenched in Black media criticism (Dates and Barlow 1990; Jhally and Lewis 1992; Riggs 1991). This is not a new concern, and it is expressed not only among academics but also in the past and present protests of Black audiences and the Black news media. The WVON audience is quick to sound off when biased coverage is sensed in mainstream news. Furthermore, most audience members I spoke with were incredulous that I even asked the question, "Do you think there is a significant difference between WVON and White-owned radio stations?" It was only common sense, one woman said to me—given the history of racism in America—to expect Whites to report and discuss Black life differently.[13] Overwhelmingly, this view of commonsense media consumption dominated interviewees' and callers' opinions of mainstream media.

During the February 9, 1998, broadcast of *World Objectives*, a caller (Ron) made the following comment to the guest, a Black television producer:

> Usually when they discuss the Black community, they deal with—what I guess I'm looking at is like the two different extremes: when you talk about those who may be dealing with a lot of the poverty, a lot of the problems there, and [then] you look at those who are (like you mentioned, Cliff) the "talented ten[th]." But I think that our community is just like society as a WHOLE; that the stability rests in the middle. The

> working class . . . a lot of times I don't find that area [of the community]
> to be represented [in mainstream media]. (Kelley 1998a)

Ron's critique matches that of many scholars who claim that mainstream
media, in collusion with other cultural forces, assumes that the only "true"
Black identity emerges from the inner city (Dent and Wallace 1992; West
1993). The other extreme is the "super Black" who has somehow transcended the negatives of Blackness (thereby becoming essentially NOT
Black) through financial means or celebrity.

During some interviews I asked the question, "Are there any other
things you'd like to say about mainstream media or WVON?" One fifty-six-
year-old male listener replied, "WVON brings out the positives and negatives that relate to Blacks. The White media in most cases only [brings out]
negatives." As with Ron, this man finds that White media are not concerned
with showing a spectrum of Black life, only the "pathological" elements of
Black experience. Another listener, a thirty-eight-year-old machinist, had
even more to say about this imbalance in coverage.

> White-owned media reduces major stories about Black people to a sound
> bite. An old Southern saying, "One drop of Black blood makes you
> Black." It must hold true for the White-owned media: one well con-
> structed and caring story too often about Black people might make the
> White-owned media Black! It can only be expected in the month of
> February, then after February you can stop. The White-owned media
> feels they have given Blacks their share of positive images—a full twenty-
> eight days! "There's no need to teach White children about Black people
> in school; they can learn it in the month of February or from our water-
> down [*sic*] version of Blacks in slavery from *Roots*."

It is very clear that this audience member feels that all the "positive" coverage given to Blacks is condensed into one month. He also hypothesizes that
White reporters assume writing a positive story about Blacks implies solidarity with Blacks, a perception that Black reporters working in White
newsrooms often find undermines their status (Wilson 1991).

Many interviewees and callers were convinced that White reporters
don't go beyond stereotypes to fully investigate and explain the stories they
cover. These reporters are also accused of not going to Black sources for information or bothering to learn about Black people and events. As a fifty-
eight-year-old female business owner responded:

> White owned media seems to view the problems facing the Black com-

munity as being the fault of the people, their lack of ethics . . . apathy. In actuality, these characteristics are most often rooted in economic deficits which give "birth" to illiteracy, crime, homelessness—but more prevalently hopelessness and a sense of despair.

This listener, a fifty-one-year-old secretary, specifically commented on coverage of the O. J. Simpson trial:

> I listened to WVON and I sometimes watched Court TV. I stopped watching the regular channels—they were very biased, very slanted, and passing on false information from the prosecutor's office.

Given the racial record of the legal system, it is no wonder that she and other WVON listeners would want reporters to get information from nongovernmental sources. But more importantly, they expect reporters to get basic facts correct, as one caller (Amina) asked Mike Miner, an editor at the *Chicago Reader* (the *Reader*), to do. Miner had recently written a very negative article about the station's dealings with a Black author and would-be advertiser, whose commercial for his book, *White Folks*, was deemed inappropriate by the station. The station refused his ad copy because it deemed its references to slave auctions offensive. Yet, the author *was* interviewed on the station twice to plug his book, and got free advertising through the interviews. In the article, Miner claimed that WVON had censored the author, yet never mentioned that he had been an on-air guest twice to discuss his book. In addition to this omission, Miner committed numerous factual errors about the station's history and scheduling, and claimed that the station "pilloried Whites from dawn till dusk" (Miner 1996). Miner was invited to be a guest on *World Objectives*. Amina called in and took Miner to task for his lack of knowledge.

> Amina: Okay, so my thing is, if you're an editor, because I have a degree in journalism, so I know that if you are . . .
> Miner: Yes.
> Amina: . . . researching information, you basically have to experience it before you write it, correct? Is that correct?
> Miner: Fair enough.
> Amina: Okay, so for you to make a—write an article, I would seem to think that you would have to listen to it a couple of—at least a couple of weeks out of the month, uh, do a little bit more in-depth, sound, uh, research to write an article, a scathing article such as the article that you had written.

Miner: A scathing article?

Amina: Yeah, I think so, it's scathing, because you can't even really defend
yourself on the radio, and you don't even listen to the radio [station]
itself. So basically, you're not really even fit to write the article. (Kelley,
1996)

As one Black editor stated, White media producers often "assume they
know everything, but a lot of editors don't pay much attention to Black culture. They never sit down and read *Essence* or *Ebony*" (Bobo 1995, 21). In
this case, they don't listen to WVON, either.

Holding Media Makers Responsible

At one point in the conversation, Miner remarked that the *Reader*'s advertisers did not want to advertise in Black neighborhoods. He defended the
advertisers citing their belief that "They [Blacks] don't come to our stores . . .
you're asking us to pay for something which does us no good whatsoever."
Kelley responded with recent statistics published in the *Wall Street Journal*
that showed that "Black people, unfortunately, spend the majority of their
money in White-owned stores." After Miner's insistence that White advertisers didn't want to pay for ad rates that would increase the *Reader*'s circulation to predominantly Black neighborhoods, Rev. Al Sampson, a local
community activist, called in to respond and suggest actions the *Reader*
should take to remedy the situation.

> I'm a chairman of the Million Man March Committee here in Chicago
> and a part of the leadership circle in Chicago, and I would just like to ask
> you to do two things. One, we really need a written apology, inside your
> paper, to hold our racial tensions down in this town. We have enough to
> do to not take this sideshow and make it a main show, this distraction,
> and make it an attraction. The second thing we'd like you to do, several of
> us on the leadership level would like to sit down with you and these White
> advertisers, because in 1996, for you to confess to us that there might be a
> White advertiser where we're putting our Black dollars in, is segregating
> the circulation of information. . . . We feel that . . . you have a corporate
> responsibility, and you have a—a—I guess you would call it White liberal
> responsibility, to stop that kind of racial gerrymandering and creating
> tension within our community while you take corporate dollars. . . . And
> for you to buy into those arrangements as if it's all-right behavior, and not
> illicit behavior, we feel . . . you ought to apologize for your misperception
> and your misconception, and your advertisers' deception.

Unfortunately, this meeting was never realized. Although the larger conversation on WVON certainly brought Miner up to speed with a range of Black opinions and introduced him to many voices in the Black audience, the *Reader* did not significantly change its circulation pattern after the show.

WVON's audience members hold media elites accountable for their representations of Blacks. In the same show, another caller (Mark) took Miner to task for the *Reader*'s past failings in both racial matters and factuality. He began by addressing a caricature of a Black alderwoman, Dorothy Tillman, that was printed in the paper a few years previously and was perceived by many as grotesquely racist.

> Mark: I would say where the real problem lies is with Mr. Miner and his staff's perception of what the community—what Chicago communities are about, whether your advertisers tell you that you—to advertise in Black communities or not, when you put your paper out, it—it gets to the Black community. . . . And the—and some of the things that you have done have been downright—downright offensive, and the—and this is—and you have a history of being offensive. I personally—I mean, the—the—it was the *Reader* where the—where the, uh, cartoon appeared with, uh, with, uh, uh . . .
>
> Miner: Dorothy Tillman?
>
> Mark: Dorothy Tillman.
>
> Kelley: Uh-huh.
>
> Mark: It was—yeah, I mean, and—and if—and that's only the beginning. As an openly gay person, the *Reader* did . . . a cover, uh, story on the first openly gay elected official, a couple of years ago, and they—and they put on the front cover, this guy, and I have nothing, you know, nothing but admiration for the person that they put on the cover, but the truth of the matter is, that [man] was not the first openly gay elected official in the state of Illinois. And the *Reader* has never done anything to try to correct the record, but only to try to rewrite the history and try to make it something else. (Kelley 1996)

One White WVON listener, Steve Sewall, wrote a long letter to the *Reader* in defense of the station, stating:

> If 'VON were a hotbed of Black racism as Miner implies, scores of regular White on-air guests, including [U.S. Senator] Paul Simon and [State Treasurer] Judy Baar Topinka, would have nothing to do with it. . . . More importantly still, most on-air callers quite plainly have bent over backwards to be on equal terms with Whites. (Sewall 1996)

Criticism of White media doesn't stop with Whites. Listeners are also quick to question how Black representatives present Black issues and views to majority White audiences. On another show, a caller (Mickey) felt that sociologist William Julius Wilson had not gone far enough in explaining the links between racism and poverty to the (assumed) White audience.

> Mickey: I heard you last week on NPR *Fresh Air* with Terry Gross, and I heard you last night on WGN with Milt Friedberg [*sic*]. And I truly appreciate your insightfulness and education of those who would think that Blacks are types of people who just want to suck this country dry. However, when you were on with Milt Friedberg, your knowledgeableness was somewhat remiss in that you didn't admonish him that Blacks entered this country far differently than any other group that he kept trying to compare our progress with. . . .
>
> Wilson: I very much appreciate your articulate comments. Let me just say that, you know, you only have so much time on these programs, and what I try to focus on are things that people don't ordinarily think about. What I did emphasize on the Milton Friedman show, for example, . . . is that Blacks are more vulnerable than other groups to a lot of these global economic changes that I'm talking about—because of the effects of historic racism. (Kelley 1996b)

Another listener (Monsong) had questions regarding a PBS documentary that featured Henry Louis Gates, Jr., on class division in the Black community. Guest Lou Turner called attention to institutional connections of featured commentators in the documentary.

> Monsong: . . . I don't know if you saw that documentary that Skip Gates did last night. And they were focusing on, you know, the class-based challenges and problems that the other America presents to us. I just wanted to know, number one, if you saw that, what did you think about what they were talking about. . . .
>
> Professor Turner: Well, I had some trouble with the piece myself. Um, I thought that the point of departure of the talented tenth, Du Bois— and I think people should know that Skip Gates is there at Harvard, and head of the Du Bois Institute there, and was part of this so-called conversation. . . . (Kelley, 1998b)

Both White and Black media figures representing Blacks in the news were subject to criticism from the WVON audience. According to the work of Detine Bowers (1996), it is just as important for Blacks to evaluate how media-picked Black "leaders" and/or "spokespersons" present Black interests and identities as it is to critique the frames and rhetorical situations set up by White media producers. WVON's wide range of guests and talk show format provides a space where Black audience members can talk about and, at times, to powerful media makers. At the same time, their individual opinions may need greater support by larger protest activities to alter the practices of mainstream media that produce these problematic, limited representations of Black life.

Framing Intergroup Tensions and Differences

Peer and Ettema found in their research of mainstream coverage of mayoral elections involving Black candidates that reporters framed the contests as driven by racial strategies. This coverage naturalized the public as "fundamentally constituted by racial and ethnic blocs," obscuring the individuality of the politicians as well as any crossover issues or common interests between groups (Peer and Ettema 1998, 255). Likewise, WVON listeners pick up on divisive frames in the news that polarize groups into eternally warring racial camps. These concerns became most clear in listeners' critiques of mainstream coverage of the Million Man March and the O. J. Simpson trial. One listener (Bob) called in to comment on a *Nightline* conversation that he deemed less than appropriate. He then reflected on the constant repetition of poll results used to represent a racial divide.

> Bob: So to speak, these are a lot of "liberal" people—You remember Ted Koppel, Tammy Bruce from the NOW organization?
>
> Kelley: Oh, she was ridiculous.
>
> Bob: These organizations all came out of the woodwork on July 13, 1994.
>
> Kelley: Yeah. . . .
>
> Bob: And played those tapes. And there's a lot—They think this is only right wing crazy people that are saying all these [racist] things. But if you listen to all the liberal media—they want to convict him. They're afraid of Tammy Bruce....
>
> And one last point, the last point Cliff. Twenty-five percent of Whites consistently supported O. J. Simpson and they support the theory that the evidence was tainted when you look at the polls. So that's about thirty or forty million people.
>
> Kelley: And about twenty-five percent of the Blacks did not support it. You know we can't forget that either.
>
> Bob: Yeah. Absolutely. That's all I wanted to say, Cliff. (Kelley 1995)

Here Bob is emphasizing that not all Whites believed O. J. was guilty. Kelley adds that not all Blacks thought he was innocent.

Listeners also adamantly criticized the media's focus on Nation of Islam leader Minister Louis Farrakhan's statements about Jews during the Million Man March.

> Caller (male): And so when you get all Black men coming under one banner of Louis Farrakhan, the Honorable Louis Farrakhan, he is the only man that I have seen that has stepped out to meet the condition of all Black men in America. . . . And the media is not giving any justi-fication—they're trying to push "Jews against Black people" and that's not true. You can see they're trying to push us together to fight, and you can see—anybody can sit back and see what's going on—they're trying to put us together to fight one another. (*Sisters at Sunrise* 1995)

The caller is criticizing the media's tendency to focus on negatives (Farrakhan's past anti-Semitic statements) as well as portray group politics in terms of ethnic competition and opposition. All morning during the broadcast, men at the Million Man March called in on cell phones and pay phones to relate their experiences and reasons for attending the march, pro-viding an alternative, personalized view of the events at the march for lis-teners. Those who were at home also rang in their support, chiding the media for implying that anyone who supported the march was pro-Farrakhan and therefore anti-Semitic. Listeners felt that the focus on Farrakhan concealed the positive statements and actions of the majority of marchers.

The Necessity of Independent Black Media

WVON listeners consume a wide range of mainstream and Black media texts. Without independent Black commentary and reporting, WVON lis-teners believe they would miss important elements of the story—and in some cases the entire story. While they are sensitive to the demands of the market, they still have high expectations for WVON and other Black-owned news media. Robert Walters, a writer and daily listener, said in an in-terview:

> I would only hope that WVON can maintain the level of independence that it has as a radio station, and remain a station that is in tune to the Black community and responsive to the needs of the Black community— and at the same time maintain the delicate balance with its goals and

purposes as a . . . business. . . . There's so much information that's provided on a daily basis, that, I think, will solve many of the problems . . .
in our community. And it's just a joy to know that we do have this one
outlet at the time of mergers and acquisitions in the, uh, media and big
corporations eating up the small ones. WVON hasn't sold out yet. But if
it happens, I wouldn't be surprised because of all the pressures and struggles that they're faced with as a business.

Another listener, a Black woman who described herself as a forty- to
fifty-five-year-old health services worker,[14] said:

> Well, the topics that they discuss, yes [are not like those discussed on
> other stations]. I don't think anyone else is bold enough to cover a lot of
> things I hear [on WVON] . . . but I tell you what: you don't hear what
> you hear on other stations because I think [WVON] callers are kind of
> bold, only because it is WVON, so I like it.

A twenty-six-year-old trucking company owner wrote in the margins
of his survey that he believes "White talk radio speaks on the behalf of its
race and not necessarily the facts of the matter which stands. Blacks on
Black talk radio deal with all sides of the matter and don't succumb to
White media peer pressure." His thinking reflects the belief that in White-
owned media venues Black reporters and commentators aren't able to give
or do not feel comfortable giving their true opinions and/or analysis of an
issue for fear of backlash.

While some may see his comments as overly pessimistic, the research
cited above supports suspicions that White news workers are not examining their assumptions or creating new frames when they write stories about
Blacks. In the Chicago market, Blacks have many reasons to be wary of the
Tribune's media empire. The paper has a historical reputation for racism
and presently focuses on White suburban readers. As one *Tribune* editor
said:

> You start to get the Northwest suburbs and DuPage and far west DuPage
> suburbs. . . . There are people there who have absolutely no affinity to the
> city of Chicago and they only want to see Chicago news if they can take a
> perverse joy out of saying, "Thank God I don't live there." (DeWerth-
> Pallmeyer 1997, 47)

Most listeners agree that Black media is a necessity in such a marketplace
and support many other Black media firms in addition to WVON.

Recently, the *Chicago Defender*, once known as the most popular Black newspaper in the country, has fallen on hard economic times. After the death of owner John Sengestacke, the paper was put into trust with Northern Trust Bank. This decision angered many Black people who wanted the paper to remain in Black hands. As the Sengestacke family and the bank were deciding how to proceed, WVON cosponsored a community discussion about the paper's future with the Community Media Workshop. The discussion was moderated by Brenda Montgomery, a WVON host, and began as a roundtable discussion. The roundtable participants included Dorothy Leavell, publisher of the *Chicago Crusader*, a small Black neighborhood paper; and Hermene Hartman, publisher of *N'Digo*, a bimonthly "magapaper" which focuses on African-American celebrities and entertainment events.[15]

The panel was in agreement that the *Chicago Defender* should be saved and rebuilt by Blacks. The audience agreed, for the most part, although they were troubled in recent lapses in quality in the paper. However, when one young man asked the panelists, "Why don't all the Black papers get together and have one?" the crowd and the panel responded loudly and negatively. Hartman responded that the Black communities in Chicago had different interests and needs, and her publication (*N'Digo*) only served the niche for human interest and entertainment news. Furthermore, she said, "the more voices there are the stronger our country is," invoking the ideal of a diverse marketplace of ideas. Others in the audience agreed. One woman used the example of a lack of Native-American voices in media partly due to lack of ownership diversity. Another man asked why it was okay for Whites to have many papers throughout the city to reflect their diversity while Blacks had to be satisfied with only one.

Hartman and other industry panelists may have had business motives for advocating multiple Black publications, but I would not be so cynical to attribute their comments only to monetary interests. One major critique of mainstream media is that Whites continually pigeonhole and stereotype Blacks, lumping us all into one (usually urban) category. The triumph of the Black press is its ability to depict wider diversity of Black life and events. Given the variety within the collective, we should not expect one publisher to show it all. This concern is not new. During one heated session of the 1847 National Negro Convention, Frederick Douglass opposed the idea of one national Black press, suggesting that Black communities should "use and support the press you already have; for it is not impossible that by catching at the shadow, you may lose the substance. You already have several newspapers. They are calling on you for support; help them rather than seek for others" (Douglass 1847). The Black audience today seems to agree with Douglass's sentiments, supporting local and national Black media producers like WVON and BET.

Concluding Remarks

Just as William Monroe Trotter got his paper's readers involved in protests against *Birth of a Nation*, so too did WVON create a forum for its listeners to respond to editor Mike Miner about his paper's suspect editorial and commercial practices. However, the latter conversations did not evince a political response. No boycott was called for, and, to my knowledge, no meetings were ever held with *Reader* executives to address racial issues. Although it is admirable that WVON and other Black-owned and -oriented media provide alternative forums, information, and views to their Black audiences, rarely do they motivate audiences to make their own criticisms of White media content, or mobilize them to take direct action. WVON has a good track record of supporting various projects such as encouraging people to vote, to protest police brutality, to write or call politicians, and the like. In terms of responses to mainstream media, though, the direct action taken by the Black audiences of the past seems to dwarf the conversations of the WVON listeners, revealing them as an example of "armchair criticism" that goes nowhere. However, within the sphere created by WVON we can see the potential for empowerment of this audience through the mechanism provided by WVON's talk shows.

Some scholars of Black media are disappointed with the consumptive orientation of Black-owned newspapers and magazines as well as their dependence on corporate advertisers, believing this turn has caused the Black press to "tone down" its criticism of racial injustices (Woseley 1990; Gandy 1998). Indeed, some scholars suggest that Black ownership is not enough to merit the label "Black media." Woseley (1990) writes that Black media must be both owned by African Americans and oriented to Black issues. But how should we define "Black issues" or "the Black audience"?

WVON fits Woseley's definition of Black media: the station is Black-owned and explicitly interested in Black issues and Black progress. The station's ability to retain its explicit focus on Black issues is due in part to its eclectic means of staying financially healthy: a combination of listener subscriptions and advertising makes up for the revenues the station might have received from large corporate advertisers. This mix of resources both insu-

lates WVON from the effects of corporate censorship feared by Black publications dependent on large advertisers and reinforces community ties.
The station also utilizes a looser—and less expensive—format than the
printed press: the talk show. Although some gatekeeping occurs in terms of
host and producer control over topics and callers, the talk show allows all
participants time to air opinions and share information, and conversations
often result in political action.

In the conversations analyzed in this chapter, however, we see that direct involvement beyond talking back to White media producers did not
occur despite listeners' displeasure with the *Reader*. It could be that the
WVON audience places media protests at a lower priority than other political activities. But, as we have seen more recently, from the NAACP-threat-
ened boycott of Hollywood, African Americans will rally against unfair
media representations and practices. Perhaps we, as media scholars dealing
with race issues, should strive to contribute our knowledge of the links between news media exposure and public opinion to Black audiences through
Black-owned media. Awareness of the connection between, say, overrepresentation of Blacks as criminals on television news and White support for
tough-on-crime laws over crime-prevention laws might motivate mobiliza-
tion against media producers who continue to overemphasize Black criminality and ignore other aspects of Black life and politics. We should also
support the development of interactive media forms for African-American
audiences via new media such as the Internet to foster more critical discussion and information sharing among communities. I feel WVON's potential for fostering such activity is strong and should be replicated if possible.

The potential for political success at WVON does not answer the larger
question raised previously: What makes media "Black" and who makes up
"the" Black audience? These questions are not asked to suggest we do not
need Black media. Indeed, Owens (1996) found that as racial oppression
increases, so too does the number of Black newspapers, signaling the importance of independent Black media for Black communities. Because
mainstream media continue to produce racially stereotypical presentations
of Black life, we need alternatives to counteract—and, perhaps, replace—
those mainstream narratives. We also need a larger spectrum of opinions
on current events to broaden and diversify discussions about racialized issues. But are these goals the sole responsibility of so-called Black media?
Are Black media institutions only those exclusively owned and operated by
African Americans? Do they produce and disseminate texts created only by

African-American writers and artists for African-American audiences? Can they target broader audiences or draw from a larger pool of creative resources?

Regardless of how these questions are answered, it is clear that no single genre of Black media can serve or reflect all Black people. In the mid-twentieth century, E. Franklin Frazier considered Black newspapers tools of a misguided Black bourgeoisie. Similarly today, news and lifestyle magazines such as *Essence*, *Ebony*, and *Black Enterprise* are seen as catering to the upper-middle class and ignoring the issues of working-class Blacks (Gandy 1998). But beyond ownership and the middle-class audience, many Black-owned media firms have screened out particular issues due in part to gender and sexuality biases. As Cathy Cohen (1999) reveals in her study of Black responses to the AIDS crisis, the Black press was negligent in their coverage of the AIDS epidemic. The Black press largely ignored the reality of HIV's and AIDS's impact on the "marginal" sectors of the Black community: gays and lesbians, IV drug users, prostitutes. The end result was a painfully delayed attempt to educate all Black audiences about transmittal, prevention, and available resources for HIV and AIDS. As this example shows, media "For Us and By Us" is tempered by the definition of "us" employed by the producers, Black or otherwise. Black magazines' and newspapers' exclusion of "gay" and "drug user" from their audiences and their vision of what are and aren't Black issues has exacted an enormous cost.

So what are "Black media"? As the AIDS example shows, Black-owned media are not immune to problematic politics of identity, just as their White counterparts are not. Tommy Lott (1997) writes that Black ownership or authorship is too restrictive a definition for Black film, because it would exclude many films made by non-Blacks that engage important questions about Black life and identity. Following his lead, I suggest that we be more specific when we speak of Black media so that we reveal the theoretical or political aims of our projects and focus on smaller subsets of the Black audiences. The term "Black media," with no other qualifiers, is too large and vague a label for analysis. Rather, we should speak of categories of Black media that signal issues of ownership and authorship without resorting to a discussion of authenticity. So, there are *Black-owned* media firms that may or may not employ a majority of Black media workers. There are *Black-oriented* media firms that are owned by Whites but target Black audiences that may or may not hire Black media workers to produce content. Then there are the media texts themselves, some created by Blacks about

Blacks, for Black audiences, some created by non-Blacks for Black audiences, and so forth. But Black ownership and/or creative control does not grant immunity from criticism; it merely defines the parameters, just as non-Black authorship does not automatically signal an inauthentic or negative Black media text.

Applying the label "Black" only to those media firms and products controlled by African Americans would reinforce a kind of essentialism that belies both the diversity within Black communities and cultures and also assumes that Blacks are the only people with insight into Black life and culture. Likewise, we should acknowledge that not all Black audience members will read or interpret media texts similarly, or even choose to consume Black-oriented media products. And not all Black media producers will target or attract the same subsets of Black people.

Because the definitions of Blackness are permeable and shifting constantly, the term "Black" should never be used to assume a single media philosophy, similar media structures, or a homogeneous audience. We can never assume that all Black-owned media share a political or editorial agenda, or that they represent all Blacks. But we can hold those Black media—Black-owned or Black-oriented—that claim to serve a Black audience to a high standard and challenge them to broaden their appeal while recognizing that commercial imperatives and fears may keep some Black-owned and/or -oriented firms from engaging in explicitly political acts. We should also support new media ventures and individual producers with promise and who look to follow the examples of past media visionaries who sought to buttress social movements through their publicity organs. Finally, we can urge Black audiences to try to use Black media as vehicles for Black activism, calling on the history of resistance as a guide and inspiration for future action.

Notes

1. For the purposes of this chapter, the term "mainstream media" refers to the large media firms that are majority-owned by Whites and dominate the media marketplace. Examples of such firms are the broadcast networks (e.g., Disney-ABC), most cable channels (e.g., CNN, HBO, Lifetime), Hollywood studios (e.g., Warner Brothers), large radio networks and syndicators, large Internet providers (e.g., AOL), and most of the major metropolitan daily newspapers (e.g., *New York Times*, *Chicago Tribune*, *Los Angeles Times*). Because mainstream media are owned and controlled by

Whites, feature White actors and events dominated by Whites, and concentrate their efforts on capturing affluent White audiences, they are often seen by respondents in my study to be "White media."

2. The letter was supposedly crafted by his advisers to give the impression that the president had not been "bullied by that 'unspeakable fellow' [Trotter]."

3. See, especially, Eric Lott's book *Love and Theft: Blackface Minstrelsy and the American Working Class* for an in-depth analysis of the history and politics of minstrelsy performance. Although many acknowledge that the minstrel tradition and its later incarnations are transformations of Black humor, these appropriations are problematic despite their "authentic" origins because of the differences in audience and emphases.

4. Black comedians freely lampooned the unsophisticated behavior of southern newcomers for segregated Black audiences, who laughed at these reflections of their communities' foibles. However, when this material was taken into White spheres, the joke was often on Blacks. "[T]hrough overexposure, shifts in emphasis, and invidious juxtaposition with 'proper' mainstream values and mores had now changed, for most of White society, to racial slurs confirming the incompetence of Blacks" (Watkins 1994, 229).

5. Bonnie Lou Ross's dissertation (1985) shows that major newspapers rarely covered Black life in the years 1910–1960. Although sharp increases occurred around civil rights events, coverage subsided after such events.

6. This deal was facilitated by liberal FCC policies that aimed to diversify ownership and content on the airwaves.

7. Although WGCI is considered "Black" or "Urban Radio," its ownership is White. The FM station is devoted to successful contemporary Black musical artists, most representing dance music. The AM station plays classic R&B and Motown-style tunes. While there are some attempts to reach out to the community, these are mostly commercially oriented.

8. At the time of this study there were only two music programs, one gospel and one blues. Both of these were on in the early morning hours (2 A.M. to 6 A.M.), whereas talk programming occupied the drive-time and early afternoon hours (6 A.M. to 1 P.M.) and late night (10 P.M. to midnight).

9. In addition to revenues from commercial advertisers, WVON has a subscription drive every year to solicit extra funds from listeners to make up for deficits in commercial ads. According to senior account executive Darryl Shelton, some businesses are unwilling to be linked with what they perceive to be "negative" or "biased" content on WVON. Although he did

not specify which races advertisers thought were being unfairly treated, it is safe to assume that the advertisers mean White people. Oftentimes Shelton has "circumvented going through the advertising agencies [where he] had gotten nowhere" and appealed directly to businesses' CEOs and presidents to convince them that "Black people shop at [their] stores" (Shelton 1998).

10. Although there are few Black-owned talk stations, other Black-owned stations, like KJLH–FM in Los Angeles, have been known to break their regular music programming formats to hold call-in discussions about pressing issues. During the turmoil after the Rodney King verdict, KJLH transformed itself from an R&B station into a lifeline for many listeners, giving information about the unrest, and providing an outlet for outraged listeners to vent and organize responses to the verdict and the violence. For three days the station did not return to its music format (Scott 1993). In a survey of Black-owned radio station managers done in 1992 by Phyllis Johnson and Thomas A. Birk (1993), over half of the respondents estimated that their level of community service activities would increase. The authors also found that Black-owned stations were very willing to be flexible with on-air programming to address community needs, and that "African American radio's partnership with the community is based upon an understanding of the urban family and culture, and its desire to succeed through education, and civic and political empowerment" (Johnson and Birk 1993). WVON, then, is not atypical of other Black-owned radio stations.

11. Two questions concerning the O. J. Simpson trial and the Million Man March were eliminated after pretesting revealed that they were too confusing to respondents.

12. I worked two days a week at the station, and recorded Cliff Kelley's drive-time show, *World Objectives*, each of those days (6 A.M. to 10 A.M.). I also recorded shows that concerned historically important events (e.g., the O. J. Simpson verdict, the Million Man March) and interviews with important national figures (e.g., Jesse Jackson, Dick Gregory, former senator Carol Moseley Braun). I transcribed and listened to the tapes for recurrent themes and controversies, paying attention to vocal emphases, to create better descriptions of the conversations I was transcribing.

13. "Common sense" here does not refer to Gramsci's definition of the term. Rather, as my grandmother would say, it means "horse sense," the sense you get in your gut when you know something isn't right.

14. Some listeners did not want to give me their names. Most were concerned that if their words were published, it might get back to their White employers or colleagues and cause friction at work.

15. My recounting of this panel comes from field notes taken while attending the Community Media Workshop's Noon Media Forum, "Future of the *Chicago Defender*," February 19, 1998 (Columbia College, Chicago, Illinois).

References

Ang, I. (1996). *Living room wars: Rethinking media audiences for a postmodern world*. London and New York: Routledge.

Bills, K. J. (1915). Facts about "Birth of a Nation" play at the Colonial. *Chicago Defender*, September 11.

"Birth of a Nation" ban made permanent. (1919). *New York Age*, March 8.

Bobo, J. (1995). *Black women as cultural readers*. New York: Columbia University Press.

Bobo, L., and J. Kluegel. (1993). Opposition to race-targeting: Self-interest, stratification ideology, or racial attitudes? *American Sociological Review* 58: 443–64.

Bowers, D. L. (1996). When outsiders encounter insiders in speaking: Oppressed collectives on the defensive. *Journal of Black Studies* (Spring): 489–502.

Brown, J., and L. Schulze. (1990). The effects of race, gender, and fandom on audience interpretations of Madonna's music videos. *Journal of Communication* 40: 88–102.

Cohen, C. J. (1999). The boundaries of Blackness: AIDS and the breakdown of Black politics. Chicago: University of Chicago Press.

Community Media Workshop. (1988). *Future of the Chicago Defender*. Noon Media Forum, February 19. Chicago: Columbia College.

Cripps, T. (1969). The reaction of the Negro to the motion picture *Birth of a Nation*. In A. Meier and E. Rudwick, eds., *The making of Black America, Volume II: The Black community in modern America* (pp. 149–64). New York: Athenaeum.

Dates, J., and W. Barlow, eds. (1990). *Split image: African Americans in the media*. Washington, D.C.: Howard University Press.

Dent, G., and M. Wallace, eds. (1992). *Black popular culture*. Seattle: Bay Press.

DeWerth-Pallmeyer, D. (1997). *The audience in the news*. Mahwah, N.J.:

Lawrence Erlbaum Associates.

Dixon, T. (2000). A social cognitive approach to studying racial stereotyping in the mass media. *Perspectives* 6: 60–68.

Dixon, T., and D. Linz. (2000). Overrepresentation and underrepresentation of African Americans and Latinos as lawbreakers on television news. *Journal of communication* 50: 131–54.

Douglass, F. (1847). *Testimony to the committee on a national press.* National Negro Convention.

Ely, M. P. (1991). *Adventures of Amos 'n' Andy: A social history of an American phenomenon.* New York: Free Press.

Entman, R. (1990). Modern racism and the images of Blacks in local television news. *Critical Studies in Mass Communication* 7: 332–45.

———. (1992). Blacks in the news: Television, modern racism, and cultural change. *Journalism Quarterly* 69: 341–61.

Frazier, E. F. (1957). *The Black bourgeoisie.* Glencoe, Ill.: Free Press.

Gandy, O. H. (1998). *Communication and race: A structural perspective.* New York and London: Oxford University Press.

Giddings, P. (1984). *When and where I enter: The impact of Black women on race and sex in America.* New York: Quill–William Morrow.

Gilens, M. (1999). *Why Americans hate welfare: Race, media, and the politics of antipoverty policy.* Chicago: University of Chicago Press.

Gilliam, F. D., and S. Iyengar. (1997). Prime suspects: Script-based reasoning about race and crime. Paper delivered at the annual meeting of the Western Political Science Association, Tucson, Ariz., March.

History making week for Afro-Americans. (1915). *Chicago Defender*, May 22.

Jhally, S., and J. Lewis. (1992). *"Enlightened racism:" The Cosby Show, audiences, and the myth of the American Dream.* Boulder: Westview Press.

Johnson, P., and T. A. Birk. (1993). Black/urban radio's community service mission: Participation in education issues and events. *Equity and Excellence in Education* 26: 41–47.

Kelley, C. (1995). *World objectives*, October 6. Chicago: WVON-AM.

———. (1996). *World objectives*, October 1. Chicago: WVON-AM.

———. (1998a). *World objectives*, February 9. Chicago: WVON-AM.

———. (1998b). *World objectives*, February 11. Chicago: WVON-AM.

Kerlin, R. (1920/1968). *The voice of the Negro, 1919.* New York: Arno Press and the *New York Times.*

Kinder, D. R., and L. M. Sanders, eds. (1996). *Divided by color: Racial poli-

tics and democratic ideals. Chicago: University of Chicago Press.

Lott, E. (1993). *Love and theft: Blackface minstrelsy and the American working class.* New York: Oxford University Press.

Lott, T. (1997). A no-theory theory of Black cinema. In V. Smith, ed., *Representing Blackness: Issues in film and video* (pp. 83–96). New Brunswick, N.J.: Rutgers University Press.

Miner, M. (1996). Hot type: WVON won't take the bait. *Chicago Defender,* September 27, p. 4.

Monroe Trotter and Dr. Fuller acquitted. (1915). *Chicago Defender,* May 8.

Owens, R. (1996). Entering the twenty-first century: Oppression and the African American press. In V. Berry and C. Manning-Miller, eds., *Mediated messages and African American culture: Contemporary issues* (pp. 96–116). Thousand Oaks, Calif.: Sage.

Palmer, Lu. (1995). Personal interview, March 8.

Peer, L., and J. Ettema. (1998). The mayor's race: Campaign coverage and the discourse of race in America's largest cities. *Critical Studies in Mass Communication* 15: 255–78.

Riggs, M. (1991). *Color Adjustment* [film]. San Francisco: California Newsreel.

Ross, B. L. (1985). Interpretations of the Black civil rights movement in the Black and White press. Unpublished Ph.D. diss., University of California, Irvine.

Ross, K. (1997). Two-tone telly: Black minority audiences and British television. *Communications* 22: 93–107.

Ruffin, M. (1991). Blacks talk on radio. *N'DIGO/Chicago Sun-Times Supplement,* May.

Scott, M. (1993). Can Black radio survive an industry shakeout? *Black Enterprise* (June): 254–60.

Sewall, S. (1996). Defending WVON. *The Reader,* October 4, p. 4.

Shelton, D. (1998). Personal interview, January 14.

Sisters at sunrise. (1995). Chicago: WVON, October 16.

Smith, V. (1997). Introduction. In V. Smith, ed., *Representing Blackness: Issues in film and video* (pp. 1–12). New Brunswick, N.J.: Rutgers University Press.

Spann-Cooper, M. (1996). Personal interview, October 18.

Squires, C. (1999). Searching Black voices in the Black public sphere: An alternative approach to the analysis of public spheres. Unpublished Ph.D. diss., Northwestern University.

———. (2000). Black talk radio: Defining community needs and identity. *Harvard International Journal of Press/Politics* 5: 2.

The death of a movie. (1915). *Chicago Defender*, May 1.

Time to fight bad movies is before they are shown. (1915). *Chicago Defender*, May 22.

To our patrons. (1827). *Freedom's Journal*, March 16, p. 1.

Valentino, N. (1999). Crime news and the priming of racial attitudes during evaluations of the president. *Public Opinion Quarterly* 63: 293–321.

Watkins, M. (1994). *On the real side: Laughing, lying and signifying, the underground tradition of African American humor that transformed America, from slavery to Richard Pryor.* New York: Touchstone.

Wells, I. B. (1892/1990). Preface to *Southern horrors: Lynch law in all its phases.* Salem, New Hampshire: Ayer Company Publishers.

———. (1909/1992). Lynching, our national crime. Speech given at the NAACP founding conference, 1909. Reprinted in R. J. Walker, ed., *The rhetoric of struggle: Public address by African American women.* New York: Garland.

West, C. (1993). *Race matters.* Boston: Beacon Press.

Wilson, C. II. (1991). *Black journalists in paradox: Historical perspectives and current dilemmas.* New York: Greenwood.

World to be "Americanized" by such films as "Birth of a Nation." (1919). *New York Age*, June 7.

Woseley, R. E. (1990). *The Black press, U.S.A.* Ames: Iowa State University Press.

4

Media Messages, Self-Identity, and Race Relations

Reader Evaluations of Newsmagazine Coverage

of the Million Man March

Debbie A. Owens

Introduction

During the latter part of the twentieth century, several highly publicized events propelled the horrors of racial conflict to the forefront of the American consciousness. We were bombarded by racially charged incidents that reflected an ugly side of our country's history and forced many of us to seriously contemplate where we stood on issues of race and ethnicity. For instance, police in New York faced charges in the assaults and shootings of unarmed Black men. An African-American man was tied to a truck and dragged to his death by two White men in Texas. State highway patrol officers were investigated for practicing racial profiling and targeting Black motorists. Airport customs officials were accused of disproportionately subjecting Black women travelers to invasive body searches for illegal drugs. In 1993 the nation was horrified by riotous civil disorders following the assault trial of Los Angeles police officers who had been videotaped violently beating motorist Rodney King. The National Association for the Advancement of Colored People waged an economic boycott against South Carolina to protest the prominent display of the Confederate flag at its state house. In 1995 the Million Man March and Day of Atonement, Absence, and Responsibility brought throngs of participants to Washington, D.C. These and other events have served as constant reminders to Americans of the precarious state of race relations in this country.

African-American Identity and the March

African Americans continually engage in a struggle for empowerment at all levels of society. This struggle is essential to African-American identity in a country that has historically oppressed them in one way or another. Consequently, "for African Americans, the country of oppression and the country of liberation are the same country" (Hertzberg and Gates 1996, 10). The complexities of oppression influence every aspect of African-American existence in our society. Economically, many African Americans labor tirelessly as the gap widens between a seemingly prosperous middle class and a growing disenfranchised underclass largely populating the inner cities. Politically, their voices have been all but silenced in a system where one party is often accused of ignoring Black voters while the other party vilifies them as threats to more conservative constituents. Judicially, our court system has been scrutinized for its treatment of Black offenders compared to that of White offenders who commit equal or more serious crimes. Socially, challenges to affirmative-action policies have curtailed educational and employment opportunities. Also, incidents of racial discrimination in every sector threaten to reverse many hard-won gains of the previous century.

Many of these empowerment issues are ingrained in the African-American consciousness. As noted by the planners of the 1995 Million Man March and Day of Atonement, Absence, and Responsibility, the status of African-American men in this country remains an issue of particular concern. Central to the African-American man's identity is his ability to support himself and his family. Also, for many African Americans, cultural identity is closely aligned with one's sense of spirituality, and cultural survival is deeply rooted in the church. Historically, involvement in religious activities has helped many individuals escape bondage, both literally and spiritually, in that their religious ties have allowed them to deal with living and working in a bigoted and racist society. To this extent, the church has provided opportunities for individuals to assume leadership roles, particularly within the African-American community.

In the mission statement for the march, organizers noted the timeliness of the event in the wake of "increasing racism, attacks on hard won gains, and continually deteriorating conditions for the poor and vulnerable and thus an urgent time for transformative and progressive leadership" (Karenga 1995, 4). They stated that African-American men could assume a leadership role without denying or minimizing the equal rights, role, or responsibilities of African-American women. According to Black Nationalist leader Maulana Karenga, the statement's primary author, the march was a declaration of the social and spiritual resolve of Black men, and a reaffirmation of Blacks' self-understanding as a people. In terms of Black identity, the march was considered "a galvanizing and mobilizing process to raise consciousness, cultivate commitment and lay the groundwork for increased positive social, political, and economic activity (Karenga 1995, 4). Organizers also considered the march as a platform from which to challenge members of the African-American community, the American government, and business corporations to practice responsibility in their respective venues. Such challenges centered around three basic themes: atonement, reconciliation, and responsibility.

A parallel activity to the Million Man March was the Day of Absence. African Americans were advised to stay home from school, work, businesses, and other commercially run places. They were advised to meditate, hold teach-ins, or facilitate some other group activity that included family and friends. They were encouraged to participate in voter-registration drives and contribute to the Economic Development Fund, which provided financial support for the march and subsequent community-based activities. Organizers proposed several projects that would extend beyond the demonstration. One such proposal was that African Americans keep a critical watch on the media. March planners recognized the significance of media organizations and the extent to which media images of African Americans influenced both their self-identity and their cultural identity in this country. Organizers stressed the need to continue reinforcing "efforts to reduce and eliminate negative media approaches and portrayals of Black life and culture; to organize a sustained and effective support for positive models, messages and works; to achieve adequate and dignified representation of Blacks in various media and various positions in media; to expand support for and development of independent Black media; and to challenge successful and notable African Americans in various media to support all these efforts" (Karenga 1995, 10).

Activities leading up to the day of the march were designed to rally the African-American community, particularly its men, to embrace the event as a celebration of their cultural values and a reaffirmation of the men's commitment to their families. Yet, as one journalist noted, "While atonement might be a great idea if it were only for the organizing committee, dragging a million Black men with them risks buying into the stereotypification of criminality and deviance as exclusively a 'Black male thing—and a pathological thing at that" (Williams 1995, 493). The prospect of a million Black men descending upon the nation's capital was fraught with controversy, centering mainly on Nation of Islam leader Minister Louis Farrakhan, who emerged as the self-proclaimed spokesperson for the event. Consequently, some critics denounced it as a spectacle, merely conceived to provide a forum for the minister's vitriolic and racially explosive rhetoric. Despite public denunciations by a cadre of political, religious, academic, and civic leaders, on October 16, 1995, throngs of marchers filled the Independence Mall in Washington, D.C. Major news organizations from around the globe covered the event, portions of which were broadcast live on cable news channels. Under the watchful eyes of social and cultural observers, political pundits and media producers, participants in the march joined in a public "communion" focused on atoning for their familial and spiritual transgressions, whether real or imagined. In its aftermath, several African-American leaders deemed the march as an event that was more symbolic than political and thus "fatally flawed" because it had no connection to public policy leaders (Gates 1996).

The Legacy of Negative Media Images

The 1995 Million Man March and Day of Atonement, Absence, and Responsibility provided journalists a sufficient opportunity to objectively "catalog" numerous images of African-American people and examine the impact of the march. Yet, despite the journalistic "code of objectivity," my analyses of mainstream newsmagazines revealed that numerous reports tended to be negatively biased because, among other things, many journalists were unable to effectively separate the march from Farrakhan, who is often perceived as a negative force in the Black community (Owens 1997, 1999). Historically, members of the mainstream media have been criticized for what is often viewed by African Americans as negative coverage of their community. Media coverage has ranged from that in which Blacks were "invisible" to coverage which perpetuated either distorted or stereotypical images of Blacks. Members of the Kerner Commission (1968/1998) admonished the news media to report more accurately on issues affecting the Black community and on race relations in this country. In the more than three decades since the report, researchers have observed how the media's relationship with African Americans has reversed from one of alliance to alienation (Drummond, 1990). News media coverage no longer reflects the civil rights storyline of the 1950s and mid-1960s that "ennobled the cause of the Negro." African Americans have become frustrated over their attempts to maintain their identities in the face of the "constant reminder that Blacks are being fit conveniently into a terrible new storyline: Black pathology" (Drummond 1990, 5). Media stories reinforce the impression that drugs, crime, violence, homelessness, and poverty are mostly a Black problem. African Americans feel a sense of alienation, which is partly because of the way in which the media cover the Black community and how Blacks see themselves (Drummond 1990). Media coverage reflects cultural myths embedded in media institutions (Campbell 1995). Such myths influence societal and cultural consciousness, which is in turn derived from media coverage of events and issues. Entrenched in stereotypical media images, Blacks wage a constant battle within themselves to counter the damage (Dates and Barlow 1994; Owens 1999, 38). Furthermore, researchers have found that large segments of the African-American population see themselves as having little influence on the media and consider the media as biased against them (Becker, Kosicki, and Jones 1992).

There is no doubt that journalists play a significant role in establishing the discourse about race and ethnic community affairs (Van Dijk 1991). The reports or "narratives" that journalists construct establish ready-made models through which to convey messages to media consumers (Carey 1989). Embedded in these narrative models are journalists' own cultural and ideological interpretations of news about events affecting African Americans. While recent news coverage has become more inclusive of racial and ethnic minorities, critical textual analyses of news articles have revealed that journalists tend to fall short of providing balanced, unbiased coverage of all groups of people. The press agenda remains suspect as various social and cultural themes emphasized by reporters perpetuate an inherently negative perspective of the African-American community (Owens 1997, 1999).

Representations in Newsmagazines

The analyses presented in this study are part of a broader exploration of print media coverage of the 1995 Million Man March and the construction of social reality in the African-American community. In the current project, I examine African-American readers' evaluations of mainstream news-magazine articles written about the march.

Previous research suggests that weekly newsmagazines "serve as a kind of news digest" offering a "set of visual highlights that reiterate news images of each week's events"(Griffin and Lee 1995, 814). The impact of news-magazines on the landscape of the nation's consciousness may rival that of either newspapers or television. Photographic displays are essential to the newsmagazine. The dramatic appeal of pictures is enhanced by the attention photojournalists give to elements of shot composition and photographic techniques such as framing, the use of filters, and lighting. These techniques also transmit a particular perspective on the part of the photographer's and/or the editor's bias about the subject. Thus, the resulting images are not "direct unmediated transcripts of the real world, as we have been encouraged to view them" (Schwartz 1992, 95). In the same manner, writers and editors can provide insight into the apparent meaning of an event while conveying a secondary (or interpretive) meaning of their own. Journalists achieve this "meaning construction" through strategic use of textual and literary elements such as comparisons and contrasts, wordplay, use of rhetorical questions, or emphasis on discrepancies or disparities associated with an event (Carey 1989; Lule 1993; Gitlin 1980). Journalists may employ these techniques throughout the body of an article as well as in the text of headlines and captions (or cutlines) (Van Dijk 1991; Owens 1999, 35, 36, and 44).

My analyses sought to address how African-American readers evaluated mainstream newsmagazine articles written about the 1995 Million Man March. To what extent were they able to recognize specific literary or narrative techniques used by journalists in constructing news stories? Did readers perceive journalistic reports to be accurate representations of the event that gave voice to the Black community? Did they consider the reports to be representative of the march in terms of its overall significance in the Black community? How did readers' evaluations reflect both their own sense of identity and their cultural association with the African-American community? And ultimately, what did readers think about the media's coverage of racial issues and the media's effect on race relations in America?

Methodology of the Study

The 113 African-American participants in this study included 67 men and 46 women, ages eighteen to eighty-eight. Education levels ranged from those who attended high school to those who had attained graduate and professional degrees. Annual incomes ranged from below $5,000 to above $100,000. The responses were collected between 1997 and 1999 from individuals in fourteen northeastern, midwestern, and southeastern states. Participants were asked to indicate whether they supported the march, attended the march, or knew someone who attended the event.

Participants were asked to view a total of fourteen items, seven photographs of the march and those same seven with accompanying captions and/or text. Picture number one came from the October 30, 1995, issue of *Newsweek*. It was a half-page photograph of two young men wearing suits and bow ties. In the background was the Capitol building, but it was out of focus. The headline read: "Battling for Souls." The subhead was "As more blacks warm to Islam's emphasis on order, Protestant leaders scramble to make their traditional churches more appealing to young men." Picture number two came from the October 30, 1995, issue of *U.S. News and World Report*. It was also a half-page photograph. In this one, three men are shown standing, holding hands, and praying with the Capitol building, a group of police, and a member of the Fruits-of-Islam in the background. The caption reads: "A spiritual communing. Many of the men on the Washington Mall bowed their heads in prayer and held hands during the extended rally." A smaller picture inset shows Minister Farrakhan at a microphone, flanked by members of the Fruits-of-Islam. Its caption reads: "Farrakhan. Vaulted to the top ranks of black leaders." Picture number three is from the October 30, 1995, issue of *Time*. It is a half-page photograph of a boxer wearing a T-shirt from the march and leaning against the ropes of a boxing ring at the gym where he practices. The caption reads "Contention" and is accompanied by a graphic inset of text: "I've seen a lot of death around me. The fighting has got to stop. It's time for the killing to stop." A picture inset shows autoworkers posed outside their union offices. It is accompanied by the caption "Revival." Picture number four is from *U.S. News and World Report*'s October 16, 1995, issue. It is a photograph of a group of men and women in church, holding hands in prayer with banners supporting the march behind them. The caption reads: "Supporters. This service at Chicago's Park Manor Christian Church raised more than $4,000." A picture inset shows a man selling a newspaper to a woman with a recruitment poster for the March pasted on a metal bin. Caption: "Recruiting. Talking up the March in Washington, D.C." Picture number five is from *Time*'s October 30, 1995, issue. It is a half-page photograph of three generations of fathers and sons, dressed in suits, staring stoically into the camera, with a row of well-maintained houses in the background. "Tradition" is the caption, along with the graphic inset, "I went to school on PTA night. If there was no homework, I'd get on the phone and ask why." Picture number six comes from the October 30, 1995, issue of *Newsweek*. It shows Minister Louis Farrakhan at a podium, his partially closed hands extended in front of him, his eyes closed. He is flanked by members of the Nation of Islam. In a second frame, we see his open hands extended upward and a NOI member in shadow. The headline reads: "An Angry Charmer." The subhead states, "Louis Farrakhan has always been a man of many faces. Now the calypso singer turned separatist wants to move into the mainstream of American politics. Even blacks are divided about his appeal—but they're listening." Picture seven is from the October 30, 1995, issue of *U.S. News and World Report*. It is a full-page photograph of a small boy sitting on the shoulders of a man standing among several other men. All are looking at something in the distance. Caption: "Black males formed the biggest civil rights demonstration ever. It was a peaceful event, with only one disorderly conduct arrest."

Respondents first viewed the seven photographs devoid of any identifying text or labels (headlines, captions, subheadings, stories, bylines, and magazine affiliations). The participants then viewed the same photographs as they had originally appeared with accompanying text and labels. Readers were asked to determine whether each of the fourteen items was either positive, negative, or neutral. Also, they were encouraged to elaborate on their decisions and to describe their impressions of the articles. The majority (77 percent) of these participants indicated that they had encountered media bias against African Americans either frequently or on a daily basis. And the majority (84 percent) said they were either "sometimes" satisfied or satisfied "only a few times" with the overall media coverage of issues relating to African Americans.

Findings Based on Emergent Themes

Five categories emerged from readers' evaluations of the articles. These categories reflected both the readers' self-identities and their cultural identities within the African-American community. The categories encompassed the following dominant themes and issues: empowerment versus disenfranchisement, demystification versus stereotypical images, family values versus dysfunction, spirituality, or religion, and reactions to Minister Farrakhan.

Individual interpretations of the photographs and text materials revealed that readers were critically aware of the perilous state of American race relations as represented by media accounts. Often, readers made direct mention of specific instances in which media accounts appeared to be negatively biased either against the march or against the African-American community. They recognized and labeled what they perceived as incongruities or "disconnects" between main text materials (e.g., headlines, captions) and photographs. In some cases, after reading entire articles, respondents pointed out further inconsistencies in the stories themselves. Here, six categories emerged, encompassing the following dominant themes and issues: (1) schisms or conflicts; (2) deviance or violence; (3) social problems; (4) powerlessness or disenfranchisement; (5) skewed media accounts of the event; and (6) balanced media accounts of the event.

Readers were diverse in their attitudes about the march, Minister Farrakhan, race issues, and mass media coverage of the African-American community. The majority of the newsmagazine photographs evoked comments from respondents that indicated how they related to the media portrayals and how the images reflected their culture. This was evidenced by the varied themes that emerged from their responses to the pictures and texts. In some instances, respondents attempted to "frame" or "situate" the images and texts on a broader social, political, or cultural level. In essence, they attempted to theorize about media-related issues in the context of African Americans and race relations in this country. The comments below provide insight into readers' evaluations of the articles.

Self-Identity and the African-American Community

There were many instances in which readers charged that journalists tended to perpetuate the myth of violence in African-American culture. This is also perhaps the most revealing aspect of how readers perceived themselves. Ironically, as they interpreted several of the uncaptioned photographs, they referenced situations fraught with social problems, crime, or other crises. Despite their attempts to temper the impact of negative media messages, the readers' own comments conjured up images of disruptive social misfits who threatened the normative balance of mainstream society. "The images evoke anger. The story appears to be about parental responsibility and accountability" (R. N., age thirty-three, a man from Ohio). "The image appears to be a very sad occasion, either a funeral or wake. Evidently, another Black man killed" (K. B., age thirty-four, a woman from North Carolina).

"The image looks sad. Anytime the only route out of poverty is beating someone else, or get beat, [it is] the realization that perhaps we are our own worst enemy. In effect, enough is enough" (anonymous thirty-eight-year-old man from Ohio). "The man is serious, standing in the ring, ready to do battle in the place where battles are expected to occur—the boxing ring! The message comes from a man who has seen abuse in the ring, if we consider some of the stories we've heard. The majority of killing beyond the ring puts Black males in a position where they are often abused" (M. F., age sixty-two, a woman from D.C.).

Readers turned a jaundiced eye on themselves by focusing on the sense of powerlessness and economic or political disenfranchisement among African Americans. Others criticized Black activists and politicians for their lack of effective leadership. "Heads are hung low. [It] makes the government look really powerful and Black people insignificant or small. Also, it reinforces that Black people will always be in pain as long as Whites are in power" (B. S., age twenty-four, a man from Ohio). "They are searching for order among chaotic times; self-respect, independence, love for fellow man, brotherhood, family" (M. W., age thirty-seven, a man from Georgia). "Yes, a charmer. But we the people of color have been led astray by many charmers, religiously, educationally, and politically" (C. O., age thirty-six, a woman from New York). "The term 'charmer' suggests that [someone] is attempting manipulation; 'many faces' suggests wavering positions, accommodation, politicians, et cetera" (S. W., age thirty, a woman from Ohio).

Empowerment, either as a group or on an individual basis, is central to one's sense of accomplishment and positive identity. Several of the comments focused on political, economic, or social gains within the African-American community, or they criticized political leaders. Some readers sought to embrace the legacy of Black individual achievement while others recognized the role of economics as a source of empowerment in this country. "The image strikes a chord that is correct both historically and socially. The blurred image of the Capitol built by a Black man in the past— Benjamin Banneker—and the clear focus of the future of Black men" (S. O., age thirty-seven, a man from North Carolina). "It's always positive to note that Black people are willing to finance our struggle; raising money from within the community provides independence" (M. R., age forty-six, a man from Ohio). "Seeing two Black men with their heads held up high, with expressions of confidence . . . despite living in a racist world, is encouraging and positive" (P. S., age thirty-two, a man from Ohio).

Some readers attempted to demystify stereotypes of African-American men. They focused on positive portrayals in which the men expressed self-pride and attempted to effect change despite living in hostile surroundings. "It captures the mood of the men—neat, solemn, disciplined, respect, no hate or disrespect, and no negative conduct" (W. M., age sixty-nine, a man from North Carolina). "Good picture of Black males on a mission—a serious one . . . because they were participating in the raising of male children in a hostile environment" (E. S., age fifty-eight, a woman from Michigan). "It shows me that a large group of Black men can come together in peace, with the goal of reconciliation of their differences and redevotion to God" (D. P., age twenty-four, a man from Ohio). "Whenever I see Blacks I think it positive, though my feelings have proven to be the minority" (D. N., age twenty-eight, a man from North Carolina).

Other comments related to the readers' own foundation of core family values. They focused on issues of responsibility, support and love of children, male/female unity, positive role models, and an emphasis on education in the African-American community. "[I'm] proud to see a grandfather with two generations 'raising up' and developing the growth of the younger males" (C. M., age forty-six, a man from Ohio). "These fathers are interested in the young boys' education and are active and supportive of them" (N. M., age twenty-six, a woman from Ohio). "More parents need to be more involved in schoolwork because if parents show an interest, maybe it will rub off on the children" (K. B., age thirty-four, a woman from North Carolina). "This meeting was well organized [and] a message to all fathers to help their sons and each other" (R. B., age eighty-eight, a man from Pennsylvania).

In their comments about religious involvement, readers appreciated the sense of spirituality among African Americans and their connectedness to a higher entity. While some readers reflected upon the significance of the church, others questioned its role in the African-American community: "The church has in some way let them down" (B. S., age thirty-six, a man from Georgia). Also, "[it's] saying basically Christians are not doing much of anything for our young Black men" (T. K., age thirty-one, a man from Georgia. "That's our goal to battle for souls; so it's not [an issue] for debate as to its power"(W. H., age twenty-eight, a man from Georgia). "Religion should not be a battle for anyone's soul; it's what you feel in your heart" (L. A., age thirty, a woman from North Carolina). "This picture is a positive image because the people [are] bowing and speaking to someone; the message is still the same, we pray to get results no matter who we pray with" (K. B., age fifty-four, a woman from Ohio). "It shows positive images of Christians and Muslims, working together toward the same goal. It also shows that many Black women supported the march" (M. R., age forty-six, a man from Ohio). "There is a true message that we must atone for our sins as a people and take the moral high road; that is a good thing" (S. O., age thirty-seven, a man from North Carolina).

Photographs of Minister Louis Farrakhan evoked comments from readers who reacted solely to his presence in terms of his racial rhetoric and political posturing. "The peaceful, prayerful young men are canceled out by media assertion that Farrakhan is a top Black leader, while he is not" (G. L., age fifty-eight, a woman from Georgia). "Because of the 'whom' in the picture, most times I have a neutral stance on Farrakhan . . . many Blacks are divided over him" (T. S., age forty-one, a woman from Ohio). "Mr. Farrakhan's rhetoric as perceived by both Blacks and Whites provides a balanced point of division versus unity in what the march was all about" (J. W., age fifty-nine, a man from California). "If you have followed the views of Farrakhan, even just a little bit, he feels we have a lot to be angry about" (Y. B., age thirty, a woman from North Carolina).

Media Coverage of Race Relations in America

When readers addressed the issue of media coverage, they noted how journalists too often focused on racial strife between Blacks and Whites as well as the media's overemphasis on internal antagonisms within the African-American community. Understandably, no community should be portrayed as being monolithic in terms of the beliefs and attitudes of its citizens. Yet these readers expressed concerns that the media did not accurately portray what the march represented as far as overall experiences among African Americans. "The title 'Battling for Souls' starts with a warrior tone . . . a polarization of Protestant-Christian numbers being used to attack the appeal of Islam" (S. O., age thirty-seven, a man from North Carolina). "It gives a false impression of the march and its purpose; an attempt to create a conflict and gap among Black Americans" (W. M., age sixty-nine, a man from North Carolina). "Neither Farrakhan nor religion was the focus of the march; for this day the cause was the same for all—nothing can separate the brothers" (C. B, age forty-one, a man from New York).

A large proportion of comments fell under the category of skewed media accounts, particularly in regards to the misrepresentation of African

Americans. It was here that journalistic credibility came into question. Readers scrutinized what they considered to be negative editorial commentary, or rhetorical wordplay used by journalists. They questioned the use of photographic techniques such as framing, and the incongruity between dominant visual elements and text. For instance, while N. W., a twenty-three-year-old New York woman, did not support the march, she was critical of how the media misrepresented African Americans and perhaps encouraged tense racial relations in this country:

> [The picture is] a very positive image of brothers making a better future for our young boys. In a nutshell [the caption] shows that White America really believes that Blacks are so violent. The caption seems to [indicate] surprise that the whole event was peaceful, . . . they used it with a great and peaceful picture to make such negative remarks. . . . It's sad but true what they think we as a people are. It's a narrow, ignorant view . . . White America has about Black America.

Other readers also noted that journalists may have overemphasized conflicts associated with either the march or the African-American community. Generally, items in this category were assessed as negative. "This headline makes it seem as though Black Christians and Black Moslems are divided and are fighting with each other for young Black male membership; I don't believe this is the case" (P. S., age thirty-two, a man from Ohio). "There are untruths and generalized statements; also the ones that are true are misleading and deceptive; on the surface it looks good but underneath it is a deadly serpent" (P. J., age forty-six, a man from Georgia). "This message makes it seem like Islam is a fad that is just surfacing in America, as though it were a religion to go to when you are not accepted anywhere else" (A. D., age eighteen, a woman from New York). "The author makes it seem as though Islam is not as strong or as good as Christianity. Both are building strong Black men" (J. W., age twenty, a man from North Carolina). "The man appears angry and ready to fight. Could he mean that the march inspired him to commit more of the same? Why is he pictured in his boxing gear, saying these words?" (anonymous, age thirty-two, Ohio man who attended the march). "Black economic power is a good thing, but that's not the emphasis here. The emphasis is financial, in the caption, where it should be spiritual" (P. S., age thirty-two, a man from Ohio).

Comments further evidenced the readers' awareness of the incongruities between photographs and graphics, photographs and captions, and headlines and the contexts of the articles they accompanied. "The caption and picture reflect opposites for me. It does, however, get my attention and prompt me to check the article out" (M. W., age fifty-three, a woman from Ohio). "[The picture] illustrates and reflects sincerity and humbleness; [the headline] reeks of sarcasm; I don't like it" (M. P., age forty-one, a woman from Ohio). "He seems to be appealing to the people to make a change; they [media] feel that some of the people are divided about his message" (C. R., age forty-four, a man from South Carolina). "Farrakhan is usually pictured pointing his finger, yelling, frowning, or scowling. Here, he seems to be in a passionate prayer. No one would have guessed he was angry!" (S. W., age thirty, a woman from Ohio). "Angry is not what I saw when I saw this picture; White media only see what they want to believe" (R. H., age twenty-eight, a man from Ohio). "The closed eyes and clenched hands suggest that Farrakhan is reaching deep into his soul for the words of his message. The words describe an angry, confused, insincere individual" (M. D., age forty-seven, a woman from Georgia). "With only one disorderly conduct arrest, it sounds like we can't do anything without an arrest of some sort. In fact, only one arrest is good" (T. J., age twenty-three, a man from Maryland). "Why must they [media] try to put the disorderly conduct arrest in there? I'm sure it happened in some other demonstrations and they didn't mention it [then]" (S. J., age twenty, a woman from New Jersey). "It is both positive to see us united for a cause, but negative [in] that they expected to have more violence because there were so many Black men" (Y. W., age forty-six, a woman from New York). "It was an event for Black males–we didn't need to be concerned with disorderly conduct because there was none that I heard of" (G. S., age fifty-four, a woman from Ohio). Similarly, J. J., age twenty-four, a woman from Iowa, stated, "It's giving credit to the Million Man March as the biggest civil rights demonstration ever and highlighting its nonviolence and spiritual nature. Also, highlighting the one arrest—why was it necessary?"

Even when readers credited the media for reporting balanced, presumably nonbiased accounts of the march, they noted some instances in which photographic representations of African Americans appeared to be framed to support the stereotypes of African Americans as potentially disruptive or violent people. "Police are in the background looking for violence to erupt even though the men are praying and holding hands" (E. B., age twenty-seven, a woman from North Carolina). "Praying men! In spite of onlooking police officers, they have freedom of worship; there is public unity"(D. P., age forty-three, a man from Ohio). "The close-up shot of the

Black men in prayer and the force of authority in the background; the Capitol shown in the background overshadows everyone and looks larger than life" (B. S., age twenty-four, a man from Ohio). "I see unity, then I see security [personnel], and in a place of unity, security should not be a factor" (R. G., age forty, a man from Ohio).

Conclusions and Implications

Ultimately, these reader evaluations have provided a degree of insight into how some African Americans interpret media messages with respect to self-identity and cultural awareness. Readers were able to recognize and label inconsistencies within the newsmagazine articles. They related these incongruities to troubling "disconnects" between media portrayals of African Americans and what actually happens in their communities. Furthermore, as a result of their examinations of newsmagazine photographs and the accompanying texts, readers recognized various journalistic techniques used to construct meaning about the 1995 Million Man March and to discuss its impact on both the African-American community and race relations in America. The comments from readers were not merely reflective of their subjective viewpoints. Many of them also addressed broader issues and challenged stereotypes and "cultural myths" embedded in the articles (Campbell 1995); and many of their responses indicated attempts to counter the damage exacted by such myths (Dates and Barlow 1994). Readers also referred to the storyline of "Black pathology," which, as suggested by Drummond (1990), alienates African Americans from the larger society. Consider these evaluations in conjunction with the fact that the overwhelming majority of readers indicated they frequently encountered media bias against African Americans and were only occasionally satisfied with the overall media coverage of issues relating to the African-American community. People want to read and view news media reports that are comprehensive yet truly representative of their experiences. When journalists' reports fall short of this expectation, it raises the question of their credibility, or lack thereof, especially among those from communities traditionally marginalized by the mainstream media. This should concern all media consumers who expect no less than accurate, complete accounts of events and issues that have a significant impact on society. Coverage of the 1995 Million Man March by the three mainstream newsmagazines examined here leaves much to be desired in terms of portrayals of the African-American community and contributions to race relations in this country.

References

Becker, L., G. Kosicki, and F. Jones. (1992). Racial differences in evaluations of the mass media. *Journalism Quarterly* 69: 124–34.

Campbell, C. (1995). *Race, myth and the news.* California: Sage.

Carey, J. (1989). *Communication as culture: Essays on media and society.* Boston: Unwin Press.

Dates, J. L., and W. Barlow, eds. (1994). *Split image: African Americans in the mass media.* 2d ed. Washington, D.C.: Howard University Press.

Drummond, W. (1990). About face from alliance to alienation: Blacks and the news media. *American Enterprise* 1: 2–29.

Finenman, H., and V. Smith. (1995). An angry charmer. *Newsweek,* October 30, p. 32.

Gates, H. L. (1995/1996). How Black academics viewed the Million Man March. *Journal of Blacks in Higher Education* (winter): 59–63.

———. (1996). After the revolution. *The New Yorker,* April 29 and May 6, pp. 116–31.

Gitlin, T. (1980). *The whole world is watching.* Berkeley: University of California Press.

Griffin, M., J. and Lee. (1995). Picturing the Gulf War: Constructing an image of war in *Time, Newsweek,* and *U.S. News and World Report. Journalism and Mass Communication Quarterly* 72: 813–25.

Hertzberg, H., and H. L. Gates. (1996). The African-American century. *The New Yorker,* April 29 and May 6, pp. 9–10.

Karenga, M. (1995). The Million Man March/Day of Absence mission statement. *The Black Scholar* 25: 2–11.

Kerner Commission Report (1968/1998). *The national advisory commission on civil disorders.* Washington, D.C.: U.S. Government Printing Office, pp. 362–88.

Lule, J. (1993). News strategies and the death of Huey Newton. *Journalism Quarterly* 70: 287–99.

Minerbrook, S. (1995). Mission on the mall: Save the children. *U.S. News and World Report,* October 30, pp. 11, 34.

Owens, D. A. (1997). A comparative analysis of news magazine photo coverage of the Million Man March. Paper presented at the Annual Research Association of Minority Professors Conference, Houston, Texas, February.

———. (1999). Images of the Million Man March: A comparative analysis of news magazine photo coverage. *Journal of Communication and Minority Issues* 5: 33–49.

Power, C., and A. Samuels. (1995). Battling for souls. *Newsweek*, October 30, p. 46.

Recruiting. (1995). *U.S. News and World Report*, October 16, p. 59.

Schwartz, D. (1992). To tell the truth: Codes of objectivity in photojournalism. *Communication* 13: 95–109.

Smolowe, J. (1995). Marching home. *Time*, October 30, pp. 46, 50.

Supporters. (1995). *U.S. News and World Report*, October 16, p. 59.

Van Dijk, T. A. (1991). *Racism and the press*. New York: Routledge.

Williams, P. (1995). The million man atonement: Different drummer please, marchers! *The Nation*, October 30, 493–94.

! 5

House Negro versus Field Negro

The Inscribed Image of Race in Television News

Representations of African-American Identity

Jennifer F. Wood

> *I don't think that Black people fit anywhere in the media, either we are*
> *the perfect imagery of slavery—the good Black or the bad Black—or either*
> *the Uncle Tom or the Nat Turner. That's it!*
>
> —Karol, participant

The above participant's statement captures the sentiments of African-American audience members who believe that there is what could be called an "inscribed image" of racism that permeates American media discourse. This comment illustrates the dismal state of Black images in media, implicitly acknowledging a troubling racist ideology that centers on minority tokenism and stereotypes of the deficient or deviant.

In media, racial identity remains an important part of social appraisal, which continues to disadvantage Blacks while benefiting Whites (Gabriel 1998; Delgado and Stefancic 1997; Kinder and Sanders 1990; Winant 1994). This dilemma about mediated racial identity in the United States is attended to on two levels of research. First is the scholarly literature that focuses on the impact of mass media representations on an individual's perceptions of the value of the racial group and their cultural practices in terms of in-group perceptions and out-group perceptions (Stroman 1991). Second, research has examined the relationship between race and media in industry and representational arenas and how the two inform our societal discourse (National Advisory Commission on Civil Disorders 1968). Additionally, a significant amount of research has focused on images of African Americans in television (Bogle 1994; Berry 1992; MacDonald 1992; Evoleocha and Ugbah 1989; Gray 1989). Mass-media images of African Americans also have been critiqued in contexts such as cartoons (McLean 1998), magazine advertising (Seiter 1990), pornography (Mayall and Russell 1995), and newspapers (Byrd 1997; Martindale and Dunlap 1997). As for news, the focal genre of this study, the Roper Organization (1993) reports that most Americans (a) continue to turn to television instead of newspapers for their news; (b) find television news more credible than newspaper news; and (c) believe that television journalists perform their jobs more ably. As for African Americans' participation in news, "it was a Black news event that helped to foster the ritual of the American family gathered round the television set for the evening news. The story was the real recurring drama of the struggle for desegregation that began with an act of defiance by a Black seamstress—an act that inspired the young preacher Martin Luther King, Jr., to lead a yearlong bus boycott in Montgomery, Alabama" (Dates and Barlow 1993, 420). Thus, United States media representations of Blackness have historically played a crucial role in American culture.

In the present study I work to unite the two concerns—individual identity and societal discourse—to document how African Americans name and talk about African-American identity in news media. Through an analysis of this talk I am able to present my interpretations of the participants' sense making of patterns of racist ideologies that they believe are inscribed in news presentations.

More positive—whole, rounded, diverse—images of African Americans existed in early mainstream television news and news documentary programming. Specifically, I argue that an exemplar for the positive can be found in the reporting style of CBS news reporter Edward R. Murrow. Murrow was a 1940s–1960s television journalist noted for presenting more full images of African Americans in his news program *See It Now* and his weekly feature *Person to Person*. In *Person to Person* Murrow visited the homes of Black celebrities discussing matters of celebrity as well as identity politics issues. Audience members were provided with rare, candid inside moments with sports figures like Althea Gibson, Sugar Ray Robinson, Joe Louis, Jesse Owens, and Don Newcombe; musical talents like Eartha Kitt, Mahalia Jackson, Duke Ellington, Cab Calloway, W. C. Handy, and Ethel Waters; and statesmen such as Ralph Bunche and Walter White (MacDonald 1983).

Murrow was somewhat of an anomaly because of his unique commentary on social events. Upon his exit from news reporting, so, too, went his inclusive reporting style. In its place was offered a standard for news coverage in mainstream media of Black life and culture. This standard is what the participants in my study describe, and I define, as the "inscribed image" of Blacks in the United States. It is a frequent image of "traditional" racism that casts African Americans as deficient, and of "modern" racism that hails certain moments in Blackness that are thought to be unique in their ability to shed the assumed defiance of Blackness, thereby moving closer to the center of Whiteness (Campbell 1995). Menelik, of Baltimore, a male in his mid-thirties, best captures the notion of the "inscribed image":

> There is an image that they have engraved in the news formula . . . I dislike the formula. There is a problem with the formula. . . . There is a distinct problem when our entire group is associated with negatives such as crime, homelessness, welfare fraud, homicide, and things of that nature. . . . I believe that there is also a problem when a member of our group—an individual—is lauded. The news gives the impression that this individual has denied his or her "natural tendencies" and in some way suppressed their natural desire to be a criminal, natural desire to be a welfare mother, natural desire to be a thief, hustler, murderer, drug dealer, drug addict, et cetera, in order to become successful.

Methodology

The use of the phrase "standard news coverage" suggests that an established set of rules (narrative presentation, focal topic, production techniques) has been set. Therefore, for this study I did not select any specific broadcast news text for respondents to view. Rather, I relied upon each participant's emergent constructions of their salient news media encounters as they focused on the representation of Black identity and the dominant ideologies that inform such representations. As a means of interpreting these responses, I drew upon the tenets and assumptions of interpretive research. Interpretive research seeks to tap the lived experiences of human actors and make sense of the meanings they attach to their social world (Lindlof 1995). I also drew on the general principles of the constructivist research paradigm as detailed by Guba and Lincoln (1981).

This research project employed purposeful sampling in which participants were purposively identified to take part in a study. The participants here consisted of six African Americans—three females and three males—from two major U.S. coastal cities, San Jose and Baltimore. Feasibility considerations on my part prompted the selection of these locales. The six responded to a call for participants and lived in communities near the universities where I was employed. They represented diversity in interpretation of news, as well as income level ($11,000 to $50,000), age (twenties to sixties), and viewing frequency (light-moderate to heavy). I conducted individual, in-depth interviews with the six. Though they were not shown a specific text, the focal genre and the form of news presentation were defined. The participants were told they could respond to any television news, including local news, network news, and newsmagazine programs such as *20/20* and *60 Minutes*.

The participants devised their constructions by participating in interviews and thus, through transactional dialogue, created themes about images of African Americans in the news. The themes represent the meanings produced in response to news media representations of race. Guba and Lincoln (1994, 11) argue that "constructions are no more or less true, in any absolute sense, but simply more or less informed and/or sophisticated, and are alterable as are their associated realities." The selected quotes presented here and used to illustrate the emergent themes are indicative of positive redundancy among the study participants. In other words, the participant quotes are not exhaustive of all participant utterances but serve to exemplify emergent themes.

African Americans' Discernment of Racist Ideology in News

By 1968, the "standard" news coverage that emerged and took up the dominant industry position with the death of Murrow's positive imagery of Blacks was immediately criticized for its pattern of racist discourse. The 1968 report of the National Advisory Commission on Civil Disorders, also known as the Kerner Commission report, specifically criticized the American news media in four areas: the media failed to adequately report race relations and urban problems, were biased or racist in their coverage of news about Blacks, had a dismal record for employing Blacks, and treated Blacks as if they were not part of American society. These criticisms pointed to the fact that news media contribute "to the Black-White schism in this country" (National Advisory Commission on Civil Disorders 1968, 211).

Today, some four decades later, the participants in my study believe that such "standard" news coverage of race remains firmly in place, and, as a result, so too does the schism. They identify, however, a new divide in news that not only separates Blacks and Whites, in the symbolic, as the groups struggle over gaining/maintaining control and power, but also turns Blacks on one another in a quest for individual dominance. Rodney, a male in his mid-thirties from Baltimore, summarizes this best when he states, "It is the same ideological thinking developed with slavery, that of the field Negro and the house Negro."

The field and house Negro today are colloquialisms used to describe the division of Blacks during slavery. As the terms suggest, field Negroes were those who labored in the fields; house Negroes were those selected for more prized work in the shelter of the slave owners' homes. I argue that this "either/or" relegation of Blacks to the center or to the margins has become accepted and expressed in many overt and covert ways within the United States, including media. The participants believed that this dichotomy is played out in media images when Blacks in news representations are *either* presented as ignorant, criminal, poor, and drug addicted, *or* as someone allowed in the media industry's "house" (like Bryant Gumble or Oprah Winfrey). Karol, a Baltimore resident in her early thirties, expressed the either/or dichotomy as being an image of either a "good" Black or a "bad" Black:

> I think you are either going to have the good Black or the bad Black. The good Black is like the Bryant Gumble. The good Black! The bad Black is—oh it's too many to name. . . . Everybody else! Think about it, even the good Blacks, like the little token Black Oprah . . . are still stuck in slavery because they [Whites] are thinking she has some kind of mammy-giving advice hold on them.

Michael, in his mid-thirties, and from San Jose, described the either/or ideological pattern of thinking as permeating societal beliefs of African Americans in terms of the rare good "token," or the more common, bad, deficient masses:

> In the dominant culture there is a recognition that people are diverse—that is, there are some good people and some bad people . . . but with Blacks . . . it seems that you are either this or you are that. You are either the token, really good in your area, or you are like the mass majority—you are lazy, shiftless, you know all those things, all those negative things, but there is no accounting for people being in the middle somewhere. Just as in slavery there is no being average.

Whether the difference was described in terms of field or house Negro, good or bad, token or mass majority, the participants believed that the dichotomy was deeply rooted in American society. This polarization is the standard of news coverage offered today.

Media's Framing of Race

It is the dominant ideology that is the "standard image" in media representations of Blackness. It is this image that serves as a frame of Blackness against which the participants struggle. Media framing is the process by which a communication source, such as a news organization, defines and constructs political issues or public controversy (Gamson and Modigliani 1989). Studies about television news (Roberts 1971, 1975) have found that Blacks often do not appear in speaking roles, are seen in blue-collar jobs, are shown in connection with "struggle"—civil rights issues, school busing— and are presented as perpetrators or victims of crime. The participants agree that African Americans must resist the circulation of discourses and construct a more favorable social identity for Blackness so as to not be cast as "the other" against and for Whites.

The inscribed images described by the participants are not new. In terms of the images that capture the field Negro extreme, the American news media have been criticized for framing Black Americans as poor, criminal, drug addicted, and dysfunctional, and for presenting the most victimized and hurting segment of the Black community as the norm (Raybon 1989). On the other hand, the images that capture the house Negro extreme have also been criticized. For example, Entman and Rojecki (2000, 206) argue that although there is a growing number of Black Americans entering the middle class, few provide highly visible symbols of success: "The success stories validate the culturally venerated qualities (hard work, restraint, disciplined) that elevated these exceptional African Americans. The implicit argument is that such qualities are all Blacks need." On this point, Rodney observed:

> The one extreme with Blacks getting arrested and the handcuffs—that is thrown in for the Whites view of us in order to show them a better self-opinion about themselves. They'll say, look, they [Blacks] are no good. . . . So it makes the Whites feel better about themselves because they see the Blacks not achieving anything. So for their self-esteem. The other end, showing the Oprah Winfreys is a decoy. It is thrown in to mentally control Blacks . . . to show that things aren't as bad as they think they are, as

bad as we portray them to you.

The participants argue that the dichotomous frame has a deleterious impact on self-identity within Black communities because it locks in not only the mythical house Negro and field Negro division, but encourages a self-fulfilling prophecy of failure. Rodney summarized the dichotomous ideology ingrained in the dominant culture's social construction of race:

> Race is a social construct just like the caste system is done in India. Set up for all time for our time to keep their [Whites] status quo going. . . . In fact, there is a book out, I can't remember the name of it, but it is a book that was given to the slaveowners back in the 1800s that tells them how to control slaves. It gives slaveowners different things that slaves can be given in order to control slaves as a mass working through the control of their collective. Control of the collective. . . . The same ideas are being used today to control society. To control Black society! They have controlled the minds of Blacks since slavery with the same exact construct that they want us to think about today.

Likewise, Alma, a female in her sixties from San Jose, provided an example of how this social construction around division, and with its focus on Black popular culture icons, is played out. Specifically, she discussed her perspective in terms of how the social construct of race is evident in the response from Whites about athletes such as O. J. Simpson and Tiger Woods:

> As long as O. J. was in the limelight and he was a football player, they [Whites] were just like gung ho for him . . . the same thing for Tiger, as long as he is up there playing golf . . . yet the slightest thing that he says that they [Whites] can twist like the comment about his ethnicity. . . . The fact that he is of mixed heritage, they want him to be either the one-drop effect—either say he is Black or African-American or if he doesn't say that then he is denying his race. . . . So they try to get you to define ethnicity in terms that they can understand, terms that are acceptable to them so they can now pigeonhole you and then its okay.

Terrell, a female in her late twenties from Baltimore, identified news stories in which the *absence* of Blacks in the coverage implies the same divisive dichotomy. She employed the Columbine High School shootings as an example:

> Well, the Columbine thing last year—I didn't like the way they focused so much on some of the children that died. I mean, they kind of talked about, his last name was Shoels, Isaiah was his first name I think; he didn't

seem to get as much play as everyone else did and it was just as important. Yet he was Black. I am not saying that any of the others should have
been downplayed. I am just saying that they should have treated him
equal. Their [society's] way holds.

A 1971 study by Johnson and Sears focused on the underrepresenta-
tions of minorities in news media. They argued that by perpetuating Black
invisibility, the news media embodied institutional racism that resulted in a
failure to combat stereotyping. The U.S. Commission on Civil Rights
(1977) reported that (a) stories reported by minority newscasters generally
dealt with minority problems; (b) minority men in the news were usually
criminals or public figures; and (c) non-White women in the news usually
were experiencing some economic deprivation. Even more recent studies
reveal the institutional level of racism and the neglect of news organizations
to combat ignorance about it. For example, Entman and Rojecki (2000, 77)
argue:

> The news does not usually reflect any conscious efforts by journalists to
> cultivate their audiences' accurate understanding of racial matters.
> Rather, the news embodies the efforts of tacitly obeying norms and fol-
> lowing cultural patterns of which journalists are only imperfectly aware,
> and of responding to pressures from elites and markets which news or-
> ganizations are disinclined to challenge.

Thus, it can be argued that the imperfect awareness of journalists about cultural patterns contributes to the media's role of "locking" a construction of
Black identity into standard news coverage. In other words, the participants
in this study believe that the news media have offered the field Negro/house
Negro frame as "what Americans should think about."

You Must Think about This

Researchers like Van Dijk (1988, 207) argue that the role and the effect of
media portrayals of minorities "indirectly favor the development of stereotypical, prejudiced, or racist interpretive frameworks among the public at
large." Participants viewed this locked-in identity within the media frame as
an "agenda-setting function" (McCombs and Shaw 1972). Agenda setting is
"the idea that media, by their display of news, come to determine the issues
that the public thinks about and talks about" (Severin and Tankard 1988,
264). In relation to racial minorities, Van Dijk (1988, 208) argues that "the
media may not always tell us *what* to think about minorities (although they

often do), but rather they define the communicative situation and the social context that dictates *how* most of their users think about minority groups."

A social issue often used to study the media agenda-setting function is crime. Gilliam, Iyengar, Simon, and Wright (1996) conducted a thirteen-month study of large-market television news stations' local news programs. The scholars found that local news programs are distorted in two respects. First, the programs project the idea that "crime," by definition, is violent (certainly not "white collar") and that criminals are African Americans. Thus, viewers are primed to consider crime through the lens of racial stereotypes. Second, the researchers found that the news producers preferred to present crime as a Black-and-White issue, in spite of the fact that urban areas increasingly house a minority population that includes expanding immigrant populations. Studies also have shown that racial representations on television do not appear to match crime statistics; rather, local news tends to overrepresent Black perpetrators, underrepresent Black victims, and overrepresent White victims (Romer, Jamieson, and de Coteau 1998; Romer et al. 1997; Gilliam et al. 1996).

Menelik, too, identified a "standard"—a racially biased formula, captured in the frame, and thereby setting society's discursive agenda around Blackness—when African Americans are reported:

> I dislike the biased nature. I dislike the formula. I believe that it is a formula that represents many people of color in a verbally and visually subhuman manner. . . . Coverage is slanted to show Blacks as criminals, infidels, subhuman mindless monsters and I resent that particular designation because we are human. . . . They [the media] feel that the formula that's out there right now is just fine and it doesn't need to be altered and Blacks need to somehow conform to it. Deny their culture. Deny their way of being. Just conform to this structure that the dominant culture created.

Rodney's experience of the agenda-setting function hit close to home when his younger sister did not get the lead coverage for her perfect attendance from kindergarten through high school:

> My sister was one of the few students who never missed a day of school from kindergarten to twelfth grade and her picture didn't get in the news, but another student that was White who missed one day of school got her picture in the news. . . . That wasn't fair! . . . All the media did was call her [my sister], they didn't come out or anything; they just called for

a telephone interview. . . . Then they just used her name. . . . They had
the White student's name and picture saying she had missed only a day
in school through all her ages of school. . . . They didn't want to be out-
done. This little Black thing didn't miss a day of school at all. It just can't
be a Black person! It just can't be!

Many studies conducted by Entman (1989, 1992, 1993, 1994a, 1994b)
reinforce the notion that the choices made by television journalists appear
to feed racial stereotypes. For example, Entman has found that television
paints a picture of Blacks as: (1) violent and threatening to Whites; (2) self-
interested and demanding toward the body of politics; and (3) continually
causing problems for the law-abiding, taxpaying majority (Entman 1994b).
He also notes in his 1992 study that television news programs suggest that
racism may be encouraged by crime coverage that depicts Blacks as more
physically threatening, and by political coverage that casts Black politicians
as far more demanding and disgruntled than comparable White leaders. In
short, Entman's studies suggest that newsroom policies and practices often
frame Blackness as deficient, and thus encourage a negative stereotype
about Blacks that is all the more powerful coming from a genre that promises to represent the "real" of our social world (1994a). The perceived credibility of news, coupled with fictive, entertainment texts that can also
introduce these images, creates an imagistic "double bind" that unduly fet-
ters racial representations.

Give Me That Old-Time Tradition:
Countering Hegemony with Afrocentric Talk

All the participants believed that African-American industry professionals
need to be included in news decision making. More ownership is the ideal.
Karol emphasized that "we need to control the machines that generate the
images and perpetuate the images. . . . We need to generate our own images." Menelik agreed as he stated his perspective as the need for each Black
to "influence each other to either make a change or create a system of our
own." Terrell emphasized the reason why anchors and reporters are just not
enough when she stated, "it really doesn't make much difference that they
are Black if they are saying the story the same way that a White person
would. So, I would change how many Black directors, producers, and owners we have."

Although the participants believed that Black ownership is one way to
counter the standard, inscribed images of Blackness they viewed in news,

they believed such counteraction would be a daunting task. Rodney addressed this notion when he emphasized that African Americans who seek this ownership are often held up as an example:

> In slavery times, whenever a Negro would escape the plantation they would always hang him to make an example to the rest of the Negroes, as in "don't do anything wrong or this will happen to you." So they [Whites] always try to make him look as bad as he could so that they could keep all the other Negroes in check or subservient on the plantation. They do the same thing in the media. So when you have someone like Bill Cosby, who tries to buy NBC, all of a sudden his son shows up missing and killed in a car accident mysteriously. This is actually a subliminal signal to Blacks as to not get too uppity to buy our property because we'll hurt your family and make an example of you.

Thus, media ownership may not be an accessible way to effectively counter the hegemonic ideology. The notion of ideological hegemony suggests that a subordinate group is constantly in a process of struggle against the dominant or, in this case, the inscribed. Participants believed that this resistance can take place by African Americans creating their own space for presenting more racially balanced news, constructing the news for themselves. Terrell used the example of news coverage about cancer:

> Unless you are watching, like, Tavis Smiley or something, news coverage is from the White perspective. Like, if you were talking about cancer then usually the mainstream will talk about it in terms of the number of White men who get it and don't really focus on the higher risk factor for us. . . . Whereas, you listen to the Tom Joyner *Morning Show* or watch BET news and they will talk about the issues and our risk, as well as talk about it more sensitively.

Afrocentrism describes the placing of African ideals at the center of an indvidual's epistemological vantage point. According to Asante (1988), there are several key elements that constitute an Afrocentric perspective. These include: (1) a continuous process that emphasizes a strong sense of spirituality; (2) a profound respect for tradition; (3) harmony with nature; (4) the paramount centrality of community; (5) life as a series of passages; (6) the importance of elders; and (7) the creation of self-identity and dignity. The participants of my study focused on three Afrocentric principles: the profound respect for tradition, the paramount centrality of community, and the creation of self-identity and dignity. As part of the respect for tradition comes a celebration of the oral tradition—storytelling, elaborate narrative construction, and interpersonal encounters.

The participants rely heavily on this oral tradition, reporting that the mainstay of making sense of their world is engaging in critical and analytic discursive encounters with other members of their racial community. I describe this practice as "Afrocentric talk." I believe that Afrocentric talk serves as a catalyst toward community building and the creation of self-identity and dignity. Therefore, Afrocentric talk is a shield against racism, both societal and internalized racism. Yamato (1995, 73) summarizes internalized racism as something that "influences the way I see or don't see myself, limits what I expect of myself and others like me. It results in my acceptance of mistreatment, leads me to believe that being treated with less than absolute respect, at least this once, is to be expected because I am Black, because I am not White." The participants believed that, historically, their talk has been their protection against internalized racism, including the symbols of the house and field Negroes. Karol summarizes all respondent comments and explains the nature of the historical response that Blacks have when dealing with the dominant ideology around race:

> That goes back to slavery and the songs. You have the house people and the field people, and there was no in between and so you had to create your own form of communication. Create your own world to live in. . . . We had to talk to each other because we are a collective. When you were by yourself you were silent. We had to talk to give ourselves codes. That's why we know the songs (spirituals) no matter where we are from, no matter if we were in the house or the field. . . . When you look at our talk, there are underlying messages just like spirituals. You know, White people thought we were singing because we were happy to be picking cotton or breast-feeding little Sally or shining massa's shoes; you weren't happy doing that! You were singing them songs because you were telling so and so we are going to have a meeting on the big hill tonight at twelve o'clock under the stars. They [Whites] thought we were talking about, you know, singing about cotton needs a pickin' so bad or whatever; or some kind of scripture, you know, look at them happy Negroes they happy pickin' my cotton. Dummy! They wasn't happy! Those were disguised messages that was Morse code back in the day. They were talking about other things. So even when we get to television, a lot of shows when you see the Black actors; the old black-and-white TV shows a lot of times if you'll see the Sambo characters and the mammy characters

sometimes you see them smile at the screen, that was an underlying message.

Afrocentricity places considerable emphasis on an affective way of obtaining knowledge (Akbar 1984). The focus on affect does not prevent recognition and use of rationality. A common affective location for all study participants was the household kitchen. The participants believed that much of their talk took place in the kitchen because of its affective cultural symbolism. With the mass media's role in society, engaging in the talk of deconstruction and reconstruction, with a close cohort in a safe and comforting environ, is the social and cultural sustenance used to recreate a more positive discourse around identity. Alma argued that "it is important to remember that the prime times of showing the news are during the breakfast, lunch, and dinner hours." Rodney described the talk as nourishment and therefore the kitchen as the appropriate place:

> The kitchen is where you get your nourishment. So, when you are there you are also getting an educational nourishment as well . . . you are getting both forms of nourishment at the same time. . . . You will probably find that when eating our mind is more open to taking in information than other times, because if you are tired and need nourishment you won't be so open to things. Which is probably why they show the five o'-clock news then showing all the Blacks sitting on the curb being handcuffed because you have just eaten. Therefore, your mind is open to new impressions. So, therefore watching TV news can impress that you do nothing but bad.

Historically, the kitchen served as a bridge between the field Negro and the house Negro. It served as a meeting place during meal times. It served as a place to feed the soul. Karol identified the significance of the kitchen as similar to that of soul food in the Black community:

> I think the kitchen is significant to us because the cycle of life is maintained there, because you are already nourishing the body, so then what better place to nourish the mind? I mean, because it is a complete package body, soul, and mind. . . . Just like food is called soul food you know it is good for the soul. . . . So in the kitchen you sit and talk about the news or things that are happening in the world because it's nourishment. It is nourishment for the mind. It is mind food . . . not only that for us [Blacks] when we worked in the kitchen for ourselves and for our families it was an act of love. A labor of love for ourselves. . . . The kitchen for us was like a no-holds-barred and you are in there ranting and raving,

hitting your hands on the table, you can cry, you can run around, jump up and down, give each other high five, you can do anything in the kitchen—roll out the chair, kick and scream dying laughing while your momma's going to get some tea. You know, you want some cake? I got some pound cake. I mean it's just like you are always being fed. It is a constant feeding plus it is like if you want the news, if you want to talk about the latest news you know to meet in the kitchen. You can't meet in any other part of the house because the business isn't in too many places of the house. If you want to talk business or get to some serious topic you go to the kitchen.

Talk in the African-American community has been needed to deconstruct the arbitrary division and dominant extremes, as a way to reclaim cultural collectivity and to construct a whole racial self-image. As African Americans, the participants felt that the dichotomous frame offers no inbetween, therefore, talk among them must center on the "in-between." As Rodney states, their talk "helps them see past the shroud that has been put over news programs." Michael stated that the type of talk the community creates is not new:

> We have to figure out what is representative. Representation becomes the center of our talk. Whereas the dominant culture goes into either token or majority, we pull them [Blacks] out of the token or the mass majority. Just like we have to explain why we are not in the history books as the mass majority, and why it is this person in the history book.

Alma agreed that we have to create talk in between "to understand both the token and mass majority, using that as a springboard for a child you can say that person was able to acculturate or still be successful." Menelik also offered that in-between talk was necessary as it was useful for encouragement and self-esteem building: "I believe that we have a responsibility to encourage and build self-esteem . . . we have a responsibility to break down things that have been internalized, especially things that go back to the number-one problem in our community, which is low self-esteem." Michael argued that we need Afrocentric talk when engaging mainstream media as it prompts critical thinking:

> I usually don't want to hear about it in the way that they were communicating it because it's obvious that in the media things are going to be portrayed in a specific light that doesn't take everything into consideration that's really going on. They've got a message that they want to com-

municate to the public. . . . There is no middle to it (the media) so it requires just questioning what they are really communicating.

Finally, Alma discussed how talk can be used to better prepare children to
live in a world where there is overt and covert prejudice circulating:

> I myself have used [the talk about the news] as a springboard to speak, as
> a catalyst, as a reason to make sure that my daughter and son-in-law, and
> my son and daughter-in-law are conscious of things that could affect
> their children. Because they are both in biracial marriages, they some-
> times—it is possible sometimes to forget when we get involved with each
> other that once you create a child that has grown lovable and all of those
> things to you that someone else may not also see that child in the same
> light, and therefore cause problems for them.

Rodney identified the importance of Afrocentric talk because it prompts
viewers to counter imagistic misrepresentations by offering up "true" historical facts:

> We would just be a greater people knowing that we've done all of these
> things. Instead of information being so secret, they only want a few peo-
> ple knowing it, our self-esteem is not as high as it should be because we
> don't think that we are that great and we keep getting bombarded with
> negative TV images of us sitting on the curb with handcuffs behind us,
> dealing drugs or whatever. They don't show the great things we have ac-
> tually done this, this, and another. So yeah, if we knew all the great things
> we have done we'd feel a lot better about ourselves and we wouldn't feel
> so inferior. We'd probably do better in school because we'd say, oh yeah,
> the Black man invented the cell phone, there must be some worth to my
> family, there must be some worth to me because I know I can achieve
> something as great as that.

Conclusion

The "Black world," a safe haven created through Afrocentric talk, serves as
a response to the ingrained ideology that views Blacks as either house or
field Negroes. According to participants, it is the Black world that can provide a space for African Americans to present their culture as prized, it is
within the Black world that African Americans can find meaning beyond
those offered in American society through an ingrained ideology that is
perpetuated in media representations of Blackness.

CBS newsman Edward R. Murrow, I argued, tried capturing the realistic images of African Americans in his programming. However, the demise of such programming resulted in the emergence of a standard of news coverage that depicts Black racial identity as a divide between the two extremes—house and field Negro. This standard perpetuates a pattern of ideological thinking described as an either-or dichotomy embedded within the dominant American culture's beliefs about African Americans. Since the media offer a reflection of society, the African-American participants in this study believed that the ingrained ideology has become the media frame used for news coverage of African Americans.

The mass media are, indeed, pervasive and the presence of this accepted ideology in the media through news reportage or fictional representation cultivates an audience's inaccurate understanding of racial matters and a warped and incorrect perception of African Americans' realities. The media frame presents this ideology as natural rather than constructed. Therefore, news coverage frames African Americans as a problem rather than framing the ingrained false ethnic identity as the problem. Since news organizations' frames become focused on a group of people rather than the ideology itself, racism is institutionalized and enacted through news formulas and the imperfect awareness of journalists.

The African-American participants believe that the maintenance of such frameworks is rooted in the agenda of mass media organizations. This agenda plays a role in reinforcing the communicative situation or social context in American society, a context that encourages the idea that Blacks fit one of two extremes but nothing in between. Furthermore, this context is not dependent upon a single social issue. Instead, it perpetuates hegemonic language and images in general. According to the African-American participants, Black ownership would be an effective counterhegemonic response by offering an in between with realistic images. However, they also believe that ownership as a response to the hegemonic ideology may not be accessible because it has the potential to result in the elimination of Blacks. Therefore, they turn to Afrocentrism, specifically Black-centered talk, as a key part of identity reconstruction.

In doing so, African Americans cling to what they believe is distinctly of their culture. They work to craft self and social identity from outside of dominant culture inscriptions. More, the participants believe that their talk is a protection against internalized racism. Afrocentric talk is social and cultural nourishment used in the deconstruction and reconstruction of identity because it serves as a bridge between the two extremes—house and field

Negro—and offers a communicative situation or social context that focuses on the in between, that is, the realistic images of African Americans.

African Americans' use of Afrocentric talk for the deconstruction and reconstruction of inscribed news images depicting their existence must be further explored. Present actions that African Americans see as countering dichotomous imagery in the news are of key importance.

An interesting topic here would be Black talk about Black-owned media institutions such as Black Entertainment Television (BET), particularly given its merger with Viacom, one dominant media corporation. Researchers should focus on emancipatory research in an effort to inform the change of the "media frame," the "agenda," and the "standard news coverage."

References

Akbar, N. (1984). Afrocentric social sciences for human liberation. *Journal of Black Studies* 14: 395–414.

Asante, M. K. (1988). *Afrocentricity*. Trenton, N.J.: Africa World.

Berry, V. T. (1992). From *Good Times* to *The Cosby Show*: Perceptions of changing televised images among Black fathers and sons. In S. Craig, ed., *Men, masculinity, and the media* (pp. 111–23). Newbury Park, Calif.: Sage.

Berry, V.T., and C.L. Manning-Miller. (1996). *Mediated messages and African American culture: Contemporary issues.* Thousand Oaks, Calif.: Sage.

Bogle, D. (1994). *Toms, coons, mulattoes, mammies, and bucks: An interpretive history of Blacks in American films.* New York: Viking Press.

Byrd, D. (1997). Blacks, Whites in news pictures. In S. Biagi and M. Kem-Foxworth, eds., *Facing difference: Race, gender, and mass media* (pp. 95–97). Thousand Oaks, Calif.: Pine Forge Press.

Campbell, C. (1995). *Race, myth and the news.* Thousand Oaks, Calif.: Sage.

Cheney, G., and P. K. Tompkins. (1987). Coming to terms with organizational identification and commitment. *Central States Speech Journal* 38: 1–15.

Dates, J. L., and W. Barlow. (1993). *Split image: African Americans in the mass media.* Washington, D.C.: Howard University Press.

Delgado, R., and J. Stefancic. (1997). *Critical White studies: Looking behind the mirror.* Philadelphia: Temple University Press.

Entman, R. M. (1989). How the media affect what people think: An information processing approach. *Journal of Politics* 51: 347–70.

————. (1992). Blacks in the news: Television, modern racism and cultural change. *Journalism Quarterly* 69: 341–61.

————. (1993). Framing: Toward clarification of a fractured paradigm. *Journal of Communication* 43: 51–58.

————. (1994a). African Americans according to TV news. *Media Studies Journal* 8: 29–38.

————. (1994b). Representation and reality in the portrayal of Blacks on network television shows. *Journalism Quarterly* 71: 509–20.

Entman, R. M., and R. M. Rojecki. (2000). *The Black image in the White mind: Media and race in America.* Chicago: University of Chicago Press.

Evoleocha, S. U., and S. D. Ugbah. (1989). Stereotypes, counter-stereotypes, and Black television images in the 1990s. *Western Journal of Black Studies* 12: 197–205.

Gabriel, J. (1998). *Whitewash: Racialized politics and the media.* London and New York: Routledge.

Gamson, W. A., and A. Modigliani. (1989). Media discourse and public opinion on nuclear power: A constructivist approach. *American Journal of Sociology* 95: 1–37.

Gilliam, F., Jr., S. Iyengar, A. Simon, and O. Wright. (1996). Crime in Black and White. *Harvard International Journal of Press/Politics* 1: 6–23.

Gramsci, A. (1971). *Selections from the prison notebooks.* New York: International Publishers.

Gray, H. (1989). Television, Black Americans, and the American dream. *Critical Studies in Mass Communication* 6: 376–86.

————. Television, Black Americans and the American dream. In V. T. Berry and C. L. Manning-Miller, eds., *Mediated messages and African-American culture: Contemporary issues* (pp. 131–45). Thousand Oaks, Calif.: Sage Publications.

Guba, E. G., and Y. S. Lincoln. (1981). *Effective evaluation.* San Francisco: Jossey-Bass.

————. (1994). Competing paradigms in qualitative research. In N. Denzin and Y. Lincoln, eds., *Handbook of Qualitative Research* (pp. 105–17). Newbury Park, Calif.: Sage.

Iyengar, S. (1991). *Is anyone responsible? How television frames political issues.* Chicago: University of Chicago Press.

Johnson, P. B., and D. O. Sears. (1971). Black invisibility, the press, and the Los Angeles riot. *American Journal of Sociology* 76: 698–721.

Kinder, D. R., and L. M. Sanders. (1990). Mimicking political debate with survey questions: The case of White opinion on affirmative action for Blacks. *Social Cognition* 8: 73–103.

Lindlof, T. R. (1995). *Qualitative communication research methods.* Thousand Oaks, Calif.: Sage.

MacDonald, J. F. (1983). *Blacks and White TV: Afro-Americans in television since 1948.* Chicago: Nelson-Hall.

Martindale, C., and L.R. Dunlap. (1997). The African Americans. In B. A. Deepe Keever, C. Martindale, and M. A. Weston, eds., *The U.S. news coverage of racial minorities: A sourcebook, 1934–1996* (pp. 63–145). Westport, Conn.: Greenwood.

Mayall, A., and D. E. H. Russell. (1995). Racism in pornography. In G. Dines and J. M. Humez, eds., *Gender, race and class in media* (pp. 287–97). Thousand Oaks, Calif.: Sage.

McCombs, M. E., and D. L. Shaw. (1972). The agenda-setting function of mass media. *Public Opinion Quarterly* 36 (summer): 176–87.

McLean, S. (1998). Minority representation and portrayal in modern newsprint cartoons. In Y. R. Kamalipour and T. Carilli, eds., *Cultural diversity in the U.S. media* (pp. 23–38). Albany: State University of New York Press.

Means Coleman, R. R. (2000). *African American viewers and the Black situation comedy: Situating racial humor.* New York: Garland.

National Advisory Commission on Civil Disorders. (1968). *Report of the national advisory committee on civil disorders.* Washington, D.C.: Government Printing Office.

Putnam, L. L. (1983). The interpretive perspective: An alternative to functionalism. In L. Putnam and M. E. Pacanowsky, eds., *Communication and organizations: An interpretive approach* (pp. 31–54). Newbury Park, Calif.: Sage.

Raybon, P. (1989). A case of "severe bias." *Newsweek*, October 2, p. 11.

Roberts, C. (1971). The portrayal of Blacks in television network newscasts. *Journal of Broadcasting* 15: 45–53.

———. (1975). The presentation of Blacks in television network newscasts. *Journalism Quarterly* 52: 50–55.

Romer, D., K. H. Jamieson, and de Coteau. (1998). The treatment of persons of color in local television news—ethnic blame discourse of realistic group conflict? *Communication Research* 25: 286–305.

Romer, D., K. H. Jamieson, C. Riegner, M. Emori, and B. Rouson. (1997).

Blame discourse versus realistic conflict as explanations of ethnic tension in urban neighborhoods. *Political Communication* 14: 273–92.

Roper Organization. (1993). *America's watching: Public attitudes toward television.* New York: Network Television Association.

Saltzman, J. (1988). CBS and the death of television journalism. *USA Today: The Magazine of the American Scene* 117: 30–33.

Seiter, E. (1990). Different children, different dreams: Racial representation in advertising. *Journal of Communication Inquiry* 14: 31–47.

Severin, W. J., and J. W. Tankard Jr. (1988). *Communication theories: Origins, methods, uses.* White Plains, N.Y.: Longman.

Stroman, C. A. (1991). Television's role in the socialization of African American children and adolescents. *Journal of Negro Education* 60: 314–27.

U.S. Commission on Civil Rights. (1977). *Window dressing on the set: Women and minorities in television.* Washington, D.C.: Commission on Civil Rights.

Van Dijk, T. A. (1988). *News analysis: Case studies of international and national news in the press.* Hillsdale, N.J.: Lawrence Erlbaum Associates.

Winant, H. (1994). *Racial conditions: Politics, theory, comparisons.* Minneapolis: University of Minnesota Press.

Yamato, G. (1995). Something about the subject makes it hard to name. In M. L. Anderson and P. H. Collins, eds., *Race, class, and gender: An anthology* (pp. 71–75). Belmont, Calif.: Wadsworth.

!

6

DMX, Cosby, and Two Sides
of the American Dream

Chyng F. Sun, Leda Cooks, Corey Rinehart, and Stacy A. S. Williams

The study presented in this chapter assesses audience's analyses of media content as part of a system of meaning making for Black youth. In particular, our focus is on male high school students: how they construct and make (non)sense of their identities in the context of friendships, family, education, community, and popular culture. We also consider the implications of this meaning-making activity for their success as adults in a White-dominated society. Our concern is with the ways the teens voice their relationships about people who are significant in their lives, as well as about the institutions, such as the media and school, that create, reinforce, or negate their everyday lives. In our analysis, we move between an ideological analysis of media content and Black identity, and the boys' own ways of negotiating the paradox between their experiences of discrimination, alienation, and isolation and hope for their future. We begin with a discussion of ethnographic research on urban youth, bringing together several concepts important to our study: ethnic or subcultural identity, identification with dominant/mainstream values (as portrayed in the media or taught in schools), and idealism about the future. Following the discussion of theoretical and methodological considerations, we turn to our analysis of six focus groups of boys with diverse levels of academic achievement from three different high schools. We address the junctures and disjunctures between critical cultural theories of the media and Black identity and the boys' own assessments of these same concerns. Finally, we offer some conclusions and address several implications for future studies in this area and for audience research of the media in general.

Our study is concerned with signification processes and follows the audience research tradition. Our specific question is how dominant or oppositional media messages might be acted upon or re-presented in the everyday lives of Black youth in the United States. We are also interested in the relationships among media messages targeted at Black youths as opposed to other audiences; Black youths' perceptions, values, and beliefs about school (as an educating institution); Blackness and Whiteness as signifying processes and belief systems; and, most importantly, the potential of Black youth to survive and succeed as Black adults in the United States.

While we found no audience studies that looked specifically at the relationship between media texts and educational experiences and identity and potential for success among Black youth, a number of studies have been conducted that measure the beliefs of youth about education, their habits, communities, and potential for success in mainstream society. Three important studies have attempted to differentiate among socioeconomic status, achievement level in school, beliefs about identity (based on group or racial affiliation), and authority and potential for success in the future.

Paul Willis (1977) examines the relationship between hegemony and resistance in his ethnographic study of a group of male, working-class, high school students in England. The "Hammertown" boys felt that education could not provide real upward mobility and that most available work for their class background had the qualities of meaninglessness. Above all, they valued group solidarity above individualism. They rejected schoolwork because, though it encouraged individual competition, it also demanded mental activity which was considered feminine in contrast to the more superior masculine manual labor. Thus, the boys' counterschool culture encouraged them to withhold from scholastic success in order to rebel against what they saw as an irrelevant authority. Sadly, the creative resistance those boys actively engaged against dominant culture only served to trap them in a rigid class structure and perpetuate what the capitalist system actually requires of them.

In accordance with Willis's findings, Fordham (1996, 283) observed that many Black students with low academic achievement used resistance to school as a "cultural mortar to reclaim, create and expand African-

American humanness." They envisioned themselves as part of an "imagined community" of Black people fighting to regain the appropriated components of their community and their identity. Their behavior and school performance is interpreted as reflecting their estrangement from the larger society. The most widely employed tactic for the preservation of self used by Fordham's underachievers was to devalue academic learning—a strategy that was also applied by Willis's subjects. Fordham's Black students identify activities such as speaking Standard English, studying hard, getting good grades, and "putting on airs" as White. Therefore, many of them tend to do the opposite of what is considered "acting White." Subsequently, they speak Ebonics (African-American Standard English), refuse to hand in homework, and fail to study. Through these antiestablishment activities, Black teens gain group solidarity and reinforce racial identity. They also fail to acquire knowledge and skills that can help them succeed in the system.

Novek's (1995) ethnographic study of African-American students affirms Fordham's findings. She reports that students "inhabited a sociocultural realm with a distinct set of values, rules, and practice[s]" (169). Some "cool" students, though eager to learn, went to great lengths to hide their interest and good work because students who performed well were seen to "lack Blackness" (180). The teens in Novek's study were also enthusiastic consumers of popular media, which is packed with violent and stereotypi-

DMX in Romeo Must Die. *Courtesy of Photofest.*

cal Black images. Highlighting the theory of "framing," Novek states that the Black teens were conscious about the differences between themselves and their day-to-day reality and the images of Black youth in dramatic entertainment. However, the teens found themselves trapped by the confusion between reality and media imposed by the larger society. Novek notes, "Because the media and the larger society around them seemed eager to classify all Black youths as social problems, regardless of the differences the young people themselves perceived, the teens in this study felt that framing was having a negative impact on their education, their relationships with adults, their current employment, and their chances for future success" (183–84).

While Novek's study reports the youths' experiences of the media as one piece of a larger puzzle, her focus is not on the specific ways these youths identified (or did not identify) with the mediated messages pervasive in their everyday lives. Our study attempts to take up where Novek leaves off—with the idea of the media as a reflection of the paradox the students faced at home, in their school, and in their community. If, in Fordham's terms, Black students were creating an "imagined community" apart from, or in opposition to, the majority notion of success and citizenship, how might they negotiate their accomplishments (or failures) in the educational system in light of the oppositional role their Black identity might play? If race, class, and education were factors in these previous studies, we wanted to explore further the ways in which the media interact with particular contexts and experiences to create perceptions of race, class, and ability to successfully navigate the future. If the previous cultural studies research had indicated that youth built their identities in opposition to those of the dominant culture, what role might specific dominant or radical media images play in the social construction of individual and racial identities in everyday experience? Considering the socializing role that school plays in the lives of youth, would students who did well in school differ with regard to their acceptance or rejection of mainstream media texts? We were interested in understanding how students read popular media texts, the ways they articulate their racial identities, and how that articulation interacts with their social and political views as well as their academic performance.

Method of Analysis

Procedure
We selected two very different representations of Blackness: DMX's music video "What's My Name?" and an episode from *The Cosby Show*. DMX has

been one of the most popular rap stars among teenagers (Touré 2000)[1] and is known for his image of hypermasculinity and toughness. He often portrays street life in his songs and talks about his own experiences. In this particular video he repeatedly reminds the audience of his name, "DMX," with his typically tough, rough and rage-filled persona. On stage, two fierce-looking pit bulls glare and bark at each other, adding explosive and violent tension to DMX's portrayal of Black masculinity. Around the stage, an all-Black teenage audience dances, sings, and cheers.

The Cosby Show is a situation comedy about an upper-middle-class Black family, headed by Cliff Huxtable (a gynecologist and obstetrician). Other characters include his wife Claire (a lawyer), their four daughters, and a son. We selected the show for this study for several reasons. Across all audiences, The Cosby Show is considered to be the most popular long-running sitcom that has featured a Black family; it offers the first portrayal on television of a highly successful Black family; and it has been the subject of a good deal of controversy and criticism targeted at its promotion of liberal notions of equality, idealism, and the American myth of individualism. On the one hand, this is one of the first shows to portray Black people with dignity and respect. Its representations are free of the derogatory stereotypes prevalent in other mainstream media. On the other hand, the Huxtables appear to have achieved the American dream without much struggle and the show eventually sustains "the harmful myth of social mobility" (Lewis 1991, 161). It also endorses the conservative ideology that is stated in Bill Cosby's defense of the program: "This is an American family . . . and if you want to live like they do, and you're willing to work, the opportunity is there" (cited in Dyson 1989, 30).

In the segment we selected from The Cosby Show, Dr. Huxtable goes to an urban school and talks to a class of mostly Black male students. Carl, a student in the class, and the focus of that segment, has children but chooses to buy expensive sneakers instead of supporting his children. Carl complains about working in a supermarket, earning minimum wage, and being treated as if "he was at the bottom of the pile." He tells Dr. Huxtable that he wants to be more than "a statistic." Dr. Huxtable tells Carl that he could be anything that he wants to be. He just has to decide what that is and work toward that goal. Dr. Huxtable asks Carl what his dream would be. However, before answering the question, Carl squirms, steals looks toward his classmates, and finally replies, "lab technician." Dr. Huxtable promises that he will help Carl to achieve his goal. This episode touches upon the issues many Black youth encounter, such as teen pregnancy, employment, and, very subtly, racism in the workplace. It also lends itself to discussions of Blackness, Whiteness, peer pressure, and hope for the future.

DMX's image of rebellion, which goes beyond societal and legal restrictions, and Cosby's promotion of the American dream both provide opportunities for students to negotiate their position in relation to a dominant ideology. Would the students we spoke to identify with DMX's hypermasculinity and antisocial behavior? Would they disregard Cosby's advice as unrealistic or Uncle Tomish? Might they laugh at Carl's wish to have a "White" job and despise him for "acting White"? How would the students in our study respond to the peer pressure Carl was obviously concerned about? Would the respondents connect their real life experience with their readings of the media text? If so, how? Would the students use the same ideological framework to interpret the media texts as they do their personal lives?

To begin to address these questions, we conducted focus groups with Black male students with a range of G.P.A.s from a diverse array of schools (see table 1) to investigate the relationship between educational achievement and identification with the media messages shown. We analyzed the data from the focus groups in two stages. In the first stage, we grouped the responses according to those that were most common, those that showed a pattern within or between groups, and those that were unique or could not fit into any one category. In the second stage, we examined how the boys' interpretations of the media texts related to their life experiences and how the boys incorporated their racial identities with their self-identities, world views, and aspirations for the future.

Participants

We selected three high schools in a small and diverse city in western Massachusetts. The schools were a public college preparatory school (School A), a public vocational school (School B), and a small alternative school with all-Black staff and predominantly Black students (School C). School A offers challenging academic classes. School B provides job training in addition to academic courses. School C serves at-risk students who have previously dropped out of school and who wish to prepare for higher education.

To explore the relationship between academic performance and students' reading of media texts, we selected a high-G.P.A. group and a low-

Table 1
Schools where focus group interviews were conducted.

School Name	Characteristics of the school	Teachers	Student groups
School A	College prepara-tory school	Predominantly White	* 1 high-achieving group * 1 low-achieving group
School B	Vocational school	Predominantly White	* 1 high-achieving group * 1 low-achieving group
School C	An alternative school, set in a community center, for students who formerly dropped out of schools; predominantly Black students	All Black	* 1 high-achieving group * 1 low-achieving group

G.P.A. group from the same grade (juniors or seniors) in each school. In this study, high-G.P.A. group members generally had a G.P.A. average above 3, and the low-G.P.A. groups had a G.P.A. below 2 (on a 4.0 scale). In order to make students feel more comfortable while expressing themselves, Corey Rinehart, a Black man with a few years of experience teaching in urban middle schools, was the only researcher present during each group interview. (The other three researchers are female, one Chinese American, one Anglo-American, and one Jamaican American.) When the teachers re-cruited them, and before the interviews started, the students were informed that this research was about their perceptions of media. The interviews lasted ninety minutes and were conducted in both high- and low-G.P.A. groups from all three schools. Each group was designed to include six stu-dents. Though School B had fewer participants, their responses were con-sistent with the overall patterns. Two Latino students were assigned to School C's low-G.P.A. group by mistake, and their comments were not in-cluded in this paper. In summary, we conducted a total of six focus groups: three high-achieving and three low-achieving from three urban high schools. Responses from the focus groups are thematized and analyzed in the following section.

Analysis of Focus Group Comments

Dog for life
We gonna get to the bottom of this shit if it takes all night
Stop drop uh
Open up shop fake up-north niggas screaming for the cops
Ride or Die
What that means is I'll tell a nigga bye-bye and pop him
in his right eye

—DMX, "What's My Name?"

Identification with DMX

Across all groups, we found that the respondents identified more or less
with the poverty and materially deprived living conditions DMX portrayed in his songs. The students considered these conditions to be common in urban Black neighborhoods. Nonetheless, they disapproved of the
choices DMX made for survival and they criticized him for portraying too
many "negativities" about Blacks and for glorifying violence as the solution to problems. Similar to Novek's (1995) Black teens' response, our subjects universally criticized the media's portrayal of them as violent,
threatening, and shiftless, noting that the roles Blacks play in media texts
are often limited to athletes, entertainers, drug dealers, or criminals. They
also complained that the dominant media contribute to society's discrimination against them.

Charles (School C, high G.P.A.) focused upon the violence in the
lyrics: "It was mad negativity in it. 'Bye bye, pop him in his right eye.' Always
has something to do with violence. . . . He's a good rapper, but too much
negativity here." Jack (School C, high G.P.A.) also criticized the violent imagery: "I ain't got no love for him [DMX], because he talking about raping
shorties in songs . . . that murder shit . . . that I'll rape your shorty while she
sleeping." Bill (School B, low G.P.A.) considered the source of DMX's material: "It seem like that's the only material he has, that's why he's always
talking about the streets. Him talking about killing somebody, or his dogs,
or drugs."

These students distanced themselves from the themes in DMX's lyrics,
specifically the violent and negative nature of the songs. Bill mentioned that
DMX's material was limited to talk about the streets, while others discussed
the negativity of violent images in his music. Though some respondents
could identify with DMX, they did *not* see him as an idol or confuse his

image with his real life. They considered DMX's continued rapping about his past experiences of street life, poverty, and violence as a marketing strategy since he no longer lives that life. They also generally agreed that his on-stage persona was just an image and that he probably behaved very differently in real life. Jerry (School A, high G.P.A.), speculated: "I think after he blew up and got all his money, he most likely don't have all those problems he used to have. But he got to keep that image tough if he wants to keep those same number of high fans who listen to his music." Art (School C, high G.P.A.) questioned the validity of DMX's work: "I think he is like a wrestler . . . fake stuff . . . he just acts like that, it's good for records sales." Alex (School A, low G.P.A.) echoed Jerry and Art and suggested that perhaps the violence was a commercial expectation for Black rap artists: "He might just be doing this whole thing just to make a living. This whole hard thing. . . . I guess that nowadays you got to put up that front that you hard core . . . it is all about commercial styling."

The comments about DMX's "styling" led the students to examine his use of that strategy to escape the hard life, the choices that he made to be successful. Even as many of them identified with the hard life, however, they also identified a choice: to stay on the street or get out. Tom (School A, low G.P.A.) stated: "Some of the decisions he made to get out of that hard life . . . he sold drugs . . . that wouldn't be my first decision." Ian (School A, low G.P.A.) identified with DMX's background: "Well, that hard living. I mean I came out of there. I'm sure everybody else done came out of there too. You know how it is in the city, born and raised there, cousin, I know exactly how it is." Leo (School A, high G.P.A.) also understood the challenges DMX has faced: "I can relate with him in a way because . . . I see that every day . . . but I don't got to stay in it, because I live right on the outside . . . nothing like that bad going around my neighborhood. I know that all my friends is like mostly into it. . . . We see crack heads on the street but we ain't gonna . . . have 'em talking to us every day because if we want to, we can just stay home. . . . But other people who just got to walk by that same guy every day and stuff like that. So yeah, I know about it pretty good." Alex placed DMX's rap in a historical context, expressing how DMX's songs connect to the Black music tradition of voicing the Blacks' conditions and despair: "I think each generation got their own music, like my father and his father's father back in the thirties. Blues were . . . for them because they fell down because they didn't have jobs and stuff and like for us now. It's like Black music is our music. And sometimes, it got . . . sad rap songs that make you feel about how you lost your friend or how you . . . be poor, and you want the best things in life. I can vibe with him."

Although the participants in our study identified with the lyrics and images portrayed in the DMX video, identification here should not be understood as the simple reading, dominant or oppositional, of the content. Identification could be said to occur on numerous levels and in more complex ways than indicated: on one level the experiences DMX rapped about were similar to the experiences (of poverty, drugs, crime, and violence) to those of the boys in the focus groups; on another level the boys identified with the ways in which others viewed those representations as indicative of Black culture. The media and other institutions, such as schools, reinforced negative images and rarely offered positive alternative or, more importantly, hope. Many of the youths in our study readily pointed out the paradox of rap celebrity: DMX made a lot money rapping about growing up on the streets and celebrating the violence that only intensified negative images of Black urban youth.

Stuart Hall (1980) indicated that readings should not be understood as unilinear (from encoder to decoder). Because humans use symbolic forms to communicate, we are always in discourse; thus, meanings are continually produced and reproduced. For Hall, then, the three decoding options are not social categories but are positions that can be inhabited by different audience members at different times.

Along these lines, Janice Radway (1986) observes that because current notions of audience analysis allow for multiple meanings and multiple readings, ideology is not, nor should it be thought of as finished within the moment of decoding. We address the complexities of hegemony in the readings and the ideological implications of the paradoxes constructed throughout the particpants' responses in the discussion section of our chapter.

The Cosby Show

Carl: I had a job in the supermarket. It paid minimum wage and they treated me like I was at the bottom of the pile and that's where I am going to stay. I don't want to be a statistic.

Dr. Huxtable: What you got to do now is you got to learn how to want to be something. . . . Pick, that's all. The second thing you do after you pick is figure out if that's what you really want to do, what you want to be. And the next step is going out and find out how to become that. . . . Pick, what would you like to be?"

—excerpt from *The Cosby Show*

In the groups of students we spoke to, almost all the respondents considered Dr. Huxtable's advice to be good. Some of them added that they had heard the same thing "all their lives." Common interpretations of the advice included: "You can do anything that you want to do, be anything that you want to be. You just gotta set your mind to it, and meet your goals"; and (stressing the importance of being self-supporting), "Don't rely on others. You got to get up and do it yourself." Only one respondent criticized this exchange, but it was not a challenge to the underlying assumption that everyone is on an equal playing field. Rather, he pointed out that obstacles on the path to success were inevitable.

Pat (School A, low G.P.A.) commented: "I wish advice was that easy in real life . . . like just working up the ladder, you gonna have times when you get booted back down the ladder and you have to climb back up. I wish life was more simple like the words he said." Pat's use of the ladder as a metaphor for the obstacles he and others encounter in "real life" allowed him to express the experience of struggle through the use of a neutral (though enabling) device. For Pat, the ladder was not provided to some at the expense of others—anyone could use it. He just wished the climb could be easier.

While it is important to note that the two kinds of discourse, "work hard for success" and "the sky is the limit," are the two sides of the same coin in regards to the American dream, the latter phrase in particular engenders a conservative stand. "The sky is the limit" endorses a color-blind position and implies that if Blacks don't succeed it is their own fault and no one else's. This idea is articulated throughout the participants' responses.

All of the respondents picked up the visual cues of Carl's discomfort before he announced his wish for wanting to be a lab technician. Most of them interpreted Carl's reaction as a fear of being laughed at by his classmates because they might think that Carl was not capable of achieving his goal, or because Carl's friends didn't have dreams themselves and wouldn't want other people to stand out. Almost universally, they said that Carl should pursue his dream, despite the peer pressure. They also listed the support Carl may need in order to succeed, such as a good role model, concrete guidance in how to find a job, supportive friends, and child care. Alex expressed sympathy toward Carl and gave the most thoughtful analysis of the peer pressure both Carl and he may have experienced:

> He [Carl] . . . felt ashamed of that . . . he wanted to be something. That's, like, bad because how you gonna be ashamed because you want to do

something good? Sometimes you be around your boys so much where all you have to do is negative stuff and all you'll think about is like doing something that you ain't gonna happen, but you want to do. But if I said something like that, my boys would be like "yeah, that ain't happening," 'cause they know me too well and they think that I ain't gonna even think about doing something like that. . . . That is the same thing . . . he [Carl] was feeling. . . . And then when he was talking about when he was working at that shopping place and how he felt he was at the bottom and all that stuff, that's like how they make Black people feel and most Black people don't be having good jobs. Since he [Carl] said a good job like that, I think his friends might have been like, "you ain't gonna do nothing like that, you gonna be still here in the projects, smoking weed." . . . You know how sometimes your friends make you feel?

Using his own experience, Alex continued to speak about the relationship between peer pressure and teasing, and how this may hurt or hinder him from pursuing his dream.

I think people who make fun of anything that you do makes it harder. You may even tell yourself that it don't hurt you but it do, because you know sometime it will bother you. I mean as long as you are strong enough to keep doing it but it do like hit you in the head. . . . It makes you think twice about what you doing.

Like all other respondents, Alex said that Carl should discard peer pressure, because he is ultimately the person who needs to take responsibility for his own life.

Really, what people say ain't got nothing to do with what you gonna do 'cause . . . they ain't feeding Carl's kids, they ain't feeding his wife, they ain't paying the rent, so, you got to do what you got to do. But it do make it, like, harder for you to do something out of the ordinary.

In contrast to most subjects' "teasing makes it hard" sentiment, some respondents, particularly the ones in the high-achieving group at School A, articulated a "tough love" position.

Since most of the members of this group had the above attitudes toward racial issues, it may not be surprising that they displayed a harsh attitude toward Carl and adopted the "tough love" position, which was unique among the groups of respondents. Jerry felt that "Sometimes people . . . need somebody to drop real life on you, and you need to come to the realization hard. . . . You need someone to be stern with you and yell at you and get you straight . . . you may get mad and offended but then while you are at home later on, you would just sit and think about it and say 'gee, maybe I do need to change something or to try to make better of myself.'" Leo (School A, high G.P.A.) said: "I would make him [Carl] feel stupid. . . . I would have clowned him. Every time I would see him in his sneakers, I would say 'you got your baby diapers on.' I would have kept drilling it into him." Andrew (School A, high G.P.A.) said: "Some people, especially he was real deep into his stuff . . . you need a rude awakening . . . you need to smack them up a little bit and then they'll go do it real fast."

The respondents who strongly endorsed the American dream often said that race didn't matter. They implied that in the United States everyone competes on an equal playing field, and that all it takes to succeed is personal will and hard work. Therefore, by extension, when people failed, it was their own fault. Adam (School A, high G.P.A.) talked about some Black people's lack of a work ethic: "It seems like a lot of people are just looking for handouts . . . you really have to work for it. People just go through some rough times but you got to understand that help is good but if we are going to come up . . . got to get out there and do it . . . if they don't want to be oppressed anymore so to speak. . . . I am tired of hearing people's excuses or giving excuses for this and that, you just got to do it."

Some of the respondents' comments echoed both Black and White conservative sentiments when they rationalized how welfare recipients were harmed by the welfare system because it created dependency and made people lazy. Thus, cutting off welfare stipends was articulated as beneficial for the recipients because without the government to depend upon, they would be able to develop good work ethics and self-reliance. For those respondents, this logic guided their attitude toward Carl in *The Cosby Show* and Blacks in general. Though we found respondents with this position from almost all groups, the high-achieving group from School A had the strongest such voice. During their discussion of Carl, they debated whether race (which they carefully replaced with the term "culture") had anything to do with Carl's condition or, for that matter, the condition of Blacks in general. Andrew (School A, high G.P.A.) commented: "He [Carl] is so stuck inside that stereotype of what him and his friends are. He can't escape that . . . his friends are on the bottom too . . . because he has found so much solace in his friends . . . if he doesn't break away from that, he can't break away from the path he is leading to." It is interesting to note that though Andrew asserted that Carl's friends are "on the bottom" and Carl couldn't break away from the "stereotype" he and his friends are stuck with, there is nothing in the program that suggests that Carl's friends have negative characteristics. Actually, Carl's friend disapproves of his behavior and is ready to find a job to support his pregnant girlfriend. Still, Andrew's reading of the story may have supported his identification with Carl and his circumstances. This identifies two versions of the support offered by friends and community: friends may offer support and solace but they also limit growth and the potential for success. The group that defines itself and its members solely in terms of its difference from mainstream (White) culture can be both supportive and stifling for those seeking an alternative identity while attempting to retain their ties to family, community, and history.

While discussing why Carl was concerned about others' reaction to his wish to be a lab technician, Pat offered that peer pressure may have resulted from the fact that the job was considered "White": "Some people might even refer to him as becoming a White person, where that job is like you never see a Black person as a lab technician. [They may say] 'Who do you think you are?' 'Do you think you are better than who we are?' . . . So maybe he was afraid to say that when there is a room mostly with Black people in there." Pat's remark provides us with a glimpse of Black students' fear of being associated with "acting White" (Fordham 1996) or "lack[ing] Blackness" (Novek 1995, 169), which can cause them to reject academic or career success that may suggest Whiteness. However, when students explored the question "Can someone be Black but not Black enough?" many of them did associate speaking Standard English with "acting White." However, none of them connected that term negatively with professionalism or good jobs. They related "Whiteness" mainly with food (red wine and steak instead of barbecued ribs), dress codes (preppy clothes), interests (skateboarding), social customs (going to brunches), or some habits they considered as foreign or even rude, such as Charles's description of his uncle who lived in California: "When he come up here, I can't stand his ass, because he be acting too White for me. Like when we got to the Y [YMCA], after we get done working out swimming, he the only Black man I ever seen strip butt naked in the Y and take a shower. . . . That's stuff White folks do . . . come in all butt naked, dangling and hanging out, showering." Relating Whiteness to particular images, behaviors, and discursive constructions afforded students the opportunity to envision alternatives to Whiteness that were attractive and, indeed, preferable. Moreover, it provided a basis for empowerment through opposition to White culture while not limiting options for defining Black identity or success.

With each of the focus groups, the opportunity to discuss race and identity issues within the context of the media clips led to a more general discussion of the discursive structuring of Black and White imagery and the consequences this discourse had for the students' everyday lives.

Meaning and Its Consequences: On Blackness, Race, and Culture

After discussing the video clip, the focus groups were asked about the meaning of Blackness to them. Almost all the students from School A and School B theorized the literal meaning of Blackness as "nothing but a color," emphasized individual differences, put a positive spin on Blackness as being limitless and strong, without mentioning the odds they were against. Andy (School B, high G.P.A.) said: "That's my background . . . my . . . family is Black. Just a color . . . nothing else, that's it. It's just a label." Bill (School B, low G.P.A.) felt much the same way as Andy: "There's no difference just either I'm Black, somebody else White or Puerto Rican, it's like nothing." Ian (School A, low G.P.A.) said: "Black to me is nothing more than a color. Although, my mom is Italian, and my dad was Black, she don't call me Black . . . she won't say Black man, she would say brown man because nobody is Black. If people were Black at night we wouldn't even see you, you'd be seeing a bunch of clothes walking." Pat (School A, high G.P.A.) shared: "Black, I just think of it as a color. . . . I don't like Black food most of the time. . . . Just because you're Black does not mean you have to eat collard greens, or neck bones. . . . I don't think that you are what you are, just because you are Black you have to act it. You can act any way you want to. . . . I learned that from my mother where she raised me as whatever you want to be . . . or want to do . . . you go ahead and do it because you are not living your life for the Black people or for the White people. You are living your life for yourself . . . you are going to be the only one you will have to answer to." In fact, color blindness and individualism were the dominant discourse when discussing Blackness among all groups, except the ones from School C.

Pat's remark was a rejection of Black essentialism. This is a discourse that can have both progressive and conservative connotations. The progressive meaning would be used to debunk the notion that Blacks are genetically or fundamentally different from Whites (often invoked as an explanation of Black's inferiority), while the conservative meaning would be used to devoid any collectivity and group identity, and help construct an ahistorical and apolitical discourse around Blackness.

Among all the respondents in School A and School B, only one student spoke of an irreconcilable contradiction Blacks often face: no, race doesn't matter, so you are limitless and you should not have prejudice against other races, but yes, race does matter so you must work harder than Whites in order to succeed.

Alex (School A, low G.P.A.) said: "I was always taught don't judge people by their color . . . but at the same time, what I was taught is that it is going to be harder for you, you got to be twice as better. And sometimes I be trying to tell my parents that is not always true . . . I be saying race is not a big issue but . . . you never know how another person is going to be thinking." In stark contrast to School A and School B, Black meant "hardship" and "overcoming obstacles" for students from School C, and they were direct in pointing out where the obstacles were coming from. Jack (School C, high G.P.A.) stated: "My definition for Black is a hustle . . . the White men don't want to give us anything, so we got to do it on ourselves, got to hustle. . . . Keep a job, a nice little job. . . . Legal. . . . Not like do something bad." Art (School C, high G.P.A.) said: "Being Black . . . for me is to overcome the odds and to tell . . . all them people that told me that I couldn't do nothing . . . just show them through action, without words . . . when I make my speech at the graduation. . . . Yo, they [Whites] still rule, but . . . being Black, I have to find a way for their system to work for me. . . . Is to use their own system that try to keep me down, to bring me up." Charles (School C, high G.P.A.) felt that he must "overcome many challenges to achieve goals. There just too much out there, too many hills . . . for Blacks to do that. And Whites it just seems like it's a downhill. They just get on the little skateboard, and just rolling down the hill and they straight. Niggers got, we got to pedal and push and what not to go up that hill man, it's mad hard." Mike (School C, low G.P.A.) summarized the underlying sentiment of many of the School C respondents: "It's power . . . 'cause you got to go through a lot to be Black . . . a lot of struggle."

Though Frank (School C, low G.P.A.) believed that he was "making something of myself which many other people can't," he replied "true" when his classmates mentioned the difficult conditions Blacks often faced. Charles's metaphor of the skateboard (rolling downhill) used to differentiate between the uphill struggle for Blacks and the constant downhill easy path for Whites was also invoked as a symbol of Whiteness. Thus, if the skateboard is equated with Whiteness and allows a person to glide "down-hill" through life, then being Black is pedaling and pushing oneself up the hill. More importantly, the struggle is also about power and about pride.

The paradox of race could be seen here as an extension of other para-doxes in the boys' lives. You have the choice to act Black or act White, but doing either has consequences that could be viewed as undesirable. Being Black means being proud of who you are and your community, but at the same time going to school and trying to better yourself are sometimes seen as "selling out." It seems unremarkable that many of these boys identified with DMX and his lyrics, while distancing themselves from his message.

Experiencing Race and Racism

Making meaning of the term "Black" naturally led to talk about discrimi-nation, differential treatment, race and racism. Given School C's strong Black culture and the students' past experiences of failing in the regular school system, respondents from that school were most vocal about the dis-crimination they suffered as well as the stereotypes the dominant society has about them. Larry (School C, high G.P.A.) felt that "some teachers and counselors and principals [in other schools], they don't give advice like that [Dr. Huxtable's advice]. They'll just toss you aside. If everybody give advice like that, I think it would be . . . more positive . . . the majority of them [Black students in other schools], they get kicked out of school . . . and that will turn them into selling drugs . . . or something worse you never know." Mike (School C, high G.P.A.) considered the implications of the stereotypes for his daily life: "Cops . . . see you walking around late night or something, they gonna automatically think you're doing something wrong, they going to search you and stuff, that's everyday, that's all the time." One person mentioned that a caseworker told them that once he was in a police station and witnessed a White kid carrying a pound of marijuana on him, and the White policemen just let him go free. Larry also knew about that incident and responded: "The charges will be lesser on him [that White boy] than it was for either . . . a Black or Puerto Rican or Hispanic. . . . They give the White man . . . drug program, they give us five years, six years, it's crazy."

In contrast to School C's students' accounts of various kinds of racism, the high-achieving group from School A responded very differently. Though they acknowledged that there were some "culturally prejudiced" people, they explained that the problems stemmed from Whites not having opportunities to understand Blacks. Many of them wanted to break down the barriers of racial differences. Thus, those high-achieving students thought that Blacks should get out, become known to Whites and learn from each other. They also had very idealistic views about the future of Blacks and how the general public would then see them very positively.

Leo (School A, high G.P.A.) stated: "A lot of people are culturally bi-ased, but . . . a lot of people are just ignorant. I mean, it is getting better though. . . . So you have to get out there and learn about them as well as them learn about you." Pat (School A, high G.P.A.) said: "They are asking [questions about Blacks] because they really don't know, and they want to know, so that they don't make that mistake with the next person that they meet, and they want to break that barrier. So I think that for Black people we have to not get angry at times, we have to understand that is how peo-ple learn from each other." Adam (School A, high G.P.A.) felt that "They [White people] see us like different. . . . They just know about stereotypes and . . . that is what they feed on and think that's true. But there are cases where they say like they want to know . . . that is broadening their horizon." Jerry (School A, high G.P.A.) stated: "As time goes by . . . the opinion of the general public of Black people is going to get better and better . . . a lot of Black people are gonna get out there and be exposed and be seen as suc-cessful images and positive images. Then people are going to look at them and probably then base their opinion and thoughts of all Black people by them 'cause that's what happen in most cases. I think they are going to have a good feeling about us . . . you still gonna have people . . . that are biased and bigots . . . but . . . the majority of the people are gonna accept us as who we are and what we do." Leo (School A, high G.P.A.) was optimistic about the possibilities for change: "I think that in a political sense . . . we are a peo-ple on the rise . . . we still have to get that first Black president." Pat (School A, high G.P.A.) thought that "Society has been changing its perception of Black people. . . . Black people are changing their perception of other Black people and their own race . . . and people are realizing that no matter what color you are you can do whatever you want to, because that's who you are, you are an individual not a group of people, you know."

Interestingly, when we explored further, every one of the students had experienced being treated as a potential thief while shopping in stores, or rejected by White teens when the respondent invited them to play basket-ball, or ignored and assumed to be incompetent in a football camp until proving himself, or being dissuaded from taking highly challenging courses at school. Pat provided an analysis of how institutional racism worked at school, resulting in disproportionately high percentages of

Black students occupying the low-tracking classes and dropping out of school:

> Most of my classes that I take, there are not that many Black people in there. I don't think guidance counselors do it . . . consciously, but when you sign up for a course, they go "Are you sure you can handle this course load?" "Are you sure you can do this and work?" What makes you think I work after school? I don't work. My mother supports me and she wants my education to be my number-one priority. Teachers . . . will say "Are you sure you can handle this homework?" or "Are you sure you want to be in my class because I am a strict person and I am not lenient, I don't make you make-up test." And they automatically get the idea that if you are Black you must be lazy or that you don't perform as well as the White students. . . . Sometimes they just do it because . . . that's how they can weed the good students from the bad out of their class. So when you go to a class, it is either predominately White or Black. In one of my class, there was a lot of Black people in there, and if you get all Black people together they are going to act crazy in the sense that they are going to chill out together because they know each other. But then . . . the teacher says that this is my bad class. Just because they like to have fun does not necessarily mean that they are bad. But if they are always put together and they know that is why they are put together, then of course they are going to act out.

Pat was not alone in feeling institutional racism at school. It was echoed by the students at School C when they complained that in their previous schooling experience they were often "tossed aside" by White teachers and administrators. School racism has also been well-documented by educational scholars such as Kozol (1992), Oakes (1986), and Wheelock (1992). However, in spite of the discrimination experienced either at the personal or institutional level by the Black students from the School A, high-G.P.A. group, they insisted that race did not matter when they discussed what it takes to succeed. Leo (School A, high G.P.A.) said:

> Yeah! It's like where you born, you ain't learn nothing but from your mama and your daddy. If your mama think that she wasn't going nowhere and she not going nowhere, and she teach you that you not going nowhere, unless you go to school and someone else steps in and tells you that you can go somewhere, you not going to go nowhere. . . . My mom . . . went to college. . . . I see myself going to college, owning my own business but that is because my mom told me that I can do that . . .

but if my mom would just lay around in the house and worked at like McDonalds, and she didn't want me to go anywhere, she wouldn't have told me anything. She would let me skip school and not make me do my homework . . . so it has to do with who you live with and your parents.

Jerry (School A, high G.P.A.) said:

Yeah! I agree. I think it has something to do with race in there, if it is not race thing then it is culture and the way he is raised and brought up . . . maybe his parents . . . just sat around the house all day and did nothing and maybe not applied themselves and if that is all he sees and that is all he knows that's basically what he is going to do. He is going to follow suit.

And Andrew (School A, high G.P.A.) commented:

It doesn't matter what your race is, 'cause anyone can be poor. I definitely believe that, it is up to you . . . it takes that person to be driven . . . to have a dream . . . to obtain goals. . . . You should be free to see beyond color, beyond creed, beyond the environment that anything is obtainable, that nothing is forsaken because of who you are and what you look like and where you from.

A few points in the previous conversation are worth further discussion. Leo used a White working-class example to disclaim the "race" influence. He reduced the limitations imposed by race (or culture) or class to an individual's lack of vision and will. Leo's rationale was affirmed by Andrew when he pointed out that "anyone can be poor . . . it is up to you . . . to obtain goals." Both Jerry's statement ("maybe his parents . . . just sat around the house all day . . . not applied themselves and if that is all he sees. . . . He is going to follow suit.") and Leo's ("if my mom would just lay around in the house and worked at like McDonalds, and she didn't want me to go anywhere") implied that the reason why some people were not able to get good jobs was because they were lazy. They also imply that poor people damage their children's future by not being able to provide good role models for their children, thus perpetuating poverty from one generation to the next. Both Jerry and Leo attempted to differentiate between the class and race issues, but they used class confinement to dismiss racism without investigating class. This phenomenon is addressed further in the discussion section of the chapter. It may not be surprising that most of this group of students (School A, high G.P.A.) have at least one parent with a college degree and a high family income. Since these students have experienced less hardship in life, and their school performance could probably guarantee their entrance to college and middle-class jobs in the future, "reap what you sow" has been a useful motto. When they projected their own experience onto other Blacks who were less fortunate, though they may be aware of the limitation imposed by "culture" (or actually, class), they still laid the responsibility of failure onto the individual's shoulders.

Discussion: Searching for Oppositional Identities

In this preliminary and small-scale study, two media texts served as important stimuli for students to discuss their identities. DMX and *The Cosby Show* can be seen as two extremes in the spectrum of media representations of Black men. DMX glorifies hypermasculinity, violence, and street life, and *The Cosby Show* promotes responsibility, work ethics, and family life. By responding to the two texts, our subjects articulated what "Blackness" meant to them and to the dominant society, how they positioned themselves in the society that bell hooks terms "White supremacist, capitalist and patriarchal" (Jhally 1997), how they explained the current social equalities, and how they dealt with the problems.

The questions that gave impetus to our study were based on the studies of Willis (1977), Fordham (1996), and Novek (1995) that documented the phenomenon of oppositional identities among low-academic-achieving groups. Extending their conclusions, we expected to find similar results: that disenfranchised youth create ideas about who they are in opposition to the values presented by dominant culture and media texts. Instead, what we found among the low- and high-achieving students was an emphasis on family values, self-support, responsibility, and education. They also condemned violence and antisocial behavior. There are several directions that can be pursued based on these findings. The first is to assume that we found no evidence at all of oppositional identities; rather, the students all conformed to the dominant ideals expressed in *The Cosby Show*.

Fusing Race, Class, and the American Dream

In accordance with Jhally and Lewis's (1992) studies of *The Cosby Show*, we found that the "American dream" was a prominent and powerful discourse among all of our respondents. Many students, particularly at School A, replicated that myth and the notion of an equal and raceless playing field, despite the fact that they had witnessed racism on a personal or institutional level. Though students at School C were aware of society's unjustness, they nonetheless believed that an individual's hard work would surely help him or her achieve his or her goals. The myth of the American dream is powerful precisely because it is true for some people. As Jhally and Lewis (1992, 73) state in their analysis of *The Cosby Show*:

> The American Dream . . . is built on the cracks in an otherwise fairly solid class system, which ensures that most poor people will stay poor and most rich people will stay rich, in cycles that inexorably revolve from one generation to the next. The system is not, however, inexorable: the cracks in it may be too small to threaten its survival, but they are large enough to allow a few people to slip upward. These happy few are seen as confirming the American Dream, whose strange logic transforms them from exceptions to the rule, creating the idea that there are, in fact, no rules.

The ideology of education being the sure way for upward mobility could then be seen as reinforcing the status quo. People who are "good examples" help validate the system and help maintain the illusion that the United States is a land of opportunity. In addition, that ideology might keep the system intact by rewarding only some fortunate individuals while not offsetting the existing hierarchy. As the remarks of the high-G.P.A. group in School A, the college preparatory, suggested, when those successful individuals believed that society worked based on meritocracy, they would not create any systematic change even if they were in a position to do so.

Drawing on this logic, we could once again affirm the results of *The Cosby Show* audience research by Jhally and Lewis (1992), who also confirmed the fusion and confusion between race and class; they state that

> the viewers' inability to perceive the growing racial distinctions in the United States was bound up with an unawareness of the limiting effects of a class system. Most people in our survey saw racism firmly within the confines of individualism. It is not simply that they were unable to draw connections between race and class. They found it difficult to talk about the social effects of class at all. (72)

Some of our respondents from School A's high-achieving group were able to point out that poverty was not solely a Black problem. However, since individual effort was the only explanation offered for success or failure, the revelation that "Black and White can both be poor" only served to dismiss the existence of racism (since Whites can also be poor) rather than to promote further investigation into the class confinement both Blacks and Whites share. Leo (School A, high G.P.A.) mentioned how a White kid only saw his father fixing cars and so he also followed suit. It is arguable that Leo's statement demonstrates class consciousness, however. He did not address the issues of access and the institution's power to maintain the rigid class structure. In Leo's example class confinement only became a personal choice, though it may have been inevitable because of the environmental influence. Without a clear conception of how class functions and how class intersects with race, the realization that class confinement was shared by Blacks and Whites alike could be seen to further solidify the myth of individualism and the American dream.

Confusing the American Dream:
Oppositional Readings and Productive Pleasures

As mentioned earlier, another and quite different conclusion could be drawn from our research, one that strongly diverges from the implication that our participants were merely upholding dominant ideology and conforming to the status quo. While Hall's (1980) distinctions between dominant, oppositional, and negotiated readings of media texts allow for differentiation between the encoding (production) and decoding (interpretation) of media texts, the theoretical underpinnings of his model—popular culture, pleasure, and class—provide a more complex understanding of how these different readings produce multiple locations and vice versa. Therefore, as Radway (1986) and Fiske (1996) have articulated, body/mind pleasures are intimately tied to sociocultural relations, but do not have to be linked to structural or institutional reform to be productive on the level of everyday experience. Thus, to translate the students' acceptance of Cosby's message into an acceptance of the status quo is perhaps to neglect the more subtle operations of discourse that recreate identities in *moments* of interaction that constitute everyday life.

Dissing DMX: On Pleasure and Resistance

For Fiske (1996) the pleasure of reading a media text becomes productive in those examples of daily life where resistance and enjoyment commingle, where media texts offer release from societal and personal constraints and pressures while making us aware of our uniqueness and potential for creativity. Therefore, pleasure is productive when it simultaneously offers both identification with and escape from the relationships that enable and constrain personal and social choices and the consequences they might bring. Oppositional readings, from this perspective, are produced in moments of interaction between the audience and the text, as well as those (subsequent) contexts in which audience members relate the media messages to other interactions and relationships. These anticonformist readings may produce radical (for Barthes, *jouissance*) pleasurable responses to social constraints or might produce subtle changes on the discursive level (*plaisir*) that lead to consequential reordering of conversational and relational patterns.

Following this reasoning, "gangsta" rap (sung by a formal criminal) that celebrates violence, abuse against women, and drug use could produce a type of *jouissance* that is oppositional, the pleasure of evading the social order.[2] Certainly, violence, drug abuse, and the mistreatment of women all violate moral and legal dictums and thus create social disorder. While the participants in our study did not seem to experience *jouissance* or construct overt oppositional identities in relation to the song, we should not dismiss their interpretations as merely dominant readings that uphold mainstream values. Although most of the students identified somewhat with DMX and the hardships he had been through, his exploitation of stereotypes about Black culture for economic reasons without offering some solutions or hope distanced them from the pleasures they might otherwise experience in relating to the music as a basis for challenging dominant values and culture.

These students negotiated their relationships to the text through opposing the oppositional textual images that DMX re-presented. A better explanation of their complex response to the text my be found in the definition of *plaisir* offered by Fiske (1996, 54):

> *Plaisir* involves the recognition, confirmation and negotiation of a social identity, but this does not mean that it is necessarily a conformist, reactionary pleasure (though it may be). There are pleasures in conforming to the dominant ideology and the subjectivity it proposes when it is in our interest to do so; equally there are pleasures of opposing or modifying that ideology and its subjectivities when it fails to meet our interests. Insofar as people are positioned complexly in society, in simultaneous relationships of conformity and opposition to the dominant ideology, so the form of *plaisir* that will be experienced will vary from the reactionary to the subversive.

As mentioned earlier, for pleasures to be productive, they must provide the experience of identification, awareness of one's uniqueness, and some degree of escape from everyday reality. While the students identify somewhat with the experiences of the "hood" in the DMX video, they do

not identify with DMX himself or view him as a positive role model. Thus, the DMX video does not give them a sense of their uniqueness or the possibilities for options other than those he presents. They resist the imagery offered in the lyrics and video of "What's My Name?" even as they accept that some of his portrayals of the "hood" are accurate. This explanation of pleasure and resistance is as crucial to our respondents' seemingly overt dismissal of the DMX video as it is to their apparent embrace of the conformist discourse in the Cosby episode.

The Paradox of Opposition: Reading Cosby Radically

Looking back at the focus groups' responses to *The Cosby Show* episode in search of productive pleasure, or *plaisir*, we found that the participants expressed both identification and escape in their talk about the show. They identified somewhat with Carl's predicament and his dreams, and certainly with his experiences of peer pressure. The students discussed Dr. Huxtable's advice as providing options or alternatives from the dead-end situation in which Carl found himself. When Dr. Huxtable asked Carl about his dreams, the boys in our study felt that he positioned Carl as having goals that were reachable. Dr. Huxtable offered Carl a future where he (Carl) thought he had none; clearly the boys in our study saw this as a way out of their own circumstances and as going "up the ladder" as well.

In finding moments of productive pleasure in *The Cosby Show* episode, the participants constructed both conformist (dominant) and noncomformist readings of the show. While the boys in our study are most certainly *not* attempting to read the show against the grain, by identifying both with Carl's constraints and his potential for success, the participants could be said to resist dominant as well as radical portrayals of Blacks as poor, lazy, criminal, and so on. For many of our participants, the pleasure of watching *The Cosby Show* was in identifying with the isolation of wanting to succeed in an environment where success can be alienating, and in finding a way out of the situation with the support of a successful Black male role model. While on a structural level the show upheld dominant values, on the level of everyday experience for these boys, it provided options for success in the struggle for a viable future.

Conclusions: The Two Sides of the American Dream

Our study has offered two alternative readings of our findings: the two sides of the American dream. In the former explanation we can see that without

an understanding of the U.S. race and class system, even the heartfelt personal experiences of racial discrimination could not help our respondents form a coherent understanding of their social condition. The myth of the American dream further engendered the discourse of color blindness and a conservative stand promoting individualism and self-blame for personal pathology. The American dream may be an effective coping strategy for despair. If the system doesn't change, it may become the only choice besides withdrawal. This reading of our study has shown that the myth has impeded the need and even the want for social change.

The latter interpretation is a reading of our respondents' superficial conformity to the American dream as an oppositional response to the dominant negative imagery of Black males. If success is interpreted as "acting White," then non-Whites have limited options. However, the students in our study were careful to differentiate between success and behaviors that could be interpreted as degrading to the Black community. DMX, for instance, represented radical Blackness to some, but to most of our participants he had achieved his success in part through the exploitation of negative images of Black urban culture.

Limitations of the Study

This study differs from the studies we discussed earlier in the chapter in that we were unable to conduct extensive fieldwork in the high schools and among the students surveyed. Willis, Fordham, and Novek used an ethnographic approach,[3] whereas our study used focus-group interviews. We were not able to conduct in-depth interviews with individual students, or to observe the students in their natural settings, meet their friends and families, or conduct the research over a long period of time. Though no teachers or administrators were present during the discussions, it is possible that the students may have felt uncomfortable in contradicting the school ideology and thus withheld more overt demonstrations of their oppositional identities. However, we did not detect any evidence that would suggest our subjects pretended to have different views from the ones expressed. Another possibility is that students who demonstrated more overt oppositional identities were beyond the reach of the schools and thus not in our groups. Many of our respondents knew of close friends, family members, or acquaintances (or even themselves in the past) who were "potheads," had dropped out of school, or had legal problems.

Within our sample there were not as many differences between academic achievement levels as there were differences between schools. For instance, students at School C who had supportive Black teachers and mostly Black student peers were much more aware and articulate about the racial discrimination they experienced and had many fewer color-blind discourses than students in either School A or School B. This is particularly the case for the high-G.P.A. group at School C. While discussing their dreams, most of the students at School A and School B expressed the desire to go to college and have professions such as computer engineer, teacher, and surgeon. Most students in the School C low-G.P.A. group also talked about going to college, though for economic reasons the majority of them planned to go to the military first in order to pay for their college tuition. The high-G.P.A. group at School C was the most different group in terms of their dreams: none of them desired to have an institutionally bound profession. Instead, they wanted to own hotels, restaurants, or clubs, play basketball, be a rap artist, or a carpenter. Their rationale can be summed up by Alex's remarks (School A, low G.P.A.): "I hate school, like right now I wish I wasn't here but in order to do what I want to do . . . I know that I need . . . [a] diploma and then that ain't even gonna be enough because then you gonna have to go to college because now you need more . . . to always get better . . . you always got to educate yourself because you got to put yourself in a position where people gonna need you."

There are good reasons to pursue higher education. According to Wilson (1999), the average wage gap between individuals with a college degree and those without has increasingly widened, and non-college-degree jobs have also declined. In the 1950s and 1960s the average earnings of college graduates was only about 20 percent higher than that of high school graduates. By 1979 it had increased to 49 percent, and grew rapidly to 83 percent by 1992. Between 1984 and 1994, while the fraction of the male population employed increased by 1 percent for college graduates, it fell by 3 percent for high school graduates, and 10 percent for high school dropouts (Wilson 1999, 27, 29).

However, the educational system in the United States does not provide enough support for those Black students who have high aspirations but may not have the qualifications required by college admissions offices. Donaldson (1996) summarizes educators' findings that, as a result of culturally biased standardized testing and teachers' prejudices, high numbers of Black students were placed in low and non-college-bound tracks. There have been well-documented disparities between lower and higher tracking groups in terms of access to "knowledge, instructional opportunities and the classroom learning environments" (Donaldson 1996, 16). The remarks from some students that teachers "just tossed them aside" may not be ungrounded. In addition, in recent years the tide of affirmative-action backlash made some colleges and universities remove affirmative action from their admission procedures.

The implications for educators and those who shape educational policy are clear: Teachers and administrators are not reaching Black students at a time when they are most in need of support. The students in our study repeatedly articulated a desire to succeed and achieve their goals, while expressing their frustration with the isolation and alienation they felt when they tried to distance themselves from negative influences (friends, family, etc.) in their community. Perhaps most striking were the metaphors that the students used to describe their situation: peer pressures that "hit you in the head," or "too many hills . . . for Blacks" to achieve their goals while Whites "get on the little skateboard," Blacks are, "working up the ladder" but constantly getting "booted back down." These metaphors are more complex than they might at first seem. They address multiple layers of signification, as this study has shown. The use of analogy and metaphor, a sophisticated technique rarely employed by White audiences, is important to understanding the process through which the Black youths in our study construct their identities in relation to the media and significant others in their lives. Educators who listen to these metaphors are more likely to comprehend the complexities of the paradoxes that Black students often face in school, at home, and in their community. Our study has also demonstrated the urgency of helping our Black youth understand how social formations such as race, gender, and class intricately intersect, how racism functions on the institutional level beyond individual and interpersonal realms, how past history connects and influences the present, and eventually, helping Black youth envision a more fair and just system through collective effort.

Furthermore, our study pointed to the need in audience research to pay attention to the multiple levels and positions through which audiences can read texts. Both of the interpretations of reading texts offered here are useful in terms of the degree and level at which intervention is desired or expected. Attention to the ways media messages are utilized and articulated in everyday experiences is imperative to understanding how the subtle pleasures involved in accepting, negotiating, or opposing dominant culture can produce change on the personal, relational, and societal levels.

Notes

The authors would like to thank the following people for their invaluable advice and suggestions: Justin Lewis, Michael Morgan, Lolly Robinson, William Cross, Jr., and Pablo Picker. Without the enthusiasm and support of Elissa Griffith-Johnson, this study would not have happened. Last but not least, we would like to thank the participants in this study.

1. According to Touré, DMX's "It's Dark and Hell Is Hot" (released in 1998) sold 3.7 million copies in 1998, "Flesh of My Flesh . . . Blood of My Blood" (released in December 1998) sold 2.8 million, and "Then There Was X" (released in December 1999) sold 1.9 million.

2. While we did not ask questions specifically about the pleasures of viewing the texts we showed respondents, their connection to or identification with the texts and expressed like or dislike of the content are indicative of the same phenomenon.

3. The three ethnographic studies were conducted in the following ways: Willis studied a group of twelve nonacademic working-class male students "by means of observation and participant observation in class, around the school and during leisure activities, regular recorded group discussion; informal interviews and diaries" (1977, 4–5). In addition, Willis also did comparative case studies with five other groups, such as conformist or nonconformist groups from different class backgrounds or neighborhoods. Novek collaborated with an English teacher who assigned students to write "daily field notes about classroom interactions and neighborhood settings, student writings, and interviews" (1995, 185). She collected the data from ninety-seven students, between December 1991 and June 1993. Fordham did her study with thirty-three students (key informants), twelve high-achieving and twenty-one underachieving. Her sample, like ours, was also selected based on teachers' assessments of the students' performance. Her "low-achieving" group had an average grade of C or lower, which was similar to our sample. Her data included formal and informal interviews with thirty-three key informants, their peers, parents, and school officials, participant observation within and outside the school, and so on. It may also be possible that the different geographical locations of the schools were

the reason why we couldn't replicate the three researchers' results. Willis's school was in England in a typical working-class town in the 1970s, Fordham's school was in Washington, D.C., Novek's "West Urbania" school was possibly in New Jersey, and both Fordham's and Novek's studies were conducted in the 1990s. There were no indications from Fordham's and Novek's studies that their East Coast urban schools were very different from our schools.

References

Donaldson, K. (1996). *Through students' eyes: Combating racism in United States schools.* Westport/London: Praeger.

Dyson, M. (1989) "Bill Cosby and the politics of race." *Zeta*, September.

Fiske, J. (1996). *Media matters: Everyday culture and political change.* Minnesota: University of Minnesota Press.

Fordham, S. (1996). *Blacked out: Dilemmas of race, identity, and success at Capital High.* Chicago: University of Chicago Press.

Hall, S. (1980). Encoding/decoding. In S. Hall et al., eds., *Culture, media, language* (pp. 129–38). London: Hutchinson.

Jenkins, H. (1995). Out of the closet and into the universe. In J. Tulloch and H. Jenkins, eds. *Science fiction audiences* (pp. 239–65). London/New York: Routledge.

Jhally, S. (1997). *bell hooks: Cultural criticism and transformation* (video). Northhampton, Mass.: Media Education Foundation.

Jhally, S., and J. Lewis. (1992). *Enlightened racism: The Cosby Show, audiences, and the myth of the American dream.* Boulder, Colo.: Westview Press.

Kozol, J. (1992). *Savage inequalities: Children in America's schools.* New York: Harper Perennial.

Lewis, J. (1991). *The ideological octopus: An exploration of television and its audience.* New York: Routledge.

Novek, E. (1995). West Urbania: An ethnographic study of communication practices in inner-city youth culture. *Communication Studies* 46 (fall/winter): 169–86.

Oakes, J. (1986). Keeping track, Part 1: The policy and practice of curriculum inequality. *Phi Delta Kappa*, 12–17.

Radway, J. (1986). Identifying ideological seams: Mass culture, analytical method, and political practice. *Communication* 9: 93–123.

Touré. (2000). DMX reigns as the dark prince of hip hop. *Rolling Stone*, April, pp. 84–91.

Wheelock, A. (1992). *Crossing the tracks: How untracking can save America's schools.* New York: New York Press.

Willis, P. (1977). *Learning to labor: How working class kids get working class jobs.* New York: Columbia University Press.

Wilson, W. J. (1999). *The bridge over the racial divide: Rising inequality and coalition politics.* Berkeley: University of California Press.

!

7

"It's Just Like Teaching People 'Do the Right Things'"
Using TV to Become a Good and Powerful Man

JoEllen Fisherkeller

A Young Individual and Television over Time

Like now I don't really watch TV, not like I watched it before. Before I was like in the show, and like "Yeah!" But now I'm just watching it. . . . I just watch it really, really for purely entertainment now. . . . Even though shows now are becoming more realistic, like bad things happen, it's not always a happy ending and things, you know. And I like happy endings, there's noth-ing wrong with that. But you know, sometimes it's just not true to the way life really is. I watch TV differently now. Sometimes I'm watching it, but I'm not really watching it, just seeing what's going on. You know you hear the music come on and (someone) hugs someone, and then things are always better. And you have to wonder, you know. That's not how at least my life is, you know. I don't hear any music coming on and I don't hear anyone com-ing, telling me that it'll be all right.

—Christopher,[1] at seventeen years of age

This African-American youth, a resident of New York City, is an individual I met when he was twelve years old. At that time, he was a seventh grader at a public school where I was conducting an ethnographic study of young adolescents and their experiences in television culture (Fisherkeller 1995). Christopher became a focal participant in that study, and I've managed to stay in contact with him over the years, interviewing him in depth when he was twelve, thirteen, seventeen, and most recently, twenty-one years old. This chapter aims to contextualize Christopher's evolution from young adolescence to young adulthood, and to reflect on his related interactions with television culture in the United States.

What can we learn from one young person and his experiences within television culture over several years' time? It is in groups that most media audiences are investigated, as interpretive communities (Radway 1984), as popular subcultures (Hebdige 1979; McRobbie 1994; Willis 1990), and as various kinds of demographic identities, such as workers in different classes (Lembo 2000; Morley 1992), middle-class females (Press 1991), and African Americans (Means Coleman 2000). Qualitative studies of media audience groups provide a valuable sense of the meaning-making processes and contexts that are common to particular groups. Yet group studies typically situate their members at a specific point in time, and do not account for the long-term aspects of their everyday lives or for any changes in situation that might take place over time. This can be done with groups, but it is costly in terms of time and energy. Additionally, one advantage to focusing on an individual is the relative ease of following one person versus many over several years.

Yet one individual, such as Christopher, cannot represent a whole group because individual identities position people within several overlapping and interrelated groups at once so that no one is a "typical" member of any group (Clark, forthcoming). Christopher is an African American; a male; a youth; a transplanted New Yorker; the son of working-class parents who have separated and recombined their extended families in different locales; a capable student; a sometimes lonely peer; a fan of mysteries, comedies, and computers; and someone who has a file of lyrics he's written, along with melodies he's composed for them by humming into a tape recorder. Another advantage of focusing on an individual rather than on groups of viewers is that multiple identities and contexts of existence such as these can be examined and understood as they are uniquely woven together by the person. A close look at Christopher's particular experiences takes us deeper into the complexity of meaning making in everyday life. And if we investigate his unique ways of making sense of his multiple experiences over time, then we can look for continuities and discontinuities in how a single person weaves a life. Perhaps then we can begin to categorize dynamic patterns of self-development processes that might be found in other individual lives.

I believe that this is a valuable approach to take with young people in particular because of the consistent changes they experience that are age-related, and because of the formative nature of these changes. As Christopher's comments indicate, he does things differently at age seventeen than when he was twelve and thirteen. In addition, what he makes of his life as a growing adolescent is regarded as crucial to his future fulfillment and success. What this study does is describe Christopher's different experiences at different points in time, and reflect on their contributions to his development. Most importantly, this study considers how his changing experiences with television culture are associated with his developing sense of himself, others, and the social worlds of fulfillment and success.

There is a long history of concern about the roles that commercial mass media play in society and in people's lives, and especially in young people's learning and development. Studies of film viewing in the late 1920s and early 1930s in the United States (Blumer 1933) attested to the worries people had even then about how young people might be influenced by the messages and images put forth by popular media. Television's appearance in the 1950s fueled similar worries and a flurry of studies, and yet TV spread to nearly every single household by the end of the 1970s. Now many young people have TVs in their own bedrooms (Roberts 2000). At present, the spread of computers and online technologies prompts these age-old worries again.

The popularity of and access to communications media and hypothetical concerns about youth and popular media cannot tell us what specific roles media play in the everyday lives of youth, and the particular meanings youth construct from their uses of different media. I focus on television because it is a generally more pervasive medium compared to others. In addition, TV is used more regularly by young people whose economic and social circumstances are circumscribed. Certainly, industries and the global economy are computer dependent, and hype about computers and online technologies is prolific. In the United States approximately 80 percent of the middle and upper classes and suburban families and schools have computers and online access, while only about half of lower-income and poor families and schools have such access (Roberts 2000). But it is important to note that the presence of these technologies at home and school doesn't guarantee that they are used regularly, or satisfactorily (Giacquinta, Bauer, and Levin 1993; Orr Vered 1998; Sefton-Green 1998).

Rather than focus on youth and computer media, I examine young people's relationships to television culture as this culture conveys and is part of a system that more generally constitutes contemporary existence. My use of the term "culture" draws on definitions referring to patterns of meaning that are embodied in the symbols, practices, and consciousness of a people located in particular places and times (Geertz 1973, 1983). While Christopher and I may be discussing specific programs and people that appear on television screens, we are both living in a society that is not only reflected in, but also supportive of, what appears on the screen (although perhaps not explicitly, or agreeably). That is, because of the historical and current dominance of commercial forces in the United States, I assume that corporate capitalist ideas and values undergird television programming and symbolism (Fiske 1987) as well as everyday life—even though Christopher, myself, and many other viewers acknowledge that the reality on television is different from the reality of most people's everyday life (Davies 1997; Lembo 2000). Television culture is a phenomenon that exists both on and off the screen, like it or not.

By analyzing Christopher's interpretations and experiences while in middle school, high school, and college, I provide illustrations of the relationships among television culture, identity developments, and learning about the social world. These illustrations rely on my analyses of open-ended interviews with Christopher and on my knowledge of the contexts of his life at different points in time. The interviews used questions as prompts only, and allowed Christopher to discuss whatever he deemed important or pertinent in response. My questions at every meeting included: How are things at home, at school, and with friends? What are your plans for the future? What are your television viewing (and other media) routines? Which are your favorite television (or other media) programs and people, and what do you like about them? What do you think about television (and other media) more generally?

My knowledge of the contexts of Christopher's life is informed by the following: (1) direct observations of specific contexts (participating in his life at school, and visiting his home); (2) shared experiences of larger contexts (living in the same city at the same time, watching the same television programs); and (3) my reading of empirical studies and reports on the topics of youth, everyday life, and/or popular media audiences. My analyses of Christopher's words and experiences are framed simultaneously by the work of Mikhail Bakhtin (1981), Clifford Geertz (1973, 1983), and G. H.

Mead (1934/1962), all of whom assume constructivist, interpretive, and interactionist perspectives toward the language, symbolism, and social activities of humans. These perspectives are most appropriate for understanding the complexity of people's meaning making in everyday life.

About This Young Individual, through Time

I met Christopher when he was twelve, at the beginning of eighteen months of ethnographic research I conducted among his peers, teachers, and families at an alternative public school in New York City. Christopher had arrived at the school midyear, having moved in with his father and away from the South, where he had lived with his mother. Both of his parents were in working-class professions. His father, a former Army man, was a security guard, and his mother was a hospital technician. Christopher had extensive family members via both parents, though they were spread out because of his parents' separate lives. When I first met Christopher, he was an only child getting used to a new stepmother and her family that lived elsewhere in the city. Due to his family's income status, Christopher's living quarters were modest.

As there were only sixty students at Christopher's middle school when he was twelve, and ninety when he was thirteen, the faculty were able, and made a point, to get to know their students. Christopher was regarded by these teachers as academically capable and skilled. His own words at twelve years of age describe his interests at school, although they don't include all the areas in which he was deemed competent: "I like to do science, social studies, and work with computers because all of these are interesting to me. I like science because you learn new things about the earth and planets. I like social studies because you learn about different people and their cultures. I like computers because I think that the way they operate is amazing." Christopher was a good reader and writer, drawn to genres that incorporate suspense and mystery, and struggles between good and evil. The pseudonym he chose for me to use for him at twelve, "Wolverine," is the name of a star character from a comics series called *X-Men*, an animated action/adventure about a futuristic society (now a feature film as well, starring live actors). *X-Men* stars are young mutant do-gooders with superpowers—five males and four females (despite the title) who work as a team. Under the guidance and leadership of a fatherly mutant figure named "Professor," the *X-Men* characters live together in a mansion with hi-tech, sci-fi communications. From this home base they learn about situations that require their assistance and rescue, and when they go on a mission they transform their human resemblances by donning superhero costumes. Wolverine is regarded as one of the signature figures for the series, along with Cyclops and Storm.

It is telling that young adolescent Christopher would choose to name himself after a superhero character who happened to be very popular at his middle school, as evidenced by the *X-Men* Wolverine drawings, stickers, and cards that students displayed and exchanged, and by their verbal references to this character. During the period of Wolverine's popularity at school, Christopher experienced difficulties with his peer relationships. His first year at middle school was painful in part because friendship groups had been established before he arrived midyear. He was regarded as an outsider by the boys he tried to befriend. He would joke around, and talk in character-like voices, as if he were an announcer on television, or a comedian. Indeed one of the people he admired at the time was the (then) late-night talk show host Arsenio Hall, because "he's funny, [and] he knows how to relax and talk to people." Yet Christopher's peers, who were mostly Black and Latino (the majority groups at this school, and labels the students themselves used) didn't respond to his "jokey" advances.

In seventh grade Christopher wasn't participating in basketball, which was a key activity where the males in his community established their bonds of friendship as well as their status as popular. As is the case in most schools, sports participation was regarded as prestigious for the males at Christopher's school (Fine 1987). And there, in part because of the constraints of its urban locale and physical education resources, basketball was the only sport that the males deemed worthy. Christopher wasn't playing because, as he admitted at the time, he was "not that physically fit." In addition, Christopher's brown oxford shoes were not suitable for moving around on the court. Most of the boys and the girls in this school, as in many urban locations, wore sneakers with brand names, and they regarded Christopher's shoes with disdain, as they did his jeans, which a female informant told me were not in style because they were too tight and too short. Christopher's status among his peers was thus further problematized due to his being "out of it" in terms of his sports participation and his clothing.

This situation, and his home situation, changed in Christopher's next year of life, at thirteen. At home, he became more comfortable. He adjusted to the routines and relationships of his father's family arrangements and living circumstances. Indeed, Christopher felt that his father helped him adjust to home and at school, because he told Christopher to "walk straight up," and to "think good thoughts." Also, his older brother, along with one of the older sons of his stepmother, provided him with camaraderie, and some ideas about how to proceed in the world, as they were learning various realms of the business world, including the businesses of media and real estate.

In the eighth grade Christopher started to play basketball. He got sneakers (though not the expensive kind, as his father didn't regard brand names as necessary), loosely fitting jeans, and he began to work out at home in a room dedicated to this activity, which had been set up by his father for his own use. Wearing more appropriate gear and being in better physical shape helped Christopher enter the world of male peers at this urban middle school.

Christopher's sense of comfort was challenged again when he moved on to high school. His words describe the stresses he faced at seventeen, when I asked him how things had changed:

> Well, things aren't as fun as they used to be. Things have gotten harder. You have a lot to think about, the future and everything, what you're going to do with your life. You've realized things, just about life in general, about people. You know, even at [his middle school], you know, things were easier, you know, you really didn't have to deal with all the problems that are going on. But now as you get older, you see things that really didn't matter back in junior high school, but now, that really do matter now.
>
> [JoEllen: Things like what?]
>
> Everything. Really everything. College is more important now. Really finding your place, like, you know, finding your place in life really is starting to become more important than junior high school. Decisions that you have to make, because I've found that like during these past years there have been more decisions that you have to make rather good or bad.

Christopher is aware of the increased pressures associated with growing into adulthood. His comments echo some of the things he had said at twelve and thirteen, when he thought life wasn't as "simple" and easy, as it had seemed when he was a very young child, and when "People focus more on you, like you at the time. You are the main focus. But now it's like, it's spread to like, they have hundreds of people to focus on, they can't just take the time to pay attention to one person." Christopher's seventeen-year-old comments suggest that he was seriously contemplating the responsibilities of adulthood, as well as realizing the pressures of maturity.

After middle school, Christopher started at a high school that he reported was "falling apart" because of the "intruders" there who he said prompted fights, pushed drugs, robbed students, and generally made going to school unsafe for Christopher, as well as affected his studies. He reported being injured in fights, and apparently fending off pressures to drink, smoke marijuana, and engage in violence, which he said were "big things" at the first high school he attended. At the same time, he was dealing with a medical situation that called for some surgery and visits back and forth to doctors and hospitals. Because of this, according to Christopher, "I had to miss so much school; I had to fall so far behind."

Because of an injury sustained in a fight, he transferred to another school in the middle of his sophomore year. Here is his description of this new place:

> [It] is a good school. There's rarely any security problems at all. They
> have good teachers except for the math teacher. It's just a good school.
> They give you a lot of independent research, a lot of reports that you
> have to go, you know, to the library and you have to go to certain institu-
> tions, and find information. A lot of research papers. Like one time I had
> to visit a congressman and ask him these questions for the report. It was
> twenty-one pages, for this report, and turn it in. They give you a lot of—
> it's a good school. Students are, you know, civil to everyone. I haven't had
> a problem as far as students since I've been there. Since December 1994. I
> haven't had a problem since. It's about four hundred students. . . . Um,
> mostly Spanish, Black, Chinese—we have very few White students in our
> school. It's basically Hispanic, Black, Chinese. [And] we have Black
> teachers, White teachers, Indian teachers, Chinese teachers, Spanish
> teachers, it's a whole—that's one thing I've, you know, I've rarely seen,
> where, you know, they have such a mix of teachers. Usually it's like all
> Black teachers or all White teachers, but it's just, you know, a whole mix
> of teachers.

At this school Christopher made the honor roll. Economics became a new favorite subject, joining his interest in social studies. He had friendships that were satisfying, and even some romances.

Life at home turned tense at seventeen, as his relationship with his father changed. Christopher had quite a bit to say about this aspect of his life:

Communication is so bad. Why does it, you know, seem like, you know, he's like, so mean sometimes. 'Cause, honestly, I can't wait to, you know, get out on my own. It's like a dream, you know. Oh, if I could just get my own—even if it's just one room. One room. And just be on my own. . . . It's just things have changed over the years where it's like, you know, it's not really a father/son relationship anymore. It's like, you know—it's almost like "This is the guy who's going to take care of me until I can get on my own." It's really—I really hate to say that but that's the way—you know, we smile and say "hello" in the morning, but it's not, it's like really not—it's like a marriage that's gone wrong, like, you know, where just the love is gone. You're just tolerating—not really tolerating one another, but you know, 'cause, you know, you say "hello" but you know there's really nothing there. You're just being courteous. It's gotten to that point. . . . [I wish he were] more like, tolerable, like, um, the biggest dispute we have is about chores and stuff like—I mean I think I clean better than most kids on earth, but he always has to find something. It's so—I mean it's things that would really have you shocked, like he'll like open the door and go like between the area between the border and he'll be like "There's dust here." And then he's serious like, "Why didn't you clean that?" and I mean he's like, it's just like harsh. He's the kind of father you don't feel comfortable talking about almost anything with him. There's always this—I have to call him "sir." That's real—you call your boss or your teacher "sir," you know, your father. But that happened in the beginning and that just, you know, strike one. It stripped things 'cause you're gonna have to call him "sir." Then there would be times I'd forget, and he would get upset and think I'm disrespecting him by calling him "dad." So, you know, that moves us apart a little bit, having to call him "sir." He would always ask these questions like, say you forgot to take out the garbage or something, it's like, "Why didn't you take out the garbage?" "Oh, well I forgot." "Why did you forget?" and then that's where I always got stuck, because if I knew why I forgot then I wouldn't have forgotten. [And] he asks questions like "Why do I have to keep telling you how to do a better job cleaning?" or something like that. Then he's actually waiting—'cause most parents, they're just saying that—he's actually waiting for an answer. And it's like, it like drives me crazy 'cause, you know, I'm supposed to answer that question? I mean—he's really sitting there waiting for an answer, I mean it's like he's never, it's like he's never—it's like he expects me to be, like, aw man, like perfect. You know, do nothing wrong.

Dealing with such high expectations, which he often experienced as "harsh" rather than encouraging, Christopher reported that he wished he could live with an older sister, who lived nearby with kids of her own not too different in age from Christopher. "I'm almost jealous because her kids can like come and talk to her about anything. She'll help them. Just being able to talk to your parent eliminates so many problems."

Christopher's comments about his father and his sister defy some common assumptions that adolescents want to separate from their parents no matter what, and only spend time with peers. Indeed, Christopher wants a parent he can talk with—he wants a "dad," not a disciplinarian—suggesting he would like a closeness that many people might think adolescents only want with peers. His desire to be connected to a parental figure confirms research that shows how adolescents don't want adults to get completely out of their lives, although they might desire more freedoms (Feldman and Elliott 1990).

Christopher's relationship with his father grew more tense, and after high school he moved out of his father's apartment just to get away from him. Via some fortuitous connections, he later found a job within a large financial institution, and attended a local community college. After a year, he dropped the college courses, partially because of the demands of his job, which he needed to pay his apartment rent and to support himself entirely. In addition, he was excited about being involved in the world of high finance and trading.

After many months dedicated almost exclusively to working long hours, Christopher began to investigate college programs in business and finance, because he knew he would need a degree. Also, he wanted to meet more people his age and have a social life. His job supervisors agreed to provide him with some college funding plus summer employment, and encouraged him to apply to one of the Ivy League schools in the Northeast. My most recent meeting with Christopher, when he was twenty-one years old, occurred at the end of his first year of studies at one of the most prestigious universities in the United States. Due to a professor there, who had become a close mentor, Christopher was considering majoring in the study of government as well as business. Also, he reported: "I've never loved learning as much as I do now. Yeah, it's totally shifted from like um, aw, I just need a degree to like, wow! I really like doing this, I love this, you know?" He was even considering becoming a teacher or a professor.

Christopher's relationship with his father was repaired over the years.

Due to Christopher's accomplishments, "people in [his] family were just amazed" and his father "gave [him] a lot of respect." As Christopher said, "You know, getting a job, an apartment, a car, going to [an Ivy League university], he just kept saying, 'wow!' Like I guess now he sees me as an adult, as a man now." Also, Christopher described a kind of silent agreement between them that fostered an acceptance. He told me that when not spending school breaks and summer weekends with various extended family members—because he's "family-oriented"—he was talking, on the phone or in person, with the woman he had engaged to marry, after they both finish college. At twenty-one, according to Christopher, "things [had] changed dramatically, like total 180, for the better."

Christopher's Uses of Television Culture, through Time

The preceding section lays out Christopher's everyday life situations, and how he experienced these at the beginning, middle, and end of his adolescent life. The situations of his everyday life necessarily set some of the parameters for when, where, and how he engaged with television programming. At the same time, his particular ways of making sense of his everyday life have a powerful bearing on how he used television in a meaningful way. Thus the term "use" here has both functional dimensions (watching television because he can't go outside) and interpretive dimensions (constructing meaning from his viewing experiences). This section aims to describe Christopher's television habits and how they are associated with his changing life circumstances, as well as to examine his television uses as they relate to his changing sense of himself and the social worlds around him at different points in time.

When Christopher entered a new home and middle school when he was twelve, he was involuntarily inserted into some ongoing patterns of activity and expectations that made him feel uncomfortable and lonely. At home, he was required to do many chores on his own. His father worked nights and double shifts, meaning he was either not around, or exhausted, while his new stepmother was recuperating from a car accident. Christopher turned the television on because

> I like TV. Because it's entertaining, especially when you're alone. I just like to, like, if I'm here alone, and I'm like, washing dishes, I just like to hear the TV. It's like, somebody's voice, like somebody's there. It's like somebody's talking to you. It's just that you can't talk back. But you can hear somebody's voice and that's like, comforting when you're alone.

Sometimes, when he was watching television with his father before his father would go to work the night shift, television provided an activity that was familiar and common for two ostensible strangers who had been put together in a household. At many other times, Christopher was watching television because: (1) he didn't yet have friends to be with in his leisure time; (2) he didn't feel safe enough in his new neighborhood to walk around; (3) there were no other media entertainments available in his home (a VCR machine and a video game player were broken, and they did not have cable or computers); and, importantly, (4) there were no subsidized youth programs that he could attend when school was not in session (a common problem in the United States, according to Heath and McLaughlin 1993). At this time in his life, Christopher was more reliant on television as an activity that provided him with company and something to do besides his chores, homework, and being bored and lonely.

At twelve Christopher had to figure out how to make a place for himself in what were to him strange new social worlds of home and school. In that year, he especially liked to watch a show called *Quantum Leap*, a prime-time science-fiction comedy/drama. This show portrayed a man who was, by an accident of technology, leaping through time and space and who had to figure out his identity and location in history and, given that, assess how to act. Christopher said he liked the show because "He [the main character] goes through a lot of changing, with other people. And trying to save those people. And the close times he tries to save those people, the suspense." Christopher was interested to see how the main character adapted to all of his changing situations, perhaps because it helped Christopher cope with his own life's changes. In addition, he seemed attracted to the "savior" aspects of the character, in keeping with Christopher's interest in superheroes coming to the rescue.

In the eighth grade Christopher included watching basketball games in a shortened and more intermittent viewing schedule. His shift to basketball viewing corresponded with his beginning to play the sport at school. He was watching to see how the games turned out, and then discussed them with his friends and sport mates. But he also looked at different players, to learn about the various positions, and to pick up tips and strategies for playing. With this viewing, Christopher was purposefully educating himself, so that he could interact with peers and so that he could play a better game. Both of these television uses helped him build and maintain his new social status and relationships.

Because of his basketball playing, and because he had more social activities and after-school events to attend with his new set of peers, Christopher was watching less television in general, even though he then had his own television for his bedroom. He explained:

> I don't watch as much TV now. . . . After school, I would either go play basketball, um go home and maybe watch half an hour, sit down, then I would go outside for a little while, come back, and then I'll watch maybe some TV, but I wouldn't like, I don't really watch, sit down and watch shows full, like beginning to end that much. I like pop in shows, and then I will go do something else, and then I come back and look at what's going on. . . . I'll be mopping, and then I will hear something interesting [in parent's room], and then I'll just pop in and see what it is, then go back to work. Or I will turn on the TV and then see something, flip the channels around, turn it off and go do something else. I don't leave it on, I just turn it off.

The only time Christopher "just watch[ed]" television, viewing with more focus in his own room, was "at nighttime . . . let's say after nine o'clock? When all the work's done?" At this time, he also read mystery novels or adventure stories, and often simultaneously played basketball with a foam ball and net that was attached to his bureau.

At thirteen years of age Christopher had developed a set of friends playing and watching basketball, and he could walk around his neighborhood feeling stronger and taller. His father had told him, in many ways, to "walk straight up." At this time, Christopher said that Bill Cosby

> makes me laugh. I like a lot of the stories they do, things they do in the show . . . like how he can take a situation that, like say, Theo [the son character] stole something from the store, and he can make it into a situation where, you know, it'd be funny. Well, it wouldn't be funny that he stole it, but, he'd make like a little joke out of something. But at the same time he'd also be telling him that it was wrong to do what he did. [But] *Married with Children*, they would make a joke out of it but they would like, pat him on the back and say, "Oh I love you. And did you get me something?" *Married with Children* is stupid. You know it's like teaching kids that they can disobey their parents, and laugh at their parents. And *The Cosby Show* is teaching children that, you know, do something good for your parents, you know, it's about parents trying to raise their children right. And *Married with Children* is like, the parents don't even care about their children.

Bill Cosby knew how to make people "laugh without cursing," and he taught people how to do "right" things for their family—just as Christopher's father had been doing. Bill Cosby, portraying an ideal African-American television father as Cliff Huxtable in the 1980s *The Cosby Show*, supported and enhanced Christopher's own growth in confidence and sense of rightness.

The quote that opens this chapter indicates some of how Christopher's television routines changed when he was seventeen. At that time, his bedroom was the former living room of his father's apartment, because his tiny bedroom had no room for a computer. Also, he got a dog that was his responsibility, so Christopher took over the common space of the house, albeit reluctantly. Because while he had increased freedoms to be on his own, and he had more of a social life with friends, without a living room he didn't feel like he could invite friends over. Yet, in general, he was watching less television than before because of his social life outside the home, increased homework loads, and dog responsibilities.

When he was at home, television was part of his activities, even though, as he said, he was not "like *in* the show." He described his at-home routines at seventeen:

> When I come home I usually watch television first. Then, listen to music. Then either use the computer or go back to television. Usually I have the television on like almost all the time. Not even, I'm not even watching it, just, it's like, you know, hearing a voice, like say you're in an empty house, I would turn the television on as loud as I could so I could hear it all through. . . . It's like someone being there. So, watch television, listen to music, mostly. I don't even use the computer much, really. I really use it for school, not really for entertainment.

Like many other children and adolescents, and indeed many adults (Lembo 2000; Morley 1992), Christopher used television as background, and engaged in simultaneous activities. Also, as seen in Sefton-Green's (1998) studies of multimedia use at home in Britain, Christopher used computers for what are considered formal educational activities, while he used television and music as "purely entertainment." He said he would like to have used the computer for fun, but the games that came with his system were "boring," and he did not have any creative software except for word processing, which he used for homework and sometimes to input the music lyrics he had handwritten. Just like the young people in the British studies, Christopher was either disappointed in what had been promised by the hype about computer technologies, or not technically equipped to meet his desires.

At seventeen, the hit sitcom *Seinfeld* was Christopher's favorite show. He liked it

> 'Cause it's funny, it's real funny how the situations, it's not really, like in some comedy shows it's really far-out humor that's funny but you really can't relate to it. But on *Seinfeld* you can relate to some of the things that, you know, happen to them, you know . . . like um, they were on the subway one time, and everyone was looking up and then Jerry said, "Why is it that everyone looks up or doesn't look anyone right in the eye on the train?" and then Elaine was like, "Maybe because they don't want to get beat up by the person that they make eye contact with." And it's just things like that. It's really funny and it's like little things like, "Why do people eat candy bars with their—" They had this whole episode about they should use a knife and fork eating a candy bar. I mean, it's a fun show. And they had one where—say they had a friend who was getting married and they bought this friend a big-screen TV, and then they broke up and but they gave them the TV already, and they broke up, and they were like what is the precedent? Do we get the TV back or do they get to keep the TV? And then there was one time where George got dumped by his girlfriend, but they were going to a mutual friend's party and he didn't want to go but they were like, "Why should you not go? You're the one who got dumped. She's the victor. She's the one who shouldn't go." And then Elaine was like, "No, no, no. He's the loser so he shouldn't go. Because she's the victorious one she should go to the party." I mean, it's really . . . It doesn't sound that funny, but it's—so that's one of my favorite shows.

Christopher and his closest friends all watched *Seinfeld* and then came to school the next day to talk about it. It is insightful how Christopher saw similarities between his friends and the feature characters on *Seinfeld*:

> [My friend] that's like George [on the show], he, he's like, like a pessimist. He really doesn't think about the positive sides of things. You know, he's really on the negative side of things. Like he'll think the worst of something and I could say especially when it comes to things like girls. Like he doesn't, if a girl would say "yes" to go out with him, he would start worrying about "Will it last?" "When will it be over? Will she dump me because I'm short?" or something. Stuff like that. He just worries, worries, worries about things. And he's always like, not really lying, but

always, you know, trying to weasel his way out of doing things. Like, you know, we say, "Let's play basketball" or "Let's, you know, just go outside" and he'll be like "Oh, oh, oh. You know, the funniest thing's happened: I'm not able to go outside, my clothes got stuck in the laundry machine." Just this big, he would make up this, just this, instead of just saying, you know, "No. Don't feel like it," he'll make up with an excuse and every-thing. Even though we all know it's an excuse and he does, too. It be-comes like a joke all of a sudden, you know. And one of my other friends is like Kramer [on the show] because, you know, he's like really outspo-ken like, you know, um, like a daredevil. You'll dare him to drive, ride down this hill on his bike with his eyes closed and he'll probably do it. He's like funny like Kramer.

[JoEllen: And you said you're like Seinfeld?]

Mainly because I'm trying to talk both of them out of doing things that's how Seinfeld is with Kramer and George. Or either I'm trying to talk them into doing something that's good, like say he wants to um, like with my friend that's like George, it seems like it's always about girls. I say, you know, "Why don't you just go say hello?" he's like, "No I can't say hello! She hardly even knows me." "I'm not asking you to go ask her for her hand in marriage, just go say hello." And then he's—or I'm trying to talk him out of not doing something like. Just really trying to, you know, talk him out of not doing something or talk him into doing something like Jerry does with Kramer and George. But there's no Elaine. I think now, the girl I used to go out with is like Elaine now.

Christopher's adolescent friends were Black and Latino (labels he and they used), unlike the feature characters on *Seinfeld* who are all White adults. Nonetheless, he noticed similarities in how his friends responded to everyday social situations and circumstances and in how the characters on *Seinfeld* acted in response to everyday phenomena, albeit staged for comic purposes. This is not unlike his attraction to his earlier-in-life television fa-vorites. At twelve he liked the lead character Sam Becken in *Quantum Leap*, a White man moving back and forth in historical situations whose chal-lenge was to resolve the personal and social problems of the characters in the lives into which he had landed. Watching Sam, Christopher seemed bet-ter able to cope with his own problems at the time of his landing in new cir-cumstances. At thirteen Christopher liked Bill Cosby, who is Black like himself, but whose sitcom role as a doctor and whose large, upper-middle-class living quarters on television did not mirror what Christopher experienced in his life. However, while Christopher reported that he didn't know any real-life families who lived the lifestyle of the Huxtables on television, he said this television family was familiar to him "Because of the way they handled things." It was Cosby's "handling" that seemed to mirror Christopher's father's guidance, which bolstered Christopher's newfound comfort at home and school. At seventeen he enjoyed watching characters whose behaviors and attitudes paralleled those of his friends rather than family, even though his friends' identities and lives were quite different than the *Seinfeld* characters. Whether he was among friends or observing *Seinfeld* characters as they all dealt with everyday idiosyncrasies, Christopher experienced a sense of camaraderie, which he valued immensely.

Thus, while the specific surface features of the characters and situations that Christopher liked changed over the years, what remained consistent was his interest in the underlying social and emotional activity of television fictions. Christopher is not unlike the many viewers that seek some kind of "emotional realism" (Ang 1985; Buckingham 1996), as well as plausibility (Lembo 2000), in their television experiences, even though viewers acknowledge that television is "not real life," and even when viewers recognize that the surface features of a program are outlandish or impossible, as in the case of science fiction. In this way Christopher might be thought of as a typical audience member of a television viewing majority. Yet, it is important to note how this typicality breaks down in terms of the particularity of his tastes, interests, and especially his interpretations, and in how they relate to his sense of himself and his life. At twelve he looked to Sam Becken because he also was coping with changes that he had no control over, but to which he had to adjust; at thirteen he looked to Bill Cosby because his way of doing things buttressed Christopher's father's ways of "handling things" which helped Christopher feel comfortable and confident in his new life; at seventeen he looked to the *Seinfeld* characters because they reminded him of the friends that he had sought to have, and of the quirkiness of human relations.

Christopher's particular interest in the social and emotional realm of media fictions extends to his attraction to cartoons and superheroes based on comics. At seventeen Christopher was watching cartoons such as *Batman* and *The Flintstones*, just to have a laugh. However, his overall attraction to cartoons goes back in years, as evidenced by his earlier preference for the animated series *X-Men* and his choice of an alias, "Wolverine."

One of the things Christopher appreciated about many (but not all) of the cartoons he watched over the years (or live-action movies based on comics, such as the *Batman* series) was the pitting of good against evil, with good winning all the time—a long-standing human interest in storytelling. Another thing he appreciated was that while he recognized that cartoon and comics characters were sometimes "outrageous" in their good and evil actions, he liked those superheroes who provided him with some thoughtful ways of dealing with personal situations, as revealed in his explanation for liking Batman the character:

> It's something about his dual personality, you know, that a lot of people, including myself, have to have sometimes in life. Like, you know, like you can be chipper and joyful in your house but then you, especially around in my neighborhood, when you go out into the street, you know, you have to put on this, like the wall I was talking about. You have to put on this, you know, you have to just change faces sometimes. Even though that's not really who you are. That's one thing I've learned over the past few years.
>
> [JoEllen: What kinds of faces have you learned to put on?]
>
> Oh, just this, ugh, you know, kinda like, you know, "Don't mess with me" kinda routine. I really don't like it, but, you know, sometimes you have to do that so you know, no one messes with you. . . . Like then there's the one that, you know, where you say you really don't care when, deep down, you really do. . . . You know, when my father has something harsh to say, "Ahh, it doesn't bother me." But actually it really, really, really, really, really does. . . . Like, um, sometimes, just, you know, hearing what he has to say can bring me to tears because he can really be, you know, harsh.

Christopher's comments about learning to "change faces sometimes" support postmodern claims that contemporary identities are transitory rather than stabilized around a singular set of values (Kellner 1992). His comments also suggest that commercial media such as *Batman* exemplify this postmodern condition as well. The origin of Christopher's postmodern perspective is beyond the scope of this study. Yet his remarks about shifting identities are indeed reflections prompted by a character in the media, a character whose at-home self is unknown to most of those existing within the *Batman* fiction, but whose "dual personality" is known by audience members outside the fiction, such as Christopher. However, note that Christopher talks about the "faces" people have to put on sometime as "not really who you are." This indicates that, for Christopher, the changeable identities that are called forth by certain contexts exist in addition to some kind of core self that is "really who you are." Perhaps postmodern claims about the nature of contemporary identities need to be revised, to account for those like Christopher, and Batman, whose "real" selves might not be unstable, but merely hidden from view in multiple contexts that need "Don't mess with me" or "It doesn't bother me" kinds of faces?

Interweaving an Ongoing Self, Changing Images of Success, and Relations to Television Culture

Christopher's television and other media interactions and interpretations when he was twenty-one years old suggest that his fundamental values and his "real" self are at least consistent, if not stable, over the years. Because of his work, university schedule, and social life, Christopher said that when it came to watching television, "it's just I don't have the time. That was one of my pastimes." And, like at seventeen, he was using computers, as well as on-line and "new" technologies, for formal educational purposes exclusively. In his words:

> I like computers and stuff, I like the programs and stuff. I mostly use it for word processing and research. I like it that if you have a simple question, like um, What's a stapler made out of? you can go find out. It's just those kinds of things, little fleeting questions that you can actually gain knowledge of, that's what I appreciate mostly. [But] the Internet, I really don't like the Internet anymore. I really use it for e-mails, writing papers, research, that's the main thing. Sure beats digging through the library and old books, where the bats are. We have bats in the library. It sure does beat that. But I lost interest in it. In the beginning it was really cool, you know, you talk to people in Istanbul, stuff like that.
>
> [JoEllen: When did you start?]
>
> The Internet? I would say just about as soon as it came out, mid- to late '80s? 'Cause when I went to school in [the South] they were always on the cutting edge of technology. Everyone had a computer, at my school. And had access to the Internet and stuff. And it was cool then to look up sites and stuff. But um, the fascination dwindled for me. I find it a little unsettling that you can do just about everything from your house. It's an old-fashioned premise, but uh, now you can order your groceries, and you don't have to leave your house anymore. It's like, I don't enjoy

> that, I like the whole process of going to the grocery store, I like seeing
> other people, seeing people you know, going down the aisles, you know, I
> like going to the bookstore, I like browsing through things. I like going
> shopping, I like going to the mall.

Christopher's comments echo many popular criticisms of the new technologies. Critics of the new media argue that people might get so caught up
in the virtual worlds of electronic communication that they lose touch with
each other in face-to-face worlds, which are deemed better. Whether non-
virtual worlds are better is debatable depending on different criteria for
what constitutes "better" (Clark 1998), a discussion beyond the scope of
this article. But what is pertinent about Christopher's comments is that they
echo his own earlier interests in being with others in a pleasant and stimulating actual social space, rather than watching television or being stuck
alone in his apartment. This is important to acknowledge because it coun-
ters the popular claims that young people today are intensely caught up in
mediated virtual worlds to the exclusion of actual realities. While there may
be youth, and adults as well, who are involved with virtual worlds to the extent that their or others' actual lives are compromised in some way,
Christopher's relationship with virtual spaces appears reasonable and even
critically distant, at least according to his own report. In addition, his relationship with the Internet aligns with the results of studies showing that,
overall, youth in the United States are not online as frequently or as long as
they watch television (McClain 1999).

What is suggested by Christopher's comments about the Internet is
also consistent with what is suggested by his talk about his favorite television shows in the past, as well as his talk about television at the age of
twenty-one. Because of our history together, Christopher assumed we
would talk about television in our most recent interview, and he commented early when we met that he was eager to talk about media. I asked
him why he was so excited to talk about media and he reflected on his own
changes in circumstance as they related to his television-viewing habits, as
well as to the significance of certain programs:

> My mother, I lived with her up until I was about eleven years, up until I
> came to New York, and it was hard for her as a single mother, and having
> a career that demanded a lot of time, and so, a lot of times I found my-
> self at home alone, and my only friend was the television. You know my
> mother didn't want me, while she wasn't there, like, going outside, where
> I could get hurt. So she really like created the perfect environment for

me, like toys and games, use the phone whenever. I grew up on TV, and the most influential show was *The Cosby Show* for me. Like I still, while I was up at [the university], I had a lot of slack time during the afternoon, because of my class schedule. I was tempted for a while just to get extra money, but I realized that while I was there, I should just focus on school. But, in the afternoon, like about two o'clock, I watched *The Cosby Show* [reruns]. And you know it brought back a lot of memories. 'Cause I remember what I was doing when I first saw this episode in prime time. Like it didn't make me feel old, but like, times have changed so much since then, cause they would always show the year that it was on, and I was like, wow, that was 1987! You know?

Christopher went on to evaluate how *The Cosby Show* played a role in his own and his friends' developmental experiences:

And I remember seeing the last episode, when Theo [the son character] graduated from NYU. You know that TV show impacted not just me, 'cause I speak to a lot of my friends about TV and it's always like "*The Cosby Show, The Cosby Show, The Cosby Show*.". . . [But] there's no more programming that really emphasizes maturity, responsibility, growth. Like um, like with *The Cosby Show*, you really saw everyone in that house, even the parents, evolve. Move into different stages of life. Going from being offered drugs at school, to you know, what they're going to do after they graduate. To just the day-to-day things that happen, like, I could relate so much, 'cause yeah, they picked on me, too, for dressing like this or talking like that.

Discussing the importance of the 1980s Cosby program in his own and his friends' lives prompted Christopher to ponder current media and their influence with other youth:

That programming, I can't think of anything on television now that's like that. . . . TV is not so much about entertainment now as that I'm actually seeing how I've changed. How society is changing. . . . What used to be acceptable isn't acceptable now, and the impact that television is having on youth. And right now I think that a lot of television programming is just being very reckless. With their responsibility. That goes for all media, that goes for television, and especially music. Like I personally love hip-hop and I like some rap, but some of it is just a little too much, you know like with all the gangsta rap, and I can't relate to that. 'Cause to me there's no relation, I can't relate to gangsta rap at all. I'm old enough to

The Cosby Show. *Courtesy of Photofest.*

understand that um like you're not going to do everything that you hear in the music, you're not going to do everything like you hear on TV, you're not going to emulate everything you see on television. But what these producers and everyone who's writing television programs are not realizing is that they have adolescents, you have children, that are watching TV, even more now, [and] they actually—it's showing a notion of "this is how life is." And this is how we should be acting, this is what we should be saying, this is what we should be. And the producers are not taking any responsibility for what they're producing on the screen. I'm not saying that dramatic events like shouldn't be talked about, not at all, but, their context is not necessarily to educate, it's more to shock.

I argue that Christopher's values and sense of self do maintain a kind of consistency through the years, as evidenced most by his current regard for *The Cosby Show* and what it provided him and his friends as they grew. That is, *The Cosby Show* was, and still is, a representation of reality familiar to, and preferred by, Christopher (and presumably his friends) in terms of how it showed families dealing with everyday contemporary life in a positive manner (helping kids resist drugs, or figure out what to do after graduation, and so on). His regard for *The Cosby Show* echoes most viewers' appreciation, as others also found the series positive in its portrayal of family life, and Black family life in particular (Inniss and Feagin 1995 [see chapter 8 of this volume]; Jhally and Lewis 1992; Means Coleman 2000). Cosby had created his show to counter the many sitcoms of the day that showed families with inept parents and smart-aleck kids. In addition, Cosby had wanted to counter the negative stereotypes about Blacks that prevailed in the media, and to provide instead an image of success that was depicted as the norm in many sitcoms featuring White families. Christopher and many other viewers appear to have accepted the producer Cosby's intentions for his show.

Christopher's evaluation and acceptance of *The Cosby Show* is associated with his sense of the role music might play in youth's lives, perhaps his own. He says that though he loves hip-hop and some rap, he doesn't like "gangsta rap" because "there's no relation" in it to his life. What is important here, as discussed previously, is Christopher's fundamental interest in certain underlying social and emotional levels of media. He experienced the actuality of "gangstas" in his neighborhood and thus he could probably relate to the depicted reality expressed through gangsta rap. However, he didn't want to be part of actual gangster life, nor did he want this actuality to be represented in the media. As he said in the quote that opens this chapter, he likes "happy endings," and like the characters Batman and Wolverine, he wants good to prevail over evil. To him, the gangster life commented on and even glorified by some Black rappers is to be resisted, not just by music listeners, but by music producers as well, because socially or emotionally relating to these images would not result in a happy ending, or in good prevailing over evil.

Christopher's interpretations of Cosby's show and hip-hop music are among the very few that indicate his interest in media associated with Black identities and culture. At thirteen he admired Arsenio Hall, a Black comedian, as well as the television show *Roc*, a situation comedy featuring all Black characters that aired in the early 1990s. In addition, he then was watching basketball, a sport dominated by Blacks, and he was playing ball at school because the Black (and Latino) males at school had made basketball the "hip" thing for males to do. But unlike many of the audiences referenced in studies of African Americans and the media (Inniss and Feagin 1995; Jhally and Lewis 1992; Means Coleman 2000), Christopher did not mention explicitly that his interest in *The Cosby Show*, hip-hop, Arsenio, *Roc*, or basketball on television had anything to do with his being African American. It is possible that my identity as a White adult is pertinent here. Perhaps Christopher never felt comfortable enough with me to express himself completely about issues of race or "Blackness," although he noticed how "Whites are always on top" in television programming. I did not ask specific questions about race and racial representations when talking with any of the youth in my studies, just as I did not prompt the participants to talk about gender and class issues. I only followed up on any issues they themselves raised, using topics and terms that they themselves supplied.

Christopher pointed to *The Cosby Show* as important to him not necessarily because it featured characters who are African-American, although that may have contributed to his liking the show both at thirteen and at twenty-one years of age. But his own words value the show in how it represented "day to day things" that "emphasize[d] maturity, responsibility, [and] growth"—themes of a program any viewer might appreciate. Thus, over the years of this study, Christopher maintained a thread of consistency as a self, as well as a media user and meaning maker, in seeking material that was uplifting to his spirit, his possibilities, and his sense of the common good.

At the same time, Christopher recognized that such material could not uphold his standards in a simplistic manner, and that such material was hard to find, given what he understood about television in general:

> I'm not trying to be corny. It doesn't have to be like "Let's all hug and be happy" 'cause like life isn't that way. It has to be realistic. But to portray this as real life is irresponsible, 'cause it's not real life. If I could sum it up, television is showing people that you have to get yours, anyway that

you possibly can. That is what television is saying now. It's not emphasizing family, it's not emphasizing growth. You know, money money money, you got to get yours, you got to look like this, you gotta get this.

Christopher's remarks indicate his implicit awareness of dilemmas inherent in the creative and dramatic arts, which include the mass media. That is, Christopher seemed to be aware that better quality works of media should have a balance of elements that contribute to their sense of plausibility, tension, and resolution, and ultimately their artistic and social merit. But Christopher did not seem to think that television could maintain that balance, nor could it "emphasize family [or] growth," because bottom-line values often override many other social and aesthetic values. Below he acknowledges how these conflicting values have played out in his own life, and perhaps in the lives of others:

And I know, um, a lot of adolescents who are going through such terrible times, trying to conform to what they see in music videos, to what they see in ads, to what the media says is cool. The media have become so bold, like they will literally say this is cool, this is not. Go with this, don't go with that. And it's a marketing ploy. I won't necessarily knock that because, you also have to understand it's a profit motive. That's why I can't do investment banking for a living anymore because you know they'll crush anyone. If there was a choice between a school and a mall, they'll build a mall. And if it's a choice between saving a monument, or putting up some new high-rise, the monument goes. I mean it is clearly, I mean if there's anything that is quote-unquote "evil," it is investment banking. That's a powerful statement but I see they're just ruthless. It's no place for someone with a heart. There's no place for them. 'Cause that's what I had to do, I had to conform to this like, rough and gruff kind of thing. You know, cursing people out over the phone, 'cause they haven't delivered bonds. And it just wasn't me, and I just couldn't do it anymore. So. But, um, that's what television has done. And I think it's, um, I don't know what to say, there needs to be a new wave of television programming.

These and several other comments reveal both change and consistency in Christopher's sense of how to be in the world, and what is good and right for him and others. The change and consistency are complexly revealed in his evolving ideas about living "the good life" in the future. All of the years I have known Christopher, he had the goal of moving into better financial circumstances than what he had known growing up in working-class, lower-income households. Like many young people in these situations, he believed in a version of the American dream:

> I knew that for me I wanted to be comfortable in life. To maybe have a car or two. I always wanted a big family, so, you know. I just wanted to be, you know, if my wife and I wanted to go to a play maybe on the weekend, you know, wanted to go on vacation every now and then, you know, you go. And go shopping on Saturday or Sunday. Nothing really extravagant, I don't need a really huge house. Just enough space for everyone to be comfortable and a good neighborhood, you know that's the most important part, because you know living in Harlem is not the safest place in the world and you know I had a hard time when I first moved there. But um, I'd never want my kids to ever go through that again.

At twelve years of age Christopher imagined becoming "comfortable" by owning and running a cable company. He saw "how [they] made so much money" and figured he could create and distribute programming himself, to suit his tastes better. So on one level, we can see that his twenty-one-year-old awareness of the "money money money" aspects of media had a history, but as a young adolescent he imagined exploiting this system for his own financial benefit, rather than critiquing it. At the same time, he imagined his profitable cable company providing more programming about "family matters" as well as a less repetitive cycle of movies, some being produced by himself. So, on another level, we see Christopher's family orientation had a history as well.

At thirteen Christopher had abandoned this media ownership plan, and instead imagined he would run a real estate business operating on a global level. He had grand visions of buying up properties all over the world and developing them. This was the time when his father and Bill Cosby were both important figures. His father had been working to turn the apartment building they lived in into a cooperative, so the tenants could buy and gain control over their own spaces, and Christopher had witnessed many tenant meetings. It is intriguing to relate these experiences to the knowledge he then had of Bill Cosby's television studios, which covered several acres in a borough of New York City. In addition, it is at thirteen years of age that he could describe the well-appointed house that Bill Cosby actually lived in at the time, which Christopher saw on television. Perhaps Christopher made some of the same connections that I am making. That is, perhaps Christopher saw that owning physical space is a mark of success and power, and that local people as well as people in media can mark their success and power via owning and controlling the physical spaces of home as well as places of business. This pertains to later comments about young people's awareness of the power that people in the media possess.

At seventeen Christopher thought about going into music, because of the songs he was creating about "love, feelings, and emotions." But, he said, "music's kind of hard to make a living at." He knew that only a select few make it into the big time. So he maintained music only as a passionate avocation, and instead contemplated becoming a dental surgeon, because of some work he had to have done on his own mouth at the time, and the surgeon telling him that this could be a lucrative career. Yet in the years between seventeen and twenty-one, Christopher got deeply involved in the world of high finance, because of his diligence and reliability, his competence in the realm of economics, and in part because of what he called his "good luck." In these years he made a very "comfortable" living, so comfortable that he was denied financial aid when he first attempted to go back to school "just for the degree." And at this time he was intent on getting a degree in finance and business, to continue to climb this ladder of extraordinary success.

As his comments reveal at twenty-one, this ladder of success had consequences his "heart" couldn't tolerate. Indeed, then Christopher thought the worlds of finance, exemplified by his experiences in investment banking, were "evil" because "they're just ruthless. It's no place for someone with a heart. There's no place for them. 'Cause that's what I had to do, I had to conform to this like, rough and gruff kind of thing. You know, cursing people out over the phone, 'cause they haven't delivered bonds. And it just wasn't me, and I just couldn't do it anymore. So. But, um, that's what television has done. And I think it's um, I don't know what to say, there needs to be a new wave of television programming." I must point out that I did not string together these statements about Christopher's experience of the financial industry and television—he did. Before our most recent meeting, he had decided to change his degree plans so that teaching and government studies were prominent on his horizon, instead of banking or other kinds of money-making endeavors. At the same time, he had not given up on his goals of having a respectable job, a big family, and an adequate house in a safe neighborhood. In other words, his desire for the American dream remained intact, he still wanted power and success. What had changed was how Christopher wanted to flesh out his American dream. He had redefined his means toward power and success.

If Christopher were to have his way, television would adjust and redefine itself, too, while still maintaining its "profit motive." I asked Christopher how he thought "a new wave of programming" might come about.

> I would tamper a lot with a lot of scripts. That's the first part. I would be
> smart about it, because I'm not going to totally change, if I'm coming
> into [a network], I'm not going to totally change everything, you're not
> wanting to start losing ratings, or whatever. But what I would do, I would
> tamper with some of the scripts of the most popular shows. Keeping the
> premise, keeping what everyone enjoys, the broad range of people.
> Adding and subtracting, here and there, and just gauging the responses
> of the viewers, and see how it goes.

Christopher justifies this strategy by considering his own desire for a "new wave" as part of a larger public desire for better quality fare on television:

> 'Cause I think people would like more engaging television, just like, "oh,
> the phone's ringing, let the answer machine pick up," yeah, I'd like that
> kind of television, too, you know? I would try to get more of that, where,
> right to the end they're like, you know, I haven't seen a show in so long
> where right after it's over I'm still thinking about it. Like the next day,
> "Did you see that episode?" Not did you see that episode because of
> something bad that happened, but something really really important
> happened. And it can happen on comedies, it can happen on dramas, it
> doesn't necessarily have to be a drama it could be anything. A story about
> two lovers living in New York, you know? It's just the quality, really that's
> it, it's just the quality of the programming. Not corny, I definitely stay
> away from corny, I'm not gonna go back to fifties television. . . . But, um
> it has to be quality programming. And I think the public will appreciate
> it. They will appreciate it.

I also asked if Christopher were in charge of a network, how would he persuade them to make such programming? He began by proclaiming, I believe, his own philosophy of life: "Well, what I learned in life so far is that, really, fear will impede progress. In a sense you can't be afraid to fail. You always must have a great plan, but you cannot be afraid of failing. 'Cause that will impede your progress." Christopher proceeded by laying out a strategy that shows he understands how the television system is entrenched as a part of the corporate culture he knows from the inside, and that also indicates his ideas on how an entrenched system can be adjusted:

> I think, they would have to do the sneaky undermining things that they do to present this, to turn things around. They would have to actually turn the tables on the producers, the writers. They would have to actually vilify—without looking uncool—they have to vilify what the other networks are showing, but they have to actually play the game. Except in the reverse. It's not going to be simply, um, "We've decided to change our programming because we don't think . . ." No, it would have to be the same model, that killer instinct that they've done to get this out there. That's what I strongly think, otherwise, you wouldn't get people on board for it, you would basically have a CEO who's trying to do that get voted out. Just by the internal company, not the, the reviewers could actually like it, and he may not have enough time to get the feedback. But um it would have to be the same aggressive style, nature, that you would have to do, to change it around.
>
> [JoEllen: That's a really intriguing prospect. Now, stepping back further, that CEO, and those people that use these strategies—how is it that they even get convinced that they could try this?]
>
> That's the hard part. Um, I personally think it would take a CEO, or not even necessarily a CEO but whoever calls the shots on programming, they would have to come at them from a position of strength. Not like, "You are gonna do this or else," but "Jump on board, we're taking this to a different level, and if you don't want to be on board that's fine, feel free to leave." Writers know, 'cause they know it's really hard to get work somewhere else, like if you are on a sitcom, and it's got really high ratings, and the network wants to take it to another level, to make it even better, I think they would adjust their style. 'Cause a lot of times they are writing what they think people want to hear, instead of necessarily what they DO want to hear. And there's gonna have to be someone who can bring everyone to the table. He's gonna have to let—this is almost like a biblical story I was reading—he's almost gonna have to let the nay-sayers, the people who are unsure, he's gonna have to let them go. And he's just gonna have to really work with what he has. Um, he's gonna try to keep them at all costs, cause they've been the backbone of the success so far. He really has to do it from a position of strength. He cannot—as far as I'm concerned TV stations and networks can be as ruthless as oil companies, the way they operate. He can't come into this business saying, "Let's

all join hands and bring love and peace to the earth," 'cause he's gonna be chased out of town. He's gonna have to really sit in his chair—his or her chair—take control, and really change the tide. It has to be someone who is not afraid of failure. Not reckless, they are not gonna go to fail, they need to have a surefire plan, but he can't be scared like "What if this doesn't work? I could bring the whole network down with me." You have to have a good plan, and go for it. It will be a difficult thing to do. You need someone in there who can basically negotiate from a position of strength.

If I had my way, Christopher would be running that cable company he thought about at twelve, and Bill Cosby would be on the board of directors.

Implications of a Young Individual Coming of Age in a Television Culture

What have we learned by focusing on Christopher's experiences and interpretations of television culture over several years' time? This study confirms that individual lives are complex, dynamic, and defy description by only one group label. Indeed, Christopher defies many of the stereotypes that some people have about African Americans, especially African-American males. Unlike many representations of this identity in the media, Christopher is not engaged in criminal acts, he isn't a "gangsta rapper," and despite his interest in basketball, he is not involved in sports as a path to financial success and celebrity glory (Gray 1995). He is also defying stereotypes that many people have about youth, who are often seen only from a social-problem standpoint, and thought to be at risk of doing everything terrible in the world. Of course, there are youth (as well as adults) who engage in dangerous or risky activity of all kinds that deserve our concern and efforts. But as Way (1998) points out in her book *Everyday Courage*, these youth are a statistical minority who receive a great deal of media and institutional attention. The majority of youth who are progressing successfully in terms of academic achievement, healthy behaviors, and social engagement—such as Christopher—are often ignored.

   Christopher's successful progress defies some negative stereotypes attached to the environments he grew up with as well. He grew to eleven years of age in a single-parent, mother-in the-workforce household. Here, he was often alone, but given "toys and games," allowed to "use the phone whenever," and his "friend was the television." At twelve years of age he moved to Harlem, an urban neighborhood that has a rich cultural heritage, but has higher levels of poverty and crime than some other areas of New York City. Christopher sometimes saw criminal incidents from his window. This, and being harassed by neighborhood boys, threatened Christopher's sense of safety on the streets. In this situation, he again had television for "company." There are many who might predict that these environments would hinder Christopher's development and progress. Indeed, Christopher himself knew that some odds were against him, as he said at twenty-one that "things could have gone just totally the other way. Especially in my environment, too many children have the option of doing other things to make money, drug dealing, and other things that will just ruin their life."

Christopher's life was not problem-free, and he did feel the burden of some of the stereotypes attached to his identities and his living situations. But he didn't "go the other way." Indeed, given that he is enrolled in an Ivy League college, financially savvy, studying government systems, engaged to marry a young woman who is "family-oriented" like himself, thinking about devoting himself to teaching, and even reading "biblical" stories— many might say that Christopher is well on his way to fulfilling the American dream, including being an informed and community-minded citizen.

At the end of our last interview, I asked Christopher what in particular he would want me to say about him and what he'd come to. In addition, I wondered what he thought had played a role in his getting where he was, and in believing what he believed. First, he cited again the role that *The Cosby Show* played in his coming to maturity:

> One thing that I learned was that, even though sometimes I feel I was raised by television, the values that I gained, I gained a lot of them from television, what you should expect from the family. And I attribute that all to *The Cosby Show*. And uh, that really gave me a basis for what you should be expected to do as far as responsibility and maturing is concerned. 'Cause you know you actually saw people on that show mature.

Next, Christopher discussed the role his father played in his coming to maturity:

> And the one thing that I learned that was disturbing at first, it wasn't really related to television, but the one person that had the most influence on my life, after I left home, was the exact reason I left home. My father. I always thought that um—and I'm gonna link this in with television—but I always thought that he was just being mean. Just being rough and gruff. He demanded perfection, you know, but I'm a kid. I always wanted to

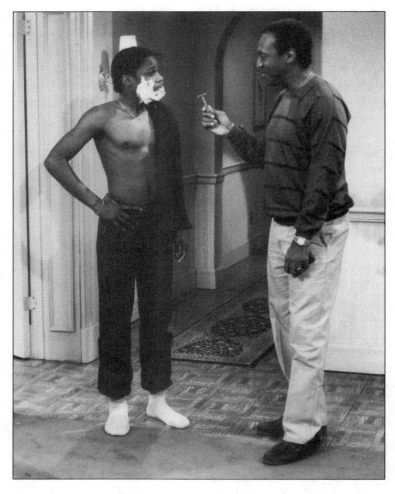

The Cosby Show. *Courtesy of Photofest.*

use that line, it's famous on television now, "I'm just a kid." But my father never accepted that. He told me simply because my last name was [*deleted*] that I had to do the best, nothing less than the best. That was his line. Always. At that point in my life I thought that was a bunch of hooey, to put it lightly. It's just an excuse to be mean. When I entered the real world, 'cause I was just thrust into it, 'cause I had to find a job, I couldn't just be a freeloader, it was, like, I was on the brink of "well, you know, we just can't have you anymore, you need to get out." Going into the workplace, the work ethic of just getting up in the morning, like um, where it's like you know, when it's time to go to school, it's time to go to school.

But Christopher then went on to say that television now is not encouraging other youth to be responsible and mature, values he says he acquired from Bill Cosby and his father:

> It's just I see now on TV that's not the case. Responsibility is not taught, maturity is not taught. You're going to have a generation that you know they are twenty-eight years old and they are not any older than they were at sexteen. They are in no shape, they have not matured. They are not capable of handling what life has to offer. And especially in African-American culture, 'cause, I think that our culture more so has been bombarded with media images that tell them what they are supposed to be. That is conforming, it shows no room for individuality, and the development of individuality is the key sign of maturity. Developing who you are, and when you're denied that, not necessarily denied that, but when it gets shown that what you think is *not* cool, and you'll get somewhat outcast, they'll suppress that, and in some respect they'll suppress their maturity.

The above quote contains the only instance (from our interviews) of Christopher discussing the role that media play in presenting messages and images to African Americans. His comments suggest that he thinks African Americans are more likely to be "conforming" to what is represented as "cool" by the media, although why he thinks his identity group would be more susceptible than others is unclear, except that he thinks they are more "bombarded." Perhaps he felt pressures to conform to what's "cool" in the media himself, yet couldn't completely adapt to that image of coolness because his father's pressures to do "nothing less than the best" opposed his conforming to media "coolness"?

Indeed, later comments revealed that Christopher sees media and parents in constant competition for young people's attentions and learning—a situation he finds unfair for parents given the everyday life realities he knows:

> The media has an enormous impact, especially living in a society where both parents have to work now. . . . And it's not necessarily that they are not paying enough attention, but, to fight, that is hard, and it's unfair. Because it's unfair that they already have to earn a living, they have to go out and earn their wage, and take care of their children, and find some

joy and happiness and purpose in their own lives. That's part of their responsibility, and it's not fair that the media will slap on their twelve-year-
old daughter sex, you know, we're showing them that it's good to get in
fights, it's good to shoot people, it's good to hate cops, it's good to be dis-
respectful, that you can get away with everything all the time. You know,
the parents shouldn't have to come home and deprogram their child.
And they shouldn't have to go to the opposite extreme, to keep them
away from television, away from the media.

For Christopher, to be raised by television is not a problem as long as what
is on television encourages the values he believes to be good for maturing
and gaining in responsibility, values that he believes parents should promote as well. He came to understand, retrospectively, that these are values
that his father had been imparting when he "demanded perfection" instead
of letting Christopher be "just a kid." These values—or "what you should be
expected to do," according to Christopher—worked for him when he "entered the real world" of the workplace. And these are values both television
and families need to encourage.

There are many media scholars and critics, policy makers, parents and
educators, and even media producers and CEOs—such as Bill Cosby—who
would agree with Christopher. However, I doubt that many of these people
have taken the time to talk with youth such as him, to find out what youth
think about television and the role it plays in their complex lives, and the
role it does, and should, play in society, except for the Cosbys (Cosby 1994).
If more of us talked with young people about these things, perhaps we
might find out that some of our worries about television and youth are dis-
placed, and that we should focus our concerns in this area differently.

We need to take note of Christopher's critical insights into the industry
of television, and his suggestions for how to change industry practices to improve the quality of television. The way Christopher described how he
would accomplish changes in television acknowledges the difficulties of
"emphasizing family [and] growth" in a capitalist system that rewards the
"killer instinct" he attributes to the business world. He argues that to create
a "new wave of programming," people who "call the shots" in the networks
are going to have to get the writers and producers of shows with "high ratings" to take those shows "to a different level" but still "play the game," a
game that involves a "profit motive." In other words, he is saying that to
change the system we need to work with the system, and not reject it entirely.

This thinking compares with that of Cosby the producer's responses to critiques that *The Cosby Show* wasn't realistic enough, as it didn't show the fictional Huxtable family dealing with issues of race relations, issues that are certainly part of actual African Americans' experiences. Cosby argued that situation comedies in general were not a suitable format for wrestling with complex social issues, and he also pointed out that situation comedies featuring White characters were not subjected to similar critiques (Inniss and Feagin 1995). Thus, while Cosby's program took portrayals of Black family life "to a different level," he played the sitcom game, thus leaving the television system unchanged at the structural level.

Christopher's thinking about Cosby's show, as well as his thinking about television programming and the system in general, suggests that he believes in a predominant story about the United States, a story about how anyone can make it if they learn to play the game. It is not clear if he sees his own racial identity as getting in the way of his own making it in the system. However, his comments about "other" African Americans being bombarded with media messages that can lead them to conform to images of "cool" rather than develop into responsible individuals who can think for themselves might suggest that he struggled with being "cool versus responsible" himself, and that his struggle may have involved his own racial identity. I cannot be certain about this, as again, my White identity—as well as my adult authority status—might have constrained Christopher's explicit expressions about his experience of being African American. This is a discussion I intend to have with him in the future.

What is clearly represented in Christopher's comments are the key roles both *The Cosby Show* and his father played in forming his beliefs that he can make it in the system. And what is most intriguing here is how his viewing of *The Cosby Show* reruns encouraged his reflection on the importance of this program in his development. At twenty-one he is viewing television reruns that provide him with a means of comparing his present self to the self he had as a young adolescent, and his present life to his life in the past. And what he sees is that he has become a good and powerful man because of this program's messages about responsibility and maturity, messages that aligned with those of Christopher's father, even though Christopher saw Cliff Huxtable as funny, while he thought of his father as harsh. This suggests an area of research in media studies, identity development, and cultural learning that is currently not undertaken. What do other young adults make of their encounters with reruns that they first saw as young adolescents? Other in-depth investigations of young adults' responses to programs they watched when younger should be conducted to find out more about how youth themselves evaluate how television programs (and other media) from their past have played a meaningful role in their being who they are, and in believing what they believe.

What is also clearly represented in Christopher's comments are the potential roles youth can play in developing programming that they themselves will find meaningful and important to their developing selves and their lives. In a culture that supports and nurtures not only media consumption but also media production as a fundamental aspect of its political economy, we must take seriously youth's understandings about media. Young people experience media as powerful through their own encounters with media messages and images that are meaningful, pleasurable, and educative, even if they don't explicitly realize the meanings, pleasures, and teachings of media, or don't until they are older, like Christopher. In addition, youth are aware, at least implicitly, that media are a pervasive and popular presence in most people's lives, as they see their family, friends, and others engaged in multiple media encounters every day. Furthermore, like Christopher, many young people know that the actual people who are involved in making media messages and images have power as celebrities, as financial moguls, as trendsetters, and even as political figures. That is, they know that the very real industry of media construction and distribution provides a powerful means of success in the United States. Given their knowledge of this means of success, we need to include youth as actual people involved in making media messages and images, especially those youth who are part of those groups whose participation in circles of power is constrained due to historical and social forces that marginalize them.

In other words, our challenge is to help all young people "play the game" successfully, while encouraging them to take the system "to a different level." This is no easy task in a world where the existence of a capitalist marketplace is often mistakenly equated with the existence of democracy and humanity. But perhaps if we talk with, and listen to, many more young individuals, they can inform our guidance strategies, and we can all work to "bring everyone to the table" and make a difference where necessary.

Notes

This article would not exist without Christopher, whose sharing of his time, energy, words, and experiences are much appreciated. In addition, the school and the family that allowed me access to Christopher must be thanked. Certainly, I am grateful to those in the academy who have provided me with various kinds of support, stimulation, and suggestions in this endeavor. Finally, warm regards go to the editor of this book, a friend and colleague.

1. At our last interview, when I asked if Christopher wanted me to continue using his young adolescent pseudonym "Wolverine," or a new one, he requested that I use his real name.

References

Ang, I. (1985). *Watching Dallas.* London: Methuen.

Bakhtin, M. (1981). *The dialogic imagination: Four essays by M. Bakhtin.* Austin: University of Texas Press.

Blumer, H. (1933). *Movies and conduct.* New York: Macmillan.

Buckingham, D. (1996). *Moving images: Understanding children's emotional responses to television.* Manchester, U.K.: Manchester University Press.

Clark, L. (1998). Dating on the net: Teens and the rise of 'pure' relationships. In S. Jones, ed., *Cybersociety 2.0: Revisiting computer mediated communication and community* (pp. 159–83). Thousand Oaks, Calif.: Sage.

Clark, L. S. (Forthcoming). Learning from the field: The journey from post positivist to constructivist methods. In S. Hoover, L. S. Clark, D. Alters, J. Champ, and L. Hood, eds., *Accounting for the media: The making of family identity.*

Cosby, C. (1994). *Television's imageable influences: The self-perceptions of young African Americans.* Maryland: University Press of America.

Davies, M. M. (1997). *Fake, fact and fantasy: Children's interpretations of television reality.* Mahwah, N.J.: Lawrence Erlbaum Associates.

Feldman, S. S., and G. R. Elliott, eds. (1990). *At the threshold: The developing adolescent.* Cambridge, Mass.: Harvard University Press.

Fine, G. A. (1987). *With the boys: Little league baseball and preadolescent culture.* Chicago: University of Chicago Press.

Fiske, J. (1987). *Television culture.* London: Routledge.

Fisherkeller, J. (1995). Identity work and television: Young adolescents learning in local and mediated cultures. Unpublished Ph.D. diss., University of California at Berkeley.

Geertz, C. (1973). *The interpretation of cultures.* New York: Basic Books.

———— (1983). *Local knowledge.* New York: Basic Books.

Giacquinta, J. B., J. A. Bauer, and J. E. Levin. (1993). *Beyond technologies promise: An examination of children's educational computing at home.* Cambridge and New York: Cambridge University Press.

Gray, H. (1995). *Watching race: Television and the struggle for "Blackness."* Minneapolis: University of Minnesota Press.

Heath, S. B., and M. W. McLaughlin, eds. (1993). *Identity and inner-city youth: Beyond ethnicity and gender.* New York: Teachers College Press.

Hebdige, D. (1979). *Subculture: The meaning of style.* London: Methuen.

Inniss, L., and J. Feagin. (1995). Views from the Black middle class. *Journal of Black Studies* 25: 692–711.

Jhally, S., and J. Lewis. (1992). *'Enlightened' racism: The Cosby Show, audiences, and the myth of the American dream.* Boulder: Westview Press.

Kellner, D. (1992). Popular culture and the construction of postmodern identities. In S. Lash and J. Friedman, eds., *Modernity and identity* (pp. 141–77). U.K.: Blackwell.

Lembo, R. (2000). *Thinking through television: Viewing culture and the social limits to power.* Cambridge, U.K.: Cambridge University Press.

McClain, D. L. (1999). Where is today's child? Probably watching TV. *New York Times,* December 6, p. C18.

McRobbie, A. (1994). *Postmodernism and popular culture.* London: Routledge.

Mead, G. H. (1934/1962). *Mind self, and society.* Chicago: University of Chicago Press.

Means Coleman, R. (2000). *African American viewers and the Black situation comedy: Situating racial humor.* New York: Garland.

Morley, D. (1992). *Television, audiences and cultural studies.* London: Routledge.

Orr Vered, K. (1998). Blue group boys play incredible machine, girls play hopscotch: Social discourse and gendered play at the computer. In J. Sefton-Green, ed., *Digital diversions: Youth culture in the age of multimedia.* London: UCL Press/Taylor and Francis Group.

Press, A. L. (1991). *Women watching television: Gender, class, and generation in the American television experience.* Philadelphia: University of Pennsylvania Press.

Radway, J. (1984). *Reading the romance: Women, patriarchy, and popular literature.* Chapel Hill: University of North Carolina Press.

Roberts, D. F. (2000). Media and youth: Access, exposure, and privatization. *Journal of Adolescent Health* 27S(2): 8–14.

Sefton-Green, J. (1998). Digital visions: Children's "creative" uses of multi-media technologies. In J. Sefton-Green, ed., *Digital diversions: Youth culture in the age of multimedia*. London: UCL Press/Taylor and Francis Group.

Way, N. (1998). *Everyday courage: The lives and stories of urban teenagers*. New York: New York University Press.

Willis, P. (1990). *Common culture: Symbolic work at play in the everyday cultures of the young*. Boulder, Colo.: Westview Press.

!

8

The Cosby Show

The View from the Black Middle Class

Leslie B. Inniss and Joe R. Feagin

Now that we have seen the final April 30, 1992, episode the television series *The Cosby Show*, "And So We Commence," we can examine the social and historical impact on its audiences. Commentators in the mass media have asserted that one of the show's greatest consequences was its help in improving race relations by projecting universal values that both Whites and Blacks could identify with, using the tried-and-true situation comedy format (Ehrenstein 1988; Gray 1989; Johnson 1986; Norment 1985; Stevens 1987). Believing that television mirrors society and articulates its values, proponents of this perspective point to the overwhelming popularity of the show among White viewers as well as its almost entirely positive assessment by White analysts and the White media. For many seasons, the show was highly rated and has been credited, among other consequences, with reviving the genre of the sitcom and saving the ailing NBC network (Curry 1986; Frank and Zweig 1988; Poussaint 1988; Taylor 1989).

However, a few recent researchers have suggested that, to the contrary, the show's popularity has set back race relations because its view of Black assimilation fails to take into account the context of the world outside of the four walls of the Huxtable household (Teachout, 1986), and because it allows Whites to excuse institutional discrimination and to become desensitized to racial inequality (Gates 1992). They do this by asserting that if

Black people fail, they only have themselves to blame because any White person can point out the successful, affluent Black family on *The Cosby Show* and confirm their belief that affirmative action is no longer needed because Blacks now enjoy the same opportunities as Whites (Gates 1992).

In a recent book, *Enlightened Racism* (1992), Lewis and Jhally report on White focus groups that watched *The Cosby Show* as part of the recent research project. They found a contradiction in White responses to the show. On the one hand, the show was taken by Whites as proving that anyone can make it in the United States and that Black Americans should stop complaining about discrimination. On the other, the Whites articulated the view that the Cosbys were not like most Black Americans. This contradiction is rationalized by Whites in the study by the failure and laziness of other Blacks. "The Huxtables proved that black people can succeed; yet in so doing they also prove the inferiority of black people in general (who have, in comparison with whites, failed)" (Lewis and Jhally 1992, 95).

Lewis and Jhally (1992, 113–17) also deal briefly with some Black reactions to *The Cosby Show* and other comedy shows starring Black comedians. They used a general group of mixed-status Black Americans in Springfield, Massachusetts. In the data that follow, we go beyond their brief analysis to examine the reactions to *The Cosby Show* in greater depth. And we examine the reactions of middle-class and upper-middle-class Black Americans whose class position is close to that of the Huxtables in *The Cosby Show*. How do middle-class and upper-middle-class Black Americans view the show? Is their reaction positive? Do middle-class Blacks accept *The Cosby Show* version of Black assimilation and integration into America: the color-blind society where African Americans, European Americans, Asian Americans, and Hispanic Americans can all interact as human beings without any mention of or even a hint of racial differences being problematic? Can this Black middle-class audience relate to a Black middle-class lifestyle in which neither the doctor-father nor the lawyer-mother nor any of the school-age children ever experience racism or discrimination in their everyday lives?

Or do middle-class Blacks perceive *The Cosby Show* in a more negative manner? Do they believe that the show depicts a false image of assimilation and helps to foster the backlash against affirmative action? Or perhaps, rather than totally positive or totally negative reactions, there is more of an ambivalence among middle-class Blacks. Perhaps they feel that it is good to see any Blacks on television who are shown in a positive light instead of as the usual pimps, prostitutes, and maids reflecting the "Sambo syndrome" (Fife 1974). On the other hand, they might suggest that *The Cosby Show* is an exceptionally positive portrayal in the same vein as the "*Shaft* syndrome" (referring to a popular, well-made motion picture from the 1970s with a Black cast). As such, the Cosby portrayal would be as distorting as the previously excessively negative ones, in the sense that Blacks are still being shown in an exaggerated fashion rather than as ordinary, everyday human beings, some good, some bad, with others all along the good-bad spectrum.

Given the pervasive impact of the mass media, particularly television (Asante 1976; Case and Greeley 1990; Goodlet 1974; Holz and Wright 1979; Leckenby and Surlin 1976; Stroman 1986), and especially the fact that Blacks watch more television than Whites and place more confidence in it (Bales 1986; Comstock and Cobbey 1979; Kassarjian 1973; Stroman and Becker 1978), it is important to examine the way in which Blacks have been portrayed. Television research has documented that the portrayal of Blacks in that and other mass media has always been inadequate and stereotypical, and generally has portrayed Black Americans as comedic characters (Carter 1988; Fife 1974; Gates 1992; O'Kelly and Bloomquist 1976; Seggar 1977). Moreover, research has shown the extent to which Blacks are underrepresented in all positions in the television industry. These data patterns underscore the need for a careful examination of Black middle-class responses to *The Cosby Show*.

The Debate over *The Cosby Show*

The Cosby Show began on September 20, 1984. The TV public was introduced to Dr. Heathcliff Huxtable, an obstetrician married to an attorney, played by Phylicia Rashad. The couple and their five children lived in a New York City brownstone and were clearly "Black middle class" at a time when that group was beginning to be recognized in the mass media. Indeed, they were upper middle class. The curtain-closing show, "And So We Commence," was on April 30, 1992, and had the extended Huxtable family prepare to celebrate the only son's graduation from New York University. During its eight-year, 198-episode run, *The Cosby Show* was lauded as a major milestone in popular entertainment: the first all-Black program that avoided racial stereotyping. Records reveal that the show was the top-rated show of the 1980s and the most-watched sitcom in television history. Bill Cosby, one of the show's creators, said he was returning to TV to save viewers from a "vast wasteland." He went on to explain his reasons for creating the show in an interview with Robert Johnson (1992, 57), editor of *Jet* magazine. Cosby told Johnson that he was tired of what he was seeing on television—tired of the car chases, the hookers with the Black pimps. Cosby believed that he could send vital messages along with the positive images of a Black family: Children are the same all over (Johnson 1986, 29).

Bill Cosby has responded to most criticisms lodged against his show during its eight-year run. For example, in answer to critics who urged him to deal with more racial issues, Cosby's response was that he would not let critics write his show and would not allow neoliberals to affect the image that the *Cosby* cast projects as a family (Johnson 1992, 60). Further, Cosby asserts that this criticism is unfair and holds him up to a different standard because other situation comedies are not expected to address pressing social problems such as racism. He stated that other shows, such as *Three's Company*, are not asked to deal with racism. Moreover, he feels that the show has addressed some tough social issues. For example, Cosby stated that the show consistently has addressed sexism as an issue, showing in a creative and humorous way how it should be resisted and debunked; at the same time, the show confronted the issue of machismo and promoted a richer understanding of fatherhood and a fuller meaning of manhood (Dyson 1989, 28). Additionally, whether through Cosby's wearing of collegiate sweatshirts or in the form of his spin-off program, *A Different World*, the show consistently sent out messages about the importance of Black academic institutions and the importance of Blacks supporting these institutions. This reflects Cosby's deep commitment to Black colleges surviving as an American institution (Cheers 1987, 28).

Other criticisms lodged against the show were that it was not "Black" enough because the family life being portrayed is not realistic, and that the show minimizes Black issues because it is a comedy rather than a dramatic series. In answer to critics who assert that the family being portrayed is not realistic enough, Cosby said, "I am not an expert on blackness" (Stevens 1987, 80), and that the show is about parents loving their children and giving them understanding. It is about people respecting each other (Johnson 1992, 60). He goes on to proclaim that although the show uses a new gimmick of centering on the parents rather than the children, without the children in the cast the show just would not work (Davidson 1986, 32). In support of the show, one writer has argued that a useful aspect of Cosby's dismantling of stereotyping and racial mythology is that it permits America to view Blacks as human beings, and it has shown that many concerns human beings have transcend race (Dyson 1989, 29). Alvin Poussaint (1988, 72), a Harvard psychiatrist and the show's psychological consultant, asserts that the Huxtables helped to dispel old stereotypes and to move the show's audience toward a more realistic perception of Blacks. Like Whites, Blacks should be portrayed on television in a full spectrum of roles and cultural styles and such an array of styles should not be challenged. Moreover, according to Poussaint, the Black culture of the characters comes through in their speech, intonations, and nuances; Black music, art, and dance are frequently displayed and Black roots and authors are often mentioned (74).

Finally, in response to those who complain that the show is a comedy rather than being more dramatic, Cosby maintains that each episode educates and informs even though the show's format is a situation comedy that entertains. He states that the shows are funny, with a caring, loving, feeling story line, and that the audience sitting at home will recognize themselves in the characters (Johnson 1986, 30). Moreover, one author admonishes Blacks to stop looking to TV for social liberation because "the revolution will not be televised" (Gates 1992, 317).

Our Research Study

To examine the Black middle-class response to *The Cosby Show*, we draw primarily on one hundred in-depth interviews from a larger study of 210 middle-class Black Americans in sixteen cities across the United States. The interviewing was done from 1988 to 1990. Black interviewers were used. We began with respondents known as members of the Black middle class to knowledgeable consultants in key cities. Snowball sampling from these multiple starting points was used to maximize diversity.

The questions in the research instrument were primarily designed to elicit detailed information on the general situations of the respondents and on the barriers encountered and managed in employment, education, and housing. The specific question used for this study asked about the portrayal of Blacks in the media. There were no specific questions about *The Cosby Show*—the discussion of that particular television program was volunteered in response to the general question about the media's portrayal of Black Americans. These volunteered responses signal the importance of this show. Although below we report mainly on the responses of the one hundred respondents who detailed specific reactions to *The Cosby Show*, in interpreting the Black middle-class response to *The Cosby Show* we also draw on some discussion in a larger sample of 117 interviews in which *The Cosby Show* was mentioned.

"Middle class" was defined broadly as those holding a white-collar job (including those in professional, managerial, and clerical jobs), college students preparing for white-collar jobs, and owners of successful businesses. This definition is consistent with recent analyses of the Black middle class (Landry 1987). The subsample of one hundred middle-class Blacks reporting a response to *The Cosby Show* is fairly representative of the demographic characteristics of the larger sample. The subsample's occupational distribution is broadly similar to the larger sample and includes university professors, college administrators, elementary and secondary teachers, physicians, attorneys, dentists, entrepreneurs, business managers and executives, doctoral students, and three retirees. There are roughly equal numbers of males (forty-eight) and females (fifty-two). The subsample has 23 percent younger than the age of thirty-five, 63 percent between thirty-five and fifty, and 14 percent older than fifty. All the respondents have at least a high school diploma, and 96 percent have some college, including 46 percent with advanced degrees. The modal income level is $56,000 or more, with 51 percent reporting this income. Seventeen percent report incomes between $36,000 and $55,000; 27 percent have incomes less than $35,000; and 5 percent refuse to disclose their income levels.

Viewing the Show as Unrealistic

The Black middle-class responses to *The Cosby Show* were ambivalent, reflecting both negative and positive aspects. Even the negative comments were often mixed with a positive preface, such as "I really like *The Cosby Show*, but . . ." or "I'm happy to see some positive images of Blacks on TV, but . . ." In many of the answers, there clearly is a dialectical tension, with a recognition of both the positive and the negative features of the program. For example, many negative responses centered on the show not providing a realistic portrayal of a Black family, or of a Black middle-class family. Yet many also felt that the show accurately reflected their own lifestyle and that of their friends.

Among our respondents, one common criticism of *The Cosby Show* was its lack of realism. As the following set of negative responses illustrate, the problem lies with the stereotypical nature of an upper-middle-class Black family that never experiences problems, especially racial problems. One respondent commented on the lack of tragedy this way: "And then *The*

Cosby Show, well, they just got too love-happy for me, it's just too good. They used to have real problems that they were faced with, and now, what's the problem? Someone wears someone else's dress, what is that?"

The absence of serious tragedy like that faced by Black Americans in the real world caused many to speak of the lack of realism in the program: "*Cosby* is not real. One of the things that disturbs me is this house is always immaculate, there's no maid, the mother's an attorney who works all day, the father's a doctor who works all day, the children are out of the house all day. Who does the laundry? Who cleans up the house? Who prepares the meals? You see them cook a specialty dish from time to time, that's not for real."

One aspect of the unreality is the casting of the father and mother as upper-middle-class professionals. One middle-class respondent focused on the family context, including the likelihood of doctor-lawyer heads of household: "My issue with *Cosby* is, how real is it? I mean, how many Black families do you know where the father's a doctor and the mother's a lawyer, and all the kids are wonderfully well-behaved, and they all deal at a psychological and emotional level of understanding? And so while I personally love *The Cosby Show*, I do question how real it is."

This questioning of the doctor-lawyer team came up a number of times and was connected to other issues. Another respondent noted the lack of attention to the racial trials: "I think if children, if people, if anybody looked at *The Cosby Show*, they'd think that everybody in the Black community has arrived like that, and it's just not true. I think it's wonderful that they portray a doctor and lawyer together working, and they live in a brownstone on a regular street, and they have children and everybody's hunky-dory. They never portray the trials and tribulations that families have. Or, if they do portray them, they portray them in a humorous light. But I think that it could be more realistic."

Another respondent wondered about the stereotyped character of a Black family like the Huxtables, who do not grapple with barriers like discrimination: "I think he's a doctor and she's a lawyer, so I think it's an upper-middle-class family. And it's just stereotyped. Nothing like that goes on in the family life every day. No family life runs smooth like that. You know, why not portray a family life story on television if you're going to use Blacks, and make it show the hard times that Blacks do run into? Why give it like it's all peaches and cream when it's not?"

Rather than viewing the Huxtables as role models, one father lamented the difficulty of explaining to his children why they don't live like the Cosbys: "I do know that this is just entertainment. But my kids think it's the way we should live. That is unfair. It is unfair for me to explain to my son that, no, mom is not a lawyer, dad is not a doctor, and these things don't work that way. I think that's really sad."

Blacks in Whiteface?

The unreality of the show has other dimensions, including a too-White image of Black culture. For example, one male respondent criticized the false image of assimilation to White culture as presented by *The Cosby Show*: "A false image. Again, it seems like something out of a fantasy, of people living the good life, acting assimilated, the so-called new-generation type people that really don't exist. If you walk the streets of America, you see something totally different. . . . The type of Blacks who have made it, everybody's happy, the don't-worry-be-happy type of Black people, again, it's a total farce, and they don't represent what the Black masses in this country are really like."

Another respondent accused the Huxtables of being "White people in blackface" and not a true representation of Black America: "From one extreme, you have the family on *The Cosby Show*. The happy-go-lucky Negro family that's made it. To me, all you're looking at are White people in blackface performing on television. That may be true to a certain extent, that may be going on, but it's not a true representation of the Black experience in America."

One female critic suggested that the show could be a "little less White," particularly in the area of problem-solving techniques: "Then you have the other extreme with Bill Cosby, that everybody is professional. And that's true, we have a lot of that. But the way problems are treated, I think is a little off the wall. I think it could be a little less White. I think that we just treat problems a little bit differently, because, let's face it, whether we're professional or not, we all come from nothing. And we still don't have that totally White mentality about problem solving."

This commentary adds another dimension to our understanding of the fear fostered by assimilation. This respondent may be suggesting that the history of today's Blacks would not allow them to work out problems in the same manner that Whites would. The decline of segregation has allowed Black Americans to deal with their children in ways different from the days of segregation, indeed in ways similar to those of Whites. Under segregation, Black youngsters were usually taught to be deferential and self-effacing, often through harsh child-rearing practices admonishing a child not to speak unless spoken to and not to stare anyone in the eye. Because conditions have improved somewhat, many Black parents now encourage children in the same ways that White parents do, to be assertive, independent, and curious. There may also be a suggestion here that the Black approach to problem solving in some matters is still different in unspecified ways from that of White Americans, perhaps that there is a Black culture or African background to be considered.

These examples provide insight into the character of the criticisms that see the show as unreal. The general complaint is not that the show is an unreal portrait of a family, but of a Black family. Cosby has argued that he is trying to show what true assimilation would be like, not what it already is—all racial and ethnic groups interacting as neighbors and friends without regard for physical differences.

There is a clear suggestion in our interviews that the Huxtables do not reflect most Black Americans. For many of our middle-class respondents this is problematic. Some had problems with the illusion of perfect integration whereby Black middle-class families no longer experience any racial problems and would in effect "live happily ever after." It seems that an underlying wish of these Black critics is that television shows featuring Blacks should be harder hitting and more realistic. There is a call here for greater seriousness in dealing with the Black experience, and a rejection of a happy-go-lucky stereotype of Black America. They have difficulty with a fantasy portrait of Black characters. None mentioned that if Black life as a whole is biting and difficult, then a show that is an escapist medium is useful. Only recently does there seem to be a push for seriousness and documentaries depicting only real-life dramas.

The Positive View: TV as Fantasy

In our interviews the negative responses are more than equaled by positive responses. Sometimes, particular individuals seem to be in a dialogue with themselves or their friends and relatives on these matters, for there is often an ambivalence about *The Cosby Show*.

A number of our middle-class respondents echoed Bill Cosby's response to some of his critics in regard to demanding too much in the way of realism from a show on television. "The problem I have with Cosby is the comments people make, in particular our own people, like what Black family has a doctor and a lawyer for a mom and dad and three or four well-behaved kids? They can't believe that could happen. And some White people too. And I sit and think, well, that's just as real as the Bionic Man, or Superman, or Batman and Robin. I mean, you don't see us walking around in tights with big Ss on our shirts."

"The *Cosby* sort of thing . . . isn't like most Black families. But then I'm not sure that you ought to expect television to portray anything realistically. I don't think they portray any family realistically, so why would they ever portray the Black family realistically, either?"

"It's not honest? Well, so what? So is almost everything else that you see on television. So why can't we be on television being fake? Or from that perspective, yeah, let us get somebody being fake, just like everybody else. It's an entertainment medium."

These positive assessments underscore the complexity of Black responses to Black-oriented shows. Explicit in these positive quotes is the idea that *The Cosby Show* is indeed unrealistic but so is most of television. The public does not ask other TV shows to be accurate representations of real life. In their view, because the public enjoys other shows that are just as fantasy oriented as *The Cosby Show* (for example, *The Bionic Woman* or *The Six Million Dollar Man*), it is not fair to expect that when Blacks are involved that the shows provide both entertainment and great realism.

Everyday Life and Role Models

Some of the positive comments took the form of acknowledging that the experiences on the show paralleled their own: "I think that . . . *Cosby* is an excellent example of our life and family." "*Cosby* parallels quite significantly my family life and that of my friends, particularly those who have teenagers or children of a wide variety of age ranges. And that's particularly a family joke with several of our friends, because we look at *Cosby* to see what's going to happen in our lives that week." These respondents are selecting out of the show's account of the Black experience common family problems. Others who had a positive view of the show were happy with the portrayal of Blacks in a positive light in order to counteract the many negative portrayals of Black Americans in the mass media, and thus in the White mind. "I think that it's about time that White America sees Black America in a positive, natural environment." "I wish we had more shows like . . . *Cosby* on TV, where you have a Black doctor, and the wife is a lawyer, because they do exist. I mean they're on a small scale, percentage-wise, but they do exist.

And I think we take too many negatives and blow them up." "I thought it was good that Black people, and Whites, could see that we all don't live in ghettos and projects and kill each other." "There are a lot of Black families that have doctors and lawyers and stuff like that, you just don't ever hear about them, people don't write stories about them." Clearly, these middle-class Black Americans are concerned about the tendency of the media, and White Americans, to exaggerate the image of Black Americans as criminal and deviant.

Those who affirm the show's merits see *Cosby*'s portrayal of Black men and Black families very positively: "*Cosby* is probably the only show, I think, that portrays Black men in a positive role." "I think that no question Bill Cosby has done a tremendous amount. And I think he portrays and projects a very, very positive image, what we need to see more." "Because I think it is a family together, and it shows that Black men can be leaders in their families, yet at the same time be responsible." One respondent emphasized the importance of stressing the commonality of the values of all Americans, regardless of racial and ethnic background: "I think that I am glad to see them portraying Blacks in middle-class roles, and realizing that Black people, Black middle-class people, have some of the same values as White middle class, Hispanic middle class, or Oriental middle class. It's not necessarily a race that determines it, it's just middle-class people sometimes have similar values. So I'm glad to see they are now portraying Blacks okay. *The Cosby Show* and these other shows that are coming on TV, you know, we both have some of the same values." This means that the general image of Black Americans as being like other Americans is an important contribution of *The Cosby Show*.

The Black Community

Other respondents noted the importance of *The Cosby Show* within the Black community. They enjoyed the Huxtable family portrayal because it offered Black people role models, positive values, and important messages for Black Americans. "I'm pleased with the Cosby portrayal because I think it sets a good example for younger Black children, not so much in the stereotypical 'when I grow up I'm going to be a doctor' kind of thing, but just in the overall quality of life and the values." "But I didn't see that being unrealistic, the type of family, a doctor and a lawyer. I didn't see that as being unrealistic. There's quite a few Black doctors and lawyers, so I thought that was a good image builder for the kids." "I think you could look

around this great country of America for the next 708 years, and I don't
think you're ever going to find a Huxtable family. But hey, you know, to me
it creates a dream. I've always believed that if you can see it in your mind,
it's possible. And like the Cos, he plays a doctor. Hey, a little five-year-old
Black kid, I want to be a doctor just like Heathcliff. That's cool. I like that."
To be able to see a Black female lawyer, a Black doctor, and Black youngsters
going to college is a very positive incentive for inner-city Black children
who may not see those same types in their own neighborhoods. Here the
accent is on positive role models for Black children. Others commented in
a general vein. "It's ideal. It's family structured. It's something basic. It has
good moral . . . everything you want to look for is in that show." "I do like
The Cosby Show because [it] delivers a whole bunch of messages, to African
Americans in particular. You know if you watch it, there's always a message." "Bill Cosby, I love Bill Cosby. It's not a put-on, it's a true family
setting. You've got a doctor and a lawyer, but you do have that. But they deal
with down-to-earth issues, realistic issues. So, I think that's a pretty good
image." The importance of positive role models for all Black Americans, not
just for children, is a significant theme here and in the rest of the interviews.

The Failure to Address Social Issues

Another major category of criticism is related to those just discussed, that
The Cosby Show does not address any important racial or other social issues, particularly those facing Black Americans today. The following quote
illustrates this criticism:

> They're not fully representative, that's for sure. Yes, we see the successful
> Cosby family, but that's only a slice of the average American Black family.
> The family is completely advantaged. They have both parents, they're to-
> gether. They're both fully employed. And they have a happy environ-
> ment. That family appears to be insulated from racism. Everything's
> always so wonderful on their block. Well, shoot, that doesn't happen. . . .
> So it's misleading. It leaves you with a flicker of hope that's not realistic
> and doesn't give us enough information about what to do if your family
> isn't like that, isn't ideal, isn't two-parent, or isn't really healthy. No one
> ever gets sick on *The Cosby Show*. No one has a debilitating illness. Cosby
> has not chosen to address sexual abuse. He's minimally addressed sub-
> stance abuse on there, and he's rarely talked about sex. That's not reality
> at all. None of those daughters have had unwanted pregnancies.

This respondent suggests that the show has not dealt with any of the major problems facing Black Americans, including questions of racism or unwed pregnancies. There is a tough call for the program to be more than a situation comedy. Other respondents expanded on the theme of the failure to deal with racial discrimination. "I have a problem with the fact that *The Cosby Show* will build a thirty-minute episode around Heathcliff Huxtable building a hero sandwich. Why aren't we dealing with, and I'm not saying do this every week, but every now and then why aren't we dealing with some real issues that are confronting the Black middle class. Yeah, there are some people who live like that . . . what happened to me in the courtroom, if I'm an attorney, or what racist thing happened to me in the hospital, if I'm a surgeon. That's what they come home talking about, and yes their kids go to NYU and other great universities like that, but what they come home talking about is what this racist professor said and did. And I don't see that occurring on *The Cosby Show.*" "It is not indicative of what Black life is really like. You would think that when Theo goes out he never has problems except in dealing with his buddies. Or that when his mother goes about her legal duties as a lawyer that she never confronts discrimination." On the air, the Huxtable family never faces or copes with discrimination. Although asking a comedy show to deal seriously with such issues as sexual abuse may be asking too much, these respondents do point to the serious issue of racial discrimination at the middle-class level. Upper middle-class Black Americans experience much discrimination, and it is overt, recognizable, and everyday. Because this discrimination is common and daily, it does not seem unreasonable to expect that a Black lawyer or doctor, and certainly a Black college student, would experience it and deal with it in daily life.

A Subtle Treatment of Racism

None of our respondents explicitly disagreed with the criticisms just noted. On the overt level, they agreed that *The Cosby Show* does not deal with racism and discrimination. However, at another level there is a battle going on against racism. One respondent noted that Cosby tends to approach the problem of racism in a subtle way, by allusion and indirection: "But at another level they deal with a lot of issues in a rather subtle way. There was an episode where Martin Luther King's 'I Have a Dream' speech was being watched by the family at the very end of the show, after I think there had been different family squabbles." This subtle treatment was examined eloquently by a professor: "In the show you can see a kind of intervention against racism, by the depiction of a family that is not totally constructed by racism. They have a life that speaks to Black art, Black music, including a traditionally Black college. But having said all that, the very scarcity of representations of racism means that one can look at *The Cosby Show* and decide on the basis of just that representation that everything is OK, when everything is very much not OK. So what might be itself harmless under one set of circumstances, ends up being hideously harmful under another set of circumstances."

What comes out as positive from a Black point of view—the ability to live outside of racism for a time—becomes a negative when Whites take the absence of racism to mean that things are fine for Black Americans. This problem is underscored in the study by Lewis and Jhally (1992, 110), where they conclude that for many of their White respondents "the Huxtables' achievement for the American dream leads them to a world where race no longer matters. This enables white viewers to combine an impeccable liberal attitude toward race with a deep-rooted suspicion of black people." In this way, *The Cosby Show* functions for Whites in a way much different from the way it functions for Blacks. It panders to the limits of White acceptance of Black Americans in the late twentieth century.

Black Life Only As Comedy

We have seen in the previous analyses some tendency to negatively or positively judge the show's content. The following responses are directed at the genre of the show. Similar to earlier comments, these critics feel that always seeing Blacks in situation comedies indicates that Black life and Black issues are not taken seriously. "True, *Cosby* has a great Black image, but basically, it's still a situation comedy. It's still comic. It's still laughter. It's still entertainment. It's not real, intense drama." "In terms of Black portrayals in television, it's a rather sad commentary that Blacks as clowns, or Blacks as those who laugh, continues to be the main image that's portrayed. . . . It's still clear that Blacks as humans that have to deal with a variety of serious issues doesn't seem to get across . . . it hasn't dealt seriously enough with topics that Blacks in general have to face." "*The Cosby Show* shows a set of affluent Blacks, but still it's a situation comedy. There are no shows that can deal with the Black person seriously, as a serious person. It seems like in order to discuss Black issues, you have to laugh." One respondent took a more positive approach to Cosby's achievements in his comedy show: "I'm a firm believer that the strength of the Black community is always in the family, and they're starting to show Blacks in a strong family situation. I think *The Cosby Show* started that instead of the slapstick comedy type. I think we're still not taken seriously because all of those are still in the sitcom type situation. I think it's difficult for most people to accept that Blacks have normal family problems, and they deal with them similarly as they do." A clear advantage is that *Cosby* has moved the situation comedy to a level beyond that of the more typical Sambo-type Black comedy. This puts the earlier comments into greater perspective. These last two responses seem to be arguing the case for the importance of class position over racial identity. These comments raise the important question as to why White Americans have a "comfort zone," which means that Whites will only watch those Black shows with which they feel comfortable. Because White viewers have the numbers to make or break a show and influence its sponsors, they are the ones whose interests are usually met. Why is the White comfort zone only able to encompass Blacks as comedians? One might say that to Whites, Black life and problems are not seen as serious. Or it may be something unconscious and less devious. It is doubtless linked to the old stereotypes where Blacks are seen as buffoons and Stepin Fetchits.

Conclusion

We have examined the Black middle-class response to *The Cosby Show* and found a mixed view of the show and its impact. The responses are both positive and negative in tone. Yet the interviews indicate a reluctance to be totally negative about one of the few positive portrayals of Blacks on TV. Middle-class Blacks want positive depictions of their lives. Many also want more realistic portrayals. Some feel that these realistic depictions can only be accomplished through a genre other than comedy. For them, to always portray Blacks as comedians makes light of the Black situation and indicates that Black life with all its inherent problems is not taken seriously. Our interviews highlight two significant aspects of their responses: (a) the fear that the show will render Black problems as irrelevant, and (b) the hope and optimism that with continued work the Black condition can improve.

The negative responses highlight both the ambivalence of the respondents and the fear that the show fosters the false assumption that Black problems have been solved and are no longer relevant. By showing a Black family that for all intents and purposes has fully assimilated, we are led to believe that we are indeed living in an equal-opportunity society and with a little hard work and lots of perseverance, anyone can make it. When we meet the

Huxtable grandparents, we are shown that they had a difficult life. The grandfather lived in a time of segregated armed forces and segregated music clubs where he was accepted as a musician but not as a person. But he worked hard, and now he has a doctor son, a lawyer daughter-in-law, and grandchildren in college. The overall impression is that the American dream is real for anyone who is willing to play by the rules. We are shown substantial upward mobility in only one generation and led to believe that mobility will be even more pronounced for the Huxtable children because they too are playing by the rules. We are left with the impression that they will not face any barriers or obstacles in their quest for the good life. They are decidedly upper middle class and can only go up—no discrimination or downward mobility for the Huxtables or by extension for Blacks as a group. The positive interviews highlight another significant aspect of the Black middle-class response to *The Cosby Show*: hope or optimism. Although it is true that not all Blacks are living the good life, with prestigious jobs, decent housing and living conditions, and college-bound children, one can always hope for and work toward these things. Just seeing what life like this could be like may be a tremendous motivator. It may inspire hard work and ward off discouragement. One middle-aged Black female was articulate on this point:

> Like the average woman in society is not blonde and blue-eyed, the average Black family by no means comes close to the Cosby family. But I think what it does, on the other hand, is suggest that there are some Black people and families out there that display those characteristics and qualities. . . . I think that it displays the fact that there is hope, and even if that's not a predominant condition in society, I think that just by the mere fact that it's on television says to people in this country that you can get there.

Generally, then, the opportunity cost of having positive Black television characters seems to be a lessening of the concern with the Black condition and a fostering of hope that things can get better. This is perhaps the dilemma that fosters the ambivalence in Black middle-class responses to *The Cosby Show*.

References

Asante, M. K. [A. L. Smith]. (1976). Television and Black consciousness. *Journal of Communication* 26 (4): 137–41.

Bales, F. (1986). Television use and confidence in television by Blacks and Whites in four selected years. *Journal of Black Studies* 16: 283–91.

Carter, R. G. (1988). TV's Black comfort zone for Whites. *Television*

Quarterly 23 (4): 29–34.

Case, C. E., and A. M. Greeley. (1990). Attitudes toward racial equality. *Humboldt Journal of Social Relations* 16 (1): 67–94.

Cheers, D. M. (1987). The Cosby Show goes to Spelman College for the season finale. *Jet* 72 (2): 28–30.

Comstock, G., and R. E. Cobbey. (1979). Television and the children of ethnic minorities. *Journal of Communication* 29 (1): 104–15.

Curry, J. (1986). The cloning of "Cosby." *American Film* 12 (1): 49–52.

Davidson, B. (1986). How Bill Cosby turned 4 kids into stars. *McCalls*, September.

Dyson, M. (1989). Bill Cosby and the politics of race. *Z Magazine* 2 (3): 26–30.

Ehrenstein, D. (1988). The color of laughter. *American Film*, September, pp. 8–11.

Fife, M. D. (1974). Black image in American TV: The first two decades. *Black Scholar*, November, pp. 7–15.

Frank, A. D., and J. Zweig. (1988). Who's making the big bucks? *Reader's Digest*, January, pp. 118–22.

Gates, H. L. Jr. (1992). TV's Black world turns—but stays unreal. In M. L. Andersen and P. H. Collins, eds., *Race, class, and gender: An anthology* (pp. 310–17). Belmont, Calif.: Wadsworth.

Goodlet, C. B. (1974). Mass Communications USA: His feet of clay. *Black Scholar* 6 (3): 2–6.

Gray, H. (1989). Television. Black Americans, and the American dream. *Critical Studies in Mass Communication* 6: 376–86.

Holz, J. R., and C. R. Wright. (1979). Sociology of mass communications. *Annual Review of Sociology* 5: 193–217.

Johnson, R. E. (1986). TV's top mom and dad. *Ebony* 41 (4): 29–34.

———. (1992). The Cosby Show ends after 8 years with a vital message to all young Blacks. *Jet* 82 (2): 56–61.

Kassarjian, W. (1973). Blacks as communicators and interpreters of mass communication. *Journalism Quarterly* 50: 285–91.

Landry, B. (1987). *The new Black middle class*. Berkeley: University of California Press.

Leckenby, J. D., and S. H. Surlin. (1976). Incidental social learning and viewer race: "All in the Family" and "Sanford and Son." *Journal of Broadcasting* 20: 481–94.

Lewis, J., and S. Jhally. (1992). *Enlightened racism*. Boulder, Colo.: Westview Press.

Norment, L. (1985). *The Cosby Show. Ebony* 40 (6): 27–34.

O'Kelly, C., and L. E. Bloomquist. (1976). Women and Blacks on TV. *Journal of Communication* 26 (4): 179–84.

Poussaint, A.F. (1988). The Huxtables: Fact or fantasy? *Ebony* 43 (12): 72–74.

Seggar, J. F. (1977). Television's portrayal of minorities and women: 1971–75. *Journal of Broadcasting* 21: 435–46.

Stevens, R. (1987). Blacks and Whites, days and nights. *Television Quarterly* 22 (4): 77–87.

Stroman, C. A. (1986). Television viewing and self-concept among Black children. *Journal of Broadcasting and Electronic Media* 30 (1): 87–93.

Stroman, C. A., and L. B. Becker. (1978). Racial differences in gratification. *Journalism Quarterly* 55: 767–71.

Taylor, E. (1989). From the Nelsons to the Huxtables: Genre and family imagery in American network television. *Qualitative Sociology* 12 (1): 13–28.

Teachout, T. (1986). Black, brown and beige. *National Review*, July, pp. 59–60.

Walsh, M. A. (1992). *Cosby* lauded by church officials as series ends. *Florida Catholic*, April 24, p. 14.

Williams, D. A. (1992). The prime time teachings of Dr. Cos. *Emerge* 3 (7): 22–26.

9

The Color Purple

Black Women as Cultural Readers

Jacqueline Bobo

Tony Brown, a syndicated columnist and the host of the television program *Tony Brown's Journal*, has called the film *The Color Purple* "the most racist depiction of Black men since *The Birth of a Nation* and the most anti-Black family film of the modern film era." Ishmael Reed, a Black novelist, has labeled the film and the book "a Nazi conspiracy."[1] Since its premiere in December 1985, *The Color Purple* has provoked constant controversy, debate, and appraisals of its effects on the image of Black people in the United States.

The film also has incited a face-off between Black feminist critics and Black male reviewers. The women defend the work, or more precisely, defend Alice Walker's book and the right of the film to exist. Black males vehemently denounce both works and cite the film's stereotypical representations. In the main, adverse criticism has revolved around three issues: (a) that the film does not examine class; (b) that Black men are portrayed unnecessarily as harsh and brutal, the consequence of which is to further the split between the Black female and the Black male; and (c) that Black people as a whole are depicted as perverse, sexually wanton, and irresponsible. In these days of massive cutbacks in federal support to social agencies, according to some rebukes, the film's representation of the Black family was especially harmful.

Most left-wing publications in the United States, the *Guardian*, *Frontline*, and *In These Times*, denounced the film, but mildly. *The Nation*, in fact, recommended the film and its director for fitting the work's threatening content into a safe and familiar form.[2] Articles in other publications praised particular scenes but on the whole disparaged the film for its lack of class authenticity. Black people of that era were poor, the left-wing critics stated, and Steven Spielberg failed to portray that fact. (Uh-uh, says Walker. She said she wrote here about people who owned land, property, and dealt in commerce.)

Jill Nelson, a Black journalist who reviewed the film for the *Guardian*, felt that the film's Black protestors were naive to think that "at this late date in our history . . . Hollywood would ever consciously offer Black Americans literal tools for our emancipation."[3] Furthermore, Nelson refuted the charge that the film would forever set the race back in White viewers' minds by observing that most viewers would only leave the theater commenting on whether or not they liked the film. Articles counter to Nelson's were published in a following issue of the *Guardian* and they emphasized the film's distorted perspective on class and the ideological use to which the film would be put to show the Black family's instability.

The December premiere of *The Color Purple* was picketed in Los Angeles by an activist group named the Coalition Against Black Exploitation. The group protested against the savage and brutal depiction of Black men in the film.[4] That complaint was carried further by a Black columnist in the *Washington Post*, Courtland Milloy, who wrote that some Black women would enjoy seeing Black men shown as "brutal bastards," and that furthermore the book was demeaning. Milloy stated: "I got tired, a long time ago, of white men publishing books by Black women about how screwed up Black men are."[5] Other hostile views about the film were expressed by representatives of the NAACP, Black male columnists, and a law professor, Leroy Clark of Catholic University, who called it dangerous. (When Ntozake Shange's choreopoem *For Colored Girls Who Have Considered Suicide/When the Rainbow Is Enuf* opened on Broadway in autumn 1976, the response from Black male critics was similar.)

Black female reviewers were not as critical of the film in its treatment of gender issues. Although Barbara Smith attacked the film for its class distortions, she felt that "sexual politics and sexual violence" in the Black community were matters that needed to be confronted and changed.[6] Jill Nelson, emphasizing that those who did not like what the messenger (the film) said about Black men should look at the facts, provided statistics on

The Color Purple. *Courtesy of Photofest.*

female-headed Black households, lack of child support, and so on.[7]

Michele Wallace, a professor of Afro-American literature and creative writing at the University of Oklahoma and author of *Black Macho: The Myth of the Superwoman*, stated that the film had some "positive feminist influences and some positive import for Black audiences in this country."[8]

However, in an earlier article in the *Village Voice*, 18 March 1986, Michele Wallace was less charitable to the film. Although she gives a very lucid explication of Walker's novel, citing its attempt to "reconstruct Black female experience as positive ground," Wallace wrote of the film, "Spielberg juggles film clichés and racial stereotypes fast and loose, until all signs of a Black feminist agenda are banished, or ridiculed beyond repair." Wallace also noted that the film used mostly cinematic types reminiscent of earlier films. She writes: "Instead of serious men and women encountering consequential dilemmas, we're almost always minstrels, more than a little ridiculous; we dance and sing without continuity, as if on the end of a string. It seems white people are never going to forget Stepin Fetchit, no matter how many times he dies."[9] Wallace both sees something positive in the film and points to its flaws. I agree with her in both instances, especially in her analysis of how it is predictable that the film "has given rise to controversy and debate within the Black community, ostensibly focused on the eminently printable issue of the film's image of Black men."

In an attempt to explain why people liked *The Color Purple* in spite of its sometimes clichéd characters, Donald Bogle, on the *Phil Donahue Show*, put it down to the novelty of seeing Black actors in roles not previously available to them:

> For Black viewers there is a schizophrenic reaction. You're torn in two. On the one hand you see the character of Mister and you're disturbed by the stereotype. Yet, on the other hand, and this is the basis of the appeal of that film for so many people, is that the women you see in the movie, you have never seen Black women like this put on the screen before. I'm not talking about what happens to them in the film, I'm talking about the visual statement itself. When you see Whoopi Goldberg in close-up, a loving close-up, you look at this woman, you know that in American films in the past, in the 1930s, 1940s, she would have played a maid. She would have been a comic maid. Suddenly, the camera is focusing on her and we say, "I've seen this woman some place, I know her."[10]

It appears to me that one of the problems most of the film's reviewers have in trying to analyze the film, with all of its faults, is to make sense of the overwhelming positive response from Black female viewers.

The Color Purple was a small, quiet book when it emerged on the literary scene in 1982. The subject of the book is a young, abused, uneducated Black girl who evolves into womanhood and a sense of her own worth gained by bonding with the women around her. When Alice Walker won the America Book Award and the Pulitzer Prize for Fiction in 1983, the sales of the novel increased to over two million copies, placing the book on the *New York Times* best-seller lists for a number of weeks.[11] Still, the book did not have as wide an audience or the impact the film would have. In December 1985 Steven Spielberg's *The Color Purple* exploded with the force of a land mine on the landscape of cultural production. Many commentators on the film have pointed out that the film created discussion and controversy about the image of Black people in the media, the likes of which had not been seen since the films *The Birth of a Nation* (1915) and *Gone with the Wind* (1939).

One of the reasons Alice Walker sold the screen rights was that she understood that people who would not read the book would go to see the film. Walker and her advisers thought that the book's critical message needed to be exposed to a wider audience. The readership for the novel was a very specific one and drastically different from the mass audience toward which the film is directed. However, the film is a commercial venture produced in Hollywood by a White male according to all the tenets and conventions of commercial cultural production in the United States. The manner in which an audience responds to such a film is varied, diverse, and complex. I am especially concerned with analyzing how Black women have responded.

My aim is to examine the way in which a specific audience creates meaning from a mainstream text and uses the reconstructed meaning to empower themselves and their social group. This analysis will show how Black women as audience members and cultural consumers have connected up with what has been characterized as the "renaissance of Black women writers."[12] The predominant element of this movement is the creation and maintenance of images of Black women that are based upon Black women's constructions, history, and real-life experiences.

As part of a larger study on *The Color Purple*, I conducted a group interview with selected Black women viewers of the film.[13] Statements from members of the group focused on how moved they were by the fact that Celie eventually triumphs in the film. One woman talked about the variety of emotions she experienced: "I had different feelings all the way through the film, because first I was very angry, and then I started to feel so sad I wanted to cry because of the way Celie was being treated. It just upset me the way she was being treated and the way she was so totally dominated. But gradually, as time went on, she began to realize that she could do something for herself, that she could start moving and progressing, that she could start reasoning and thinking things out for herself." Another woman stated that she was proud of Celie for her growth: "The lady was a strong lady, like I am. And she hung in there and she overcame."

One of the women in the group talked about the scene where Shug tells Celie that she has a beautiful smile and that she should stop covering up her face. This woman said that she could relate to that part because it made Celie's transformation in the film so much more powerful. At first, she said, everybody who loved Celie (Shug and Nettie), and everyone that Celie loved, kept telling her to put her hand down. The woman then pointed out "that last time that Celie put her hand down nobody told her to put her hand down. She had started coming into her own. So when she grabbed that knife she was ready to use it." This comment refers to the scene in the film at the dinner table, when Celie and Shug are about to leave for Memphis. Mister begins to chastise Celie telling her that she will be back. He says, "You ugly, you skinny, you shaped funny and you scared to open your mouth to people." Celie sits there quietly and takes Mister's verbal abuse. Then she asks him, "Any more letters come?" She is talking about Nettie's letters from Africa that Mister has been hiding from Celie and that Celie and Shug had recently found. Mister replies, "Could be, could be not." Celie jumps up at this point, grabs the knife, and sticks it to Mister's throat. The woman who found this scene significant continued: "But had she not got to that point, built up to that point [of feeling herself worthwhile], she could have grabbed the knife and turned it the other way for all that it mattered to her. She wouldn't have been any worse off. But she saw herself getting better. So when she grabbed that knife she was getting ready to use it and it wasn't on herself."

Other comments from the women were expressions of outrage at criticisms made against the film. The women were especially disturbed by vicious attacks against Alice Walker and against Black women critics and scholars who were publicly defending the film. One of the women in the interview session commented that she was surprised that there was such controversy over the film: "I had such a positive feeling about it, I couldn't imagine someone saying that they didn't like it." Another said that she was shocked at the outcry from some black men: "I didn't look at it as being stereotypically Black, or all Black men are this way" (referring to the portrayal of the character Mister). Another related a story that shows how two people can watch the same film and have opposite reactions:

> I was thinking about how men felt about it [*The Color Purple*] and I was surprised. But I related it to something that happened to me some time ago when I was married. I went to see a movie called *Three in the Attic*. I don't know if any of you ever saw it. But I remember that on the way home I thought it was funny but my husband was so angry he wouldn't even talk to me on the way home. He said, "You thought that was funny?" I said that I sure did. He felt it was really hostile because these ladies had taken this man up in the attic and made him go to bed with all of them until he was . . . blue. Because he had been running around with all of these ladies. But he [her husband] was livid because I thought it was funny. And I think now, some men I talked to had a similar reaction to *The Color Purple*. That it was . . . all the men in there were dummies or horrible. And none of the men, they felt, were portrayed in a positive light. And then I started thinking about it and I said, "Well . . . I felt that somebody had to be the hero or the heroine, and in this case it just happened to be the woman.

I have found that on the whole Black women have discovered something progressive and useful in the film. It is crucial to understand how this is possible when viewing a work made according to the encoding of dominant ideology. Black women's responses to *The Color Purple* loom as an extreme contrast to those of many other viewers. Not only is the difference in reception noteworthy, but Black women's responses confront and challenge a prevalent method of media audience analysis which insists that viewers of mainstream works have no control or influence over a cultural product. Recent developments in media audience analysis demonstrate that there is a complex process of negotiation whereby specific members of a culture construct meaning from a mainstream text that is different from the meanings others would produce. These different readings are based, in part, on viewers' various histories and experiences.

Oppositional Readings

The encoding/decoding model is useful for understanding how a cultural product can evoke such different viewer reactions. The model was developed by the University of Birmingham Centre for Contemporary Cultural Studies, under the direction of Stuart Hall, in an attempt to synthesize various perspectives on media audience analysis and to incorporate theory from sociology and cultural studies. This model is concerned with an understanding of the communication process as it operates in a specific cultural context. It analyzes ideological and cultural power and the way in which meaning is produced in that context. The researchers at the Centre felt that media analysts should not look simply at the meaning of a text but should also investigate the social and cultural framework in which communication takes place.[14]

From political sociology, the encoding/decoding model was drawn from the work of Frank Parkin, who developed a theory of meaning systems.[15] This theory delineates three potential responses to a media message: dominant, negotiated, or oppositional. A dominant (or preferred) reading of a text accepts the content of the cultural product without question. A negotiated reading questions parts of the content of the text but does not question the dominant ideology which underlies the production of the text. An oppositional response to a cultural product is one in which the recipient of the text understands that the system that produced the text is one with which he or she is fundamentally at odds.[16]

A viewer of a film (reader of a text) comes to the moment of engagement with the work with a knowledge of the world and a knowledge of other texts, or media products. What this means is that when a person comes to view a film, he or she does not leave his or her histories, whether social, cultural, economic, racial, or sexual, at the door. An audience member from a marginalized group (people of color, women, the poor, and so on) has an oppositional stance as he or she participates in mainstream media. The motivation for this counterreception is that we understand that mainstream media have never rendered our segment of the population faithfully. We have as evidence our years of watching films and television programs and reading plays and books. Out of habit, as readers of mainstream texts, we have learned to ferret out the beneficial and put up blinders against the rest.

From this wary viewing standpoint, a subversive reading of a text can occur. This alternative reading comes from something in the work that strikes the viewer as amiss, that appears "strange." Behind the idea of subversion lies a reader-oriented notion of "making strange."[17] When things appear strange to the viewer, he or she may then bring other viewpoints to bear on the watching of the film and may see things other than what the filmmakers intended. The viewer, that is, will read "against the grain" of the film.

Producers of mainstream media products are not aligned in a conspiracy against an audience. When they construct a work, they draw on their own background, experience, and social and cultural milieu. They are therefore under "ideological pressure" to reproduce the familiar.[18] When Steven Spielberg made *The Color Purple* he did not intend to make a film that would be in the mold of previous films that were directed by a successful White director and had an all-Black or mostly Black cast.

Spielberg states that he deliberately cast the characters in *The Color Purple* in a way that they would not carry the taint of negative stereotypes: "I didn't want to cast traditional Black movie stars, which I thought would create their own stereotypes. I won't mention any names because it wouldn't be kind, but there were people who wanted to play these parts very much. It would have made it seem as if these were the only Black people accepted in White world's mainstream. I didn't want to do that. That's why I cast so many unknowns like Whoopi Goldberg, Oprah Winfrey, Margaret Avery."[19] But it is interesting that while the director of the film made a conscious decision to cast against type, he could not break away from his culturally acquired conceptions of how Black people are and how they should act. Barbara Christian, professor of Afro-American Studies at the

University of California, Berkeley, contends that the most maligned figure in the film is the character Harpo. She points out that in the book he cannot become the patriarch that society demands he be.[20] Apparently Spielberg could not conceive of a man uncomfortable with the requirements of patriarchy, and consequently depicts Harpo as a buffoon. Christian comments that "the movie makes a negative statement about men who show some measure of sensitivity to women." The film uses the husband and wife characters, Harpo and Sofia, as comic relief. Some of the criticism against the film from Black viewers concerned Harpo's ineptness in repairing a roof. If the filmmakers have Harpo fall once, it seems they decided that it was even funnier if he fell three times.

In her *Village Voice* review, Michele Wallace attributed motives other than comic relief to the film's representations of the couple. Wallace considered their appearances to be the result of "white patriarchal interventions." She wrote:

> In the book Sofia is the epitome of a woman with masculine powers, the martyr to sexual injustice who eventually triumphs through the realignment of the community. In the movie she is an occasion for humor. She and Harpo are the reincarnations of Amos and Sapphire; they alternately fight and fuck their way to a house full of pickaninnies. Harpo is always falling through a roof he's chronically unable to repair. Sofia is always shoving a baby into his arms, swinging her large hips, and talking a mile a minute. Harpo, who is dying to marry Sofia in the book, seems bamboozled into marriage in the film. Sofia's only masculine power is her contentiousness. Encircled by the mayor, his wife and an angry mob, she is knocked down and her dress flies up providing us with a timely reminder that she is just a woman.[21]

The depiction of Sofia lying in the street with her dress up is almost an exact replica of a picture published in a national mass-circulation magazine of a large Black woman lying dead in her home after she had been killed by her husband in a domestic argument. Coincidence or not, this image, among others in the film, makes one wonder about Spielberg's unconscious store of associations.

Black People's Representation in Film

While a filmmaker draws on his or her background and experience, he or she also draws on a history of other films. *The Color Purple* follows in the footsteps of earlier films with a Black storyline and/or an all-Black cast that were directed by a White male for mass consumption by a White American audience. The criticisms against the film repeatedly invoked the names of such racist films as *The Birth of a Nation* (1915), *Hallelujah* (1929), and *Cabin in the Sky* (1943). One reviewer in the *Village Voice* wrote that *The Color Purple* was "a revisionist *Cabin in the Sky*, with the God-fearing, long-suffering Ethel Waters (read Celie) and the delectable temptress Lena Horne (known as Shug Avery) falling for each other rather than wrestling over the soul of feckless (here sadistic) Eddie Anderson."[22]

According to Donald Bogle in *Toms, Coons, Mulattoes, Mammies and Bucks*, Nina Mae McKinney's character in *Hallelujah* executing "gyrations and groans" and sensuous "bumps and grinds" became a standard for almost every Black "leading lady" in motion pictures, from Lena Horne in *Cabin in the Sky* to Lola Falana in *The Liberation of L. B. Jones*.[23] The corollary of the stereotype can be seen acted out by Margaret Avery as Shug in the juke joint scenes in *The Color Purple*. Here we see Shug singing in the juke joint and later leading the "jointers" singing and prancing down the road to her father's church. One viewer of *The Color Purple* wondered, in reference to this scene, if it were obligatory in every film that contained Black actors and actresses that they sing and dance.[24]

As Spielberg called on his store of media memories in making *The Color Purple*, he used a cinematic technique that made D. W. Griffith famous—crosscutting—toward the same end as Griffith: that of portraying the "savage" nature of Black people. At the beginning of *The Color Purple* the young Celie gives birth to a child fathered by the man she thinks is her father. The viewer can recall the beads of sweat on Celie's face and the blood in the pan of water as Nettie wrings out the cloth she is using to wash Celie. The next shot of blood is on the rock that one of Mister's bad kids throws and which hits the young Celie. We look at Celie and then there is a close-up of the blood on the rock. Later in the film, there is a scene of the grown Celie taking up a knife that she will use to shave Mister. It should be noted that this scene was not in the book and was entirely the film's invention. As Celie brings the knife closer to Mister's neck there is continual crosscutting with scenes of the initiation rites of Adam (Celie's son) and Pasha in Africa. This crosscutting is interspersed with shots of Shug dressed in a red dress running across a field to stop Celie from cutting Mister's throat. As the back-and-forth action of the three scenes progresses, the kids' cheeks are cut and we see a trickle of blood running down one of their faces.

In fictional filmmaking, scripts utilize what is known as the rule of threes: first there is the introduction to a concept that is significant, then the setup, then the payoff. Without reaching too hard for significance, we can see in the meaning of the shots of blood with the blood-red of Shug's dress as she runs to rescue Celie, and then the bloodletting of the African initiation rite, that these shots and their use of red culminate in the payoff: these are "savage" people. This connects up later in the film with the overall red tone to the juke-joint sequences and the red dress that Shug wears while she is performing there. As Barbara Christian put it, the gross inaccuracy of the African initiation ceremony coupled with the shots of Celie going after Mister with the sharpened knife seemed intended to depict a "primordial blood urge shared by dark peoples in Africa and Afro-Americans."

Other films that have formed the foundation of Black people's demeaning cinematic heritage are *Hearts of Dixie* (1929), *The Green Pastures* (1936), *Carmen Jones* (1954), and *Porgy and Bess* (1959). *Porgy and Bess* is especially interesting because of the similarity of its reception to that of *The Color Purple*. The playwright Lorraine Hansberry figures prominently in Black people's negative reaction to *Porgy and Bess*. Hansberry was the only Black person who confronted the director, Otto Preminger, in a public debate about the film. At the time of the debate, Hansberry was well-known because of the success of her play *A Raisin in the Sun* (1959). Hansberry's condemnation of the film and its director was the catalyst for a scathing article in *Ebony* magazine, criticizing not only the makers of the film, but also the Black stars who had defended the film as a commendable work of art.[25]

There is a sense of déjà vu in considering the success of Lorraine Hansberry, her view of Black people's representation in commercial films, and her deliberations about having her work turned into a Hollywood property. Hansberry's concern almost twenty-five years before the release of *The Color Purple* reads as if it could have been written about the contemporary film. Both Hansberry and Alice Walker were hesitant about turning their works, which were successful in another medium, over to a White director in Hollywood. Hansberry wrote about this in 1961:

> My twenty years of memory of Hollywood treatment of 'Negro material' plus the more commonly decried aspects of Hollywood tradition, led me to visualize slit skits and rolling eyeballs, with the latest night club singer playing the family's college daughter. I did not feel it was my right or duty to help present the American public with yet another latter-day minstrel show.[26]

The negative assumptions that Hansberry was confronting and that she countered in her works is the myth of the exotic primitive.[27] I label it a myth not because of the concept's falseness but because of its wide acceptance, and because of the manner in which it functions as a cultural belief system.

In contemporary terms, a myth is a narrative that accompanies an historical sequence of events or actions. A body of political writings and literature develops around this narrative. This becomes the formulated myth. The myth is constructed of images and symbols that have the force to activate a cultural belief system. This means that if a culture believes a myth to be true or operable in their society, a body of tradition, folklore, laws, and social rules is developed around this mythology. In this way myths serve to organize, unify, and clarify a culture's history in a manner that is satisfactory to a culture.

Mark Schorer, in *Myth and Mythmaking*, states that all convictions (belief systems), whether personal or societal, involve mythology. The mythology, although historically grounded, does not have to be historically accurate. The truth or falsity of the myth is not important when considering the function of the myth (that of validating history), as the cultural system of beliefs is not rational but based on the assumptions in the myth-making process. As Schorer indicates, "Belief organizes experience not because it is rational but because all belief depends on a controlling imagery and rational belief is the intellectual formalization of that imagery."[28] In other words, we believe first, and then we create a rationale for our beliefs and subsequent actions. The formal expression of our beliefs can be seen in the imagery used by a culture.

The characteristics of the myth of the exotic primitive are these: (a) Black people are naturally childlike. Thus, they adjust easily to the most unsatisfactory social conditions, which they accept readily and even happily; (b) Black people are oversexed, carnal sensualists dominated by violent passions; and (c) Black people are savages taken from a culture relatively low on the scale of human civilizaiton.[29]

As a panelist on *The Negro in American Culture*, a radio program aired on WBAI-FM in New York in January 1961, Lorraine Hansberry spoke eloquently about mainstream artists' need to portray Black people in a negative light:

> And it seems to me that one of the things that has been done in the
> American mentality is to create this escape valve of the exotic Negro,
> wherein it is possible to exalt abandon on all levels, and to imagine that
> while I am dealing with the perplexities of the universe, look over there,
> coming down from the trees is a Negro who knows none of this, and
> wouldn't it be marvelous if I could be my naked, brutal, savage self again?[30]

Knowing that this concept of exoticism underlies the products of mainstream cultural production, I think this is one of the reasons that many viewers of a film such as *The Color Purple* have what Bogle described earlier as a schizophrenic reaction. The film did have something progressive and useful for a Black audience but at the same time some of the caricatures and representations cause the viewer to wince. It is my contention that a Black audience, through a history of theater-going and film-watching, knows that at some point an expression of the exotic primitive is going to be presented to us. Since this is the case, we have one of two options available to us. One is to never indulge in media products, an impossibility in an age of media blitz. Another option, and I think this is more an unconscious reaction to and defense against racist depictions of Black people, is to filter out that which is negative and select from the work elements we can relate to.

Black Women's Response

Given the similarities of *The Color Purple* to past films that have portrayed Black people negatively, Black women's positive reaction to the film seems inconceivable. However, their stated comments and published reports prove that Black women not only like the film but have formed a strong attachment to it. The film is significant in their lives.

John Fiske provides a useful explanation of what is meant by the term "subject" in cultural analysis. The "subject" is different from the "individual." The individual is the biological being produced by nature; the "subject" is a social and theoretical construction that is used to designate individuals as they become significant in a political or theoretical sense. When considering a text—a cultural product—the subject is defined as the political being who is affected by the ideological construction of the text.[31]

Black women, as subjects for the text *The Color Purple*, have a different history and consequently a different perspective from other viewers of the film. This became evident in the controversy surrounding the film, and in the critical comments from some Black males about what they perceived as the detrimental depiction of Black men. In contrast to this view, Black women have demonstrated that they found something useful and positive in the film. Barbara Christian relates that the most frequent statement from Black women has been: "Finally, somebody says something about us."[32] This sense of identification with what is in the film would provide an impetus for Black women to form an engagement with the film. This engagement could have been either positive or negative. That it was favorable indicates something about the way in which Black women have constructed meaning from this text.

It would be too easy, I think, to categorize Black women's reaction to the film as an example of "false consciousness," to consider Black women as cultural dupes in the path of a media barrage who cannot figure out when a media product portrays them and their race in a negative manner. Black women are aware, along with others, of the oppression and harm that comes from a negative media history. But Black women are also aware that their specific experience, as Black people, as women, in a rigid class/caste state, has never been adequately dealt with in mainstream media.

One of the Black women that I interviewed talked about this cultural past and how it affected her reaction to *The Color Purple*:

> When I went to the movie, I thought, here I am. I grew up looking at Elvis Presley kissing on all these White girls. I grew up listening to "Tammy, Tammy, Tammy." [She sings the song that Debbie Reynolds sang in the movie *Tammy*] And it wasn't that I had anything projected before me on the screen to really give me something that I could grow up to be like. Or even wanted to be. Because I knew I wasn't Goldilocks, you know, and I had heard those stories all my life. So when I got to the movie, the first thing I said was "God, this is good acting." And I liked that. I felt a lot of pride in my Black brothers and sisters. . . . By the end of the movie I was totally emotionally drained. . . . The emotional things were all in the book, but the movie just took every one of my emotions. . . . Towards the end, when she looks up and sees her sister Nettie . . . I had gotten so emotionally high at that point . . . when she saw her sister, when she started to call her name and to recognize who she was, the hairs on my neck started to stick up. I had never had a movie do that to me before.

The concept of "interpellation" sheds light on the process by which Black women were able to form a positive engagement with *The Color Purple*. Interpellation is the way in which the subject is hailed by the text; it is the method by which ideological discourses constitute subjects and draw them into the text-subject relationship. John Fiske describes "hailing" as similar to hailing a cab. The viewer is hailed by a particular work; if he or she gives a cooperative response to the beckoning, then not only is he or she constructed as a subject, but the text then becomes a text, in the sense that the subject begins to construct meaning from the work and is constructed by the work.[33]

The moment of the encounter of the text and the subject is known as the "interdiscourse." David Morely explains this concept, developed by Michel Pecheux, as the space, the specific moment when subjects bring their histories to bear on meaning production in a text.[34] Within this interdiscursive space, cultural competencies come into play. A cultural competency is the repertoire of discursive strategies, the range of knowledge, that a viewer brings to the act of watching a film and creating meaning from a work. As has been stated before, the meanings of a text will be constructed differently depending on the various backgrounds of the viewers. The viewers' positions in the social structure determine, in part, what sets of discourses or interpretive strategies they will bring to their encounter with the text. A specific cultural competency will set some of the boundaries to meaning construction.

The cultural competency perspective has allowed media researchers to understand how elements in a viewer's background play a determining role in the way in which he or she interprets a text. Stuart Hall, David Morley, and others utilize the theories of Dell Hymes, Basil Bernstein, and Pierre Bourdieu for an understanding of the ways in which a social structure distributes different forms of cultural decoding strategies throughout the different sections of the media audience. These understandings are not the same for everyone in the audience because they are shaped by the individual's history, both media and cultural, and by the individual's social affiliations such as race, class, gender, and so on.[35]

As I see it, there can be two aspects to a cultural competency, or the store of understanding that a marginalized viewer brings to interpreting a cultural product. One is a positive response where the viewer constructs something useful from the work by negotiating his/her response, and/or gives a subversive reading to the work. The other is a negative response in which the viewer rejects the work. Both types of oppositional readings are prompted by the store of negative images that have come from prior mainstream media experiences—in the case of *The Color Purple*, from Black people's negative history in Hollywood films.

A positive engagement with a work could come from an intertextual cultural experience. This is true, I think, with the way in which Black women constructed meaning from *The Color Purple*. Creative works by Black women are proliferating now. This intense level of productivity is not accidental nor coincidental. It stems from a desire on the part of Black women to construct works more in keeping with their experience, their history, and with the daily lives of other Black women. And Black women, as cultural consumers, are receptive to these works. This intertextual cultural knowledge is forming black women's store of decoding strategies for films that are about them. This is the cultural competency that Black women brought to their favorable readings of *The Color Purple*.

Black Women's Writing Tradition: Community and Articulation

The historical moment in which the film *The Color Purple* was produced and received is what one Black feminist scholar has categorized as the "renaissance of Black women writers" of the 1970s and 1980s. Within this renaissance, the central concern of the writers has been the personal lives and collective histories of Black women. The writers are reconstructing a heritage that has either been distorted or ignored. In this reconstruction, Black women are both audience and subject.[36] A major difference in the current period of writing from that of the well known Harlem Renaissance of the 1920s, the protest literature of the 1940s and the Black activist literature of the 1960s, is that Black women writers are getting more exposure and recognition today, and the target of their works is different. In the earlier periods of Black writing, male writers were given dominant exposure and the audience to whom they addressed their works was White. The writers believed that because Black people's oppression was the direct result of White racism, exposing this fact to White people would result in change. By contrast, for Black women writers within the last forty years, the Black community has been the major focus of their work.

Hortense J. Spillers writes that the community of Black women writing is a vivid new fact of national life. Spillers includes in this community not only the writers but Black women critics, scholars, and audience members. This community, which Spillers labels a community of "cultural workers" is fashioning its own tradition. Its writers and its readers are, she writes, creating their works against the established canons and are excavating a legacy that is more appropriate to their lives. Spillers argues compellingly that traditions are made, not born. Traditions do not arise spontaneously out of nature, but are created social events. She insists that traditions exist not only because there are writers there to make them, but also because there is a "strategic audience of heightened consciousness prepared to read and interpret the works as such."[37] Spillers adds that traditions need to be maintained by an audience if they are to survive, and she argues that this is currently happening. She writes that "we are called upon to witness" the formation of a new social order of Black women as a community conscious of itself. This is not a random association of writers creating in isolation or readers consuming the works in a vacuum. According to Spillers, the group views itself as a community and is aware that it is creating new symbolic values and a new sense of empowerment for itself and the members of the group.

Stuart Hall has defined the principle of "articulation," developed by Ernesto Laclau, to explain how individuals within a particular society at a specific historical moment wrest control away from the dominant forces in a culture and attain authority over their lives for themselves and for others within their social group. The way in which an articulation is accomplished, and its significance, has bearing on this examination of the film *The Color Purple*. An articulation is defined as the form of a connection, a linkage, that can establish a unity among different elements within a culture, under certain conditions.[38] In the case of a cultural product such as the film *The Color Purple*, the unity that is formed links a discourse (the film) and a specific social group (Black women, or more precisely, what Spillers had defined as the Black women's writing community). Such unity is flexible, but not for all time. It must constantly be strengthened. The strength of the unity formed between a discourse and a social alliance comes from the use to which the group puts the discourse, or the cultural product. In the case of *The Color Purple*, the film has been used to give new meaning to the lives of Black women.

Articulation, as it is normally defined, can have two meanings: "joining up" in the sense of the limbs of a body or an anatomical structure, or "giving expression to."[39] Hall disagrees with the use of articulation to mean "giving expression to" because it implies that a social group shares an expressive unity, which Hall believes it does not. An articulation results from a coming together of separate discourses under certain specific conditions and at specific times. The use of articulation to mean "giving expression to" implies that the two elements that are linked are the same, but for Hall they are not. The unity formed "is not that of an identity where one structure perfectly reproduces or recapitulates" the other. The social group and the signifying text are not the same. An articulation occurs because a social alliance forms it, in a political act, which makes the group a cohesive one for a time, as long as it goes on acting for a political purpose.

When an articulation arises, old ideologies are disrupted and a cultural transformation is accomplished. The cultural transformation is not something totally new, nor does it have an unbroken line of continuity with the past. It is always in a process of becoming. But at a particular moment the reality of the cultural transformation becomes apparent. The group that is the catalyst for it recognizes that a change is occurring and that they are in the midst of a cultural transition. The formal elements of the transformation are then recognized and consolidated.

The Black women's writing tradition laid a foundation for the way in which Black women formed an articulation through which they interpreted the film *The Color Purple*. The boundaries of the tradition are set from 1850 onward. Although Black women were socially and politically active from the beginning of their enforced presence in the "new world," their writings, speeches, and lectures, their "public voice," as Hazel Carby describes it, was not being recorded and preserved. Carby makes the critical point, however, that Black women's voices were being heard.[40] The public voice of nineteenth-century Black women activists resounds now in the creative works of Black women in the 1970s and the 1980s, thus giving contemporary texts all the elements of a tradition.

Barbara Christian's *Black Women Novelists* (1980) was instrumental in identifying the presence of the tradition. In her book Christian not only demonstrated that there was indeed a Black women's writing tradition, but she also proved that the reasons that these Black women were little known was that the two established critical institutions, African-American literature and mainstream White literature, had placed Black women in the shadows of literary scholarship. She proved, as Spillers indicated, that tradition is a man-made product and that Black women had been left out.

Christian also looks at the elements of Black women's writing that foreshadowed and formed a foundation for the contemporary writers that she finds most influential: Paule Marshall, Toni Morrison, and Alice Walker. The elements of Black life that they portray seem to strike a resonance in the audience for whom the works are written—Black women. Christian argues that Black women's literature is not just a matter of discourse but is a way of acknowledging one's existence: "it has to do with giving consolation to oneself that one does exist. It is an attempt to make meaning out of that existence." And further, "The way in which I have often described this for myself, as a Black woman, is that this literature helps me to know that I am not hallucinating. Because much of one's life from the point of view of a Black woman could be seen as an hallucination from what society tells you." She said the way in which the literature connects up with the experiences of other Black women is that, in giving Black women a place as subject, it "therefore gives them a sense that their lives are in fact *real*."[41]

Toni Morrison writes of one of her characters: "She had nothing to fall back on; not maleness, not whiteness, not ladyhood, not anything. And out of the profound desolation of her reality she may well have invented herself."[42] Out of the profound desolation of Black women's reality, to paraphrase Toni Morrison, Black women cultural producers are beginning to create works more appropriate to their lives and to the daily reality of other Black women. In Ntozake Shange's choreopoem *For Colored Girls Who Have Considered Suicide/When the Rainbow Is Enuf* (1976), one of the characters, the lady in orange, tells her former boyfriend:

> ever since I realized there was someone callt
> a colored girl an evil woman a bitch or a nag
> I been trying not to be that and leave bitterness
> in somebody else's cup
> come to somebody to love me
> without deep and nasty smellin scald from lye or bein
> left screamin in a street fulla lunatics
> whisperin slut bitch bitch niggah
> get outa
> here wit alla
> that . . .

Later in the passage the lady in orange delivers what I think is a sign for Black women that the status quo is not for them and that something different is required:

> . . . but a real dead
> lovin is here for you now
> cuz I don't know anymore
> how to avoid my own face
> wet wit my tears
> cuz I had convinced
> myself colored girls had no right to sorrow
> and I lived
> and loved that way and kept sorrow on the curb
> allegedly
> for you
> but I know I did it for myself
> I cdnt stand it
> I cdnt stand bein sorry and colored at the same time it's so redundant in
> the modern world . . . [43]

"I couldn't stand it," the lady in orange says, and she issues an ultimatum that the Black woman was evolving from one place in society's conception of her to another of her own choosing. The Black woman was changing from victim to victor, was placing herself outside of the cocoon for others' constructions of her and, as Alice Walker's character Celie says in *The Color Purple*, entering into "the Creation."

Celie's declaration contains the essence of Black women's response to the film *The Color Purple*. There has been a long march from early images of the Black woman in creative works to the reconstruction of the character Celie in Alice Walker's novel. Celie tells Mister, at a turning point in the novel, that she is leaving the prison that he has created for her and entering into a freer place where she has more control over her own destiny. Black women responded to Celie's statement in their overwhelming positive reaction to both the novel and the film.

Black women's positive response to the film *The Color Purple* is not coincidental, nor is it insignificant. It is in keeping with the recent emergence of a body of critical works about the heritage of Black women writers, the recent appearance of other novels by Black women written in the same vein as *The Color Purple*, and, very importantly, the fact that there is a knowledgeable core of Black women readers of both literary and filmic texts. This community of heightened consciousness is in the process of creating new self-images and forming a force for change.

Notes

1. Phil Donahue read a quote by Tony Brown with this statement on his show, *The Phil Donahue Show*, on April 25, 1986. Brown was part of a panel along with Donald Bogle, Michele Wallace, and Willis Edwards debating the film. Ishmael Reed's statement was quoted by Tony Brown on his show *Tony Brown's Journal*, when Reed was a guest there. Reed was debating Barbara Smith on the topic of the show, "Do Black Feminist Writers Victimize Black Men?" (repeat program), November 2, 1986.

2. Andrew Kopkind, "The Color Purple," *The Nation*, February 1, 1986, p. 124. *The Guardian* is a radical journal in the United States.

3. Jill Nelson, "Spielberg's 'Purple' Is Still Black," *Guardian*, January 29, 1986, p. 1.

4. E. R. Shipp, "Blacks in Heated Debate over *The Color Purple*, *New York Times*, January 27, 1986, p. A13.

5. Courtland Milloy, "A 'Purple' Rage Over a Rip-Off," *Washington*

Post, December 24, 1985, p. B3.

6. Barbara Smith, "Color Purple Distorts Class, Lesbian Issues," *Guardian*, February 19, 1986, p. 19.

7. Jill Nelson, "Spielberg's 'Purple,'" p. 17.

8. Michele Wallace, *The Phil Donahue Show*, April 25, 1986.

9. Michele Wallace, "Blues for Mr. Spielberg," *Village Voice*, March 18, 1986, p. 27.

10. Donald Bogle, *The Phil Donahue Show*, April 25, 1986.

11. William Goldstein, "Alice Walker on the set of *The Color Purple*," *Publisher's Weekly*, September 6, 1985, p. 48.

12. Mary Helen Washington, "Book Review of Barbara Christian's *Black Women* Novelists," Signs: *Journal of Women in Culture and Society* 8, no. 1 (August 1982): 182.

13. As part of the research for my dissertation on Black women's response to the film *The Color Purple*, I conducted an ethnography of reading with selected Black women viewers of the film in December 1987 in California. All references to women interviewed come from this study. For a discussion of the issues of readers' response to texts in media audience analysis, see Ellen Seiter et al., "Don't Treat Us Like We're so Stupid and Naive: Towards an Ethnography of Soap Opera Viewers," in *Rethinking Television Audiences*, ed. Ellen Seiter (Chapel Hill: University of North Carolina Press, forthcoming). See also Seiter's use of Umberto Eco's open/closed text distinction to examine the role of the woman reader. Seiter uses Eco's narrative theory to argue for the possibility of "alternative" readings unintended by their producers in "Eco's TV Guide: The Soaps," *Tabloid*, no. 6 (1981): 36–43.

14. David Morely, "Changing Paradigms in Audience Studies," in *Rethinking Television Audiences*, ed. Seiter.

15. Ibid., p. 4.

16. Lawrence Grossberg, "Strategies of Marxist Cultural Interpretation," *Critical Studies in Mass Communication*, no. 1 (1984): 403.

17. Christine Gledhill explains the idea of "making strange" in two articles: "Developments in Feminist Film Criticism," in *Re-vision: Essays in Feminist Film Criticism*, ed. Mary Ann Doane, Patricia Mellencamp, and Linda Williams (Frederick, Md.: University Publications of America, in association with the American Film Institute, 1984), and "Klute 1: A Contemporary Film Noir and Feminist Criticism," in *Women in Film Noir*, ed. E. Ann Kaplan (London: British Film Institute, 1984).

18. Grossberg, "Strategies," p. 403.

19. Steven Spielberg, *Alice Walker and* The Color Purple, BBC documentary, 1986.

20. Barbara Christian, "De-Visioning Spielberg and Walker: *The Color Purple*—the Novel and the Film," Center for the Study of Women in Society, University of Oregon, May 20, 1986.

21. Wallace, "Blues for Mr. Spielberg," p. 25.

22. J. Hoberman, "Color Me Purple," *Village Voice*, December 24, 1985, p. 76.

23. Donald Bogle, *Toms, Coons, Mulattoes, Mammies and Bucks: An Interpretive History of Blacks in American Films* (New York: Viking Press, 1973), p. 31.

24. Julie Salamon, ". . . As Spielberg's Film Version is Released," *Wall Street Journal*, December 19, 1985, p. 20.

25. Era Bell Thompson, "Why Negroes Don't Like 'Porgy and Bess,'" *Ebony*, October 1959, p. 51. A rundown of Lorraine Hansberry's debate with Otto Preminger is also given by Jack Pitman, "Lorraine Hansberry Deplores 'Porgy,'" Variety, May 27, 1959.

26. Lorraine Hansberry, "What Could Happen Didn't," *New York Herald-Tribune*, March 26, 1961, p. 8. In this article Lorraine Hansberry writes about the experience of turning her play *A Raisin in the Sun* into a Hollywood movie. Hansberry wrote the screenplay herself and, as far as I know, was the first Black woman to have a Hollywood film based on her work. For a further examination of the political and historical significance of Hansberry, see Jacqueline Bobo, "Debunking the Myth of the Exotic Primitive: Three Plays by Lorraine Hansberry" (master's thesis, San Francisco State University, 1980).

27. Anthropologist Melville Herskovits gives a broader scope to the myth, designating it as the myth of the Negro past. The trait of exotic primitivism can be extrapolated from Herskovits's definition and considered a myth itself in that both concepts are of sufficient potency that the effect in a culture is the same: validating the social processes whereby Black people are considered inferior. Melville Herskovits, *The Myth of the Negro Past* (Boston: Beacon Press, 1958), p. 1.

28. Mark Schorer, "The Necessity of Myth," in *Myth and Mythmaking*, ed. Henry A. Murray (New York: George Braziller, 1960), p. 356.

29. Herskovits, *Myth*, p. 1.

30. Lorraine Hansberry, "The Negro in American Culture," reprinted

in *The Black American Writer*, ed. C. W. E. Bigsby (Florida: Everett/Edward, 1969), p. 93.

31. John Fiske, "British Cultural Studies and Television," in *Channels of Discourse: Television and Contemporary Criticism*, ed. Robert C. Allen (Chapel Hill: University of North Carolina Press, 1987), p. 258.

32. Christian, "De-Visioning Spielberg and Walker."

33. Fiske, "British Cultural Studies and Television," p. 258.

34. David Morely, "Texts, Readers, Subjects," in *Culture, Media, Language*, ed. Stuart Hall, Dorothy Hobson, Andrew Lowe, and Paul Willis (London: Hutchinson, 1980), p. 164.

35. David Morley, "Changing Paradigms in Audience Studies," p. 4.

36. Barbara Christian, Seminar: "Black Women's Literature and the Canon," University of Oregon, December 7, 1987.

37. Hortense J. Spillers, "Cross-Currents, Discontinuities: Black Women's Fiction," in *Conjuring: Black Women, Fiction, and Literary Tradition*, ed. Marjorie Pryse and Hortense J. Spillers (Bloomington: Indiana University Press, 1985), p. 250.

38. Stuart Hall discusses the principle of "articulation" in "Race, Articulation an Societies Structured in Dominace," in *Sociological Theories: Race and Colonialism* (UNESCO, 1980), pp. 305–45, and in Lawrence Grossberg, ed., "On Postmodernism and Articulation: An Interview with Stuart Hall, " *Journal of Communication Inquiry* 10, no. 2 (summer 1986): 45–60.

39. Hall, "Race, Articulation and Societies Structured in Dominance," p. 28.

40. Hazel V. Carby, *Reconstructing Womanhood: The Emergence of the Afro-American Woman Novelist* (New York: Oxford University Press, 1987). Other critical works that examine the Black women's writing tradition are Toni Cade, *The Black Woman* (1970); Mary Helen Washington, *Black-Eyed Susans* (1975), *Midnight Birds* (1980), and *Invented Lives* (1987); Claudia Tate, ed., *Black Women Writers at Work* (1983); Mari Evans, *Black Women Writers* (1984); and Susan Willis, *Specifying* (1987).

41. Christian, "Black Women's Literature."

42. Toni Morrison, cited in Mary Helen Washington, *Black-Eyed Susans: Classic Stories by and about Black Women*, (New York: Anchor Press/Doubleday, 1975), p. vii.

43. Ntozake Shange, *For Colored Girls Who Have Considered Suicide/When the Rainbow Is Enuf* (New York: Macmillian, 1976), p. 43.

10

"America's Worst Nightmare"

Reading the Ghetto in a Culturally Diverse Context

Celeste A. Fisher

The representation of young, Black urban males in ghettocentric street films has been the focus of widespread social concern and debate since the early 1990s. The genre has generated a great deal of interest because of its depiction of the economic and social disparity present in American society from the point of view of the disenfranchised voice seldom heard in mainstream Hollywood cinema. Adding to the controversy are several outbreaks of violence that occurred throughout the country at the time of the theatrical release of ghettocentric street films, which called attention to the impact of the genre on its audience. In an attempt to give meaning to the films and those incidents, many cultural critics, theater executives, and filmmakers have commented on the racialized responses of Black and White audiences to the genre and thus defined Black males as the producers, consumers, and perpetrators of violent activity. I, however, am interested in how viewers' responses to a particular cinematic construction of "Blackness" are shaped by their immediate social context. In other words, I am suggesting the idea that meaning can also be constructed during its expression to others in dialogue, and that the dynamics of the dialogue and the relations among the participants play a major role in the meanings readers give to texts. Specifically, I am concerned with the notion of meaning making within the context of a multicultural setting, when the readers are young adults responding to a particular construction of "Blackness" as represented in the Hood film *Menace II Society*.

The response of critics and the reaction of audiences to the ghettocentric films at the time of their theatrical release highlighted the questions of this study—questions about the roles played in audiences' meaning making and response by the messages in the text itself, the experiences audiences bring to the text, the sociocultural situation of different audiences, and the immediate social context in which meanings and responses are constructed.

The Films

After the commercial and critical success of *Boyz N the Hood* in 1991, Hollywood embraced the Black underclass. Films such as *Straight out of Brooklyn* (1991), *Juice* (1992), *Menace II Society* (1993), *Poetic Justice* (1993), *Just Another Girl on the IRT* (1993), *Clockers* (1995), and *Set It Off* (1996) soon followed. Unlike Dennis Hopper's *Colors* (1988) which examined gang life in South Central Los Angeles from a cop's point of view, ghettocentric Hood films painted a portrait of the marginalized individuals who comprise underclass African-American communities.

With the exception of *Just Another Girl on the IRT*, directed by Leslie Harris, and a few films by White directors (*Fresh*, Boaz Yakin; *South Central*, Steve Anderson), Hood films are primarily the products of Black male filmmakers. According to Manthia Diawara (1993) in "The New Black Realism," the genre was generated out of Black male masculinity—young Black men coming of age in a hostile urban environment where knowledge of the streets is essential to their survival. The characters live in impoverished neighborhoods where drugs and gang activity are a way of life. Many come from single-parent homes where the father is rarely visible. In "The New Ghetto Aesthetic," Jacquie Jones (1991) states that women in this genre generally occupy supporting roles, ranging from strong, yet flawed, single mothers to crack addicts. More often than not they are referred to as "bitches" and "hos."

As a whole, Black-on-Black crime and distrust of police are common themes in Hood films. Other themes in the genre include revenge (*Boyz N the Hood*), a boy's initiation into manhood (*Juice*), and the struggle to escape one's surroundings (*Straight out of Brooklyn*) (Diawara 1993, 20). With few exceptions, characters exhibit a feeling of helplessness and hopelessness (*Menace II Society*), as well as a need to survive their current conditions by adapting to the laws of the streets (*Juice*; *Set It Off*). Many of the films are set on the West Coast, which has been the focus of highly publicized gang activity. For the most part, the soundtracks are dominated by rap music—an art form also dominated by Black men addressing issues of importance to Black male, urban youth. Not surprisingly, rap artists also occupy central roles in the genre—such as Ice Cube in *Boyz N the Hood*, Tupac Shakur in *Juice* and *Poetic Justice*, and Queen Latifah in *Set It Off*— as the films are, for the most part, an extension of the rap video (George 1998).

The Second Wave of Blaxploitation

However dismal the depiction of Black life, in the early 1990s, ghettocentric street films generated a great deal of money at the box office. *Boyz N the Hood*, for which John Singleton was nominated for an Academy Award, took in $9.2 million in its first weekend (Landis and Stewart 1991). As a result, Hood films have been credited with helping to revitalize the film industry, and with starting the second Black movie boom since the early 1970s (Guerrero 1993).

The first wave of blaxploitation films emerged shortly after the Civil Rights movement. These were essentially fantasy films and primarily directed by White directors. The genre placed importance on the role of individuals on the fringes of society by depicting a "Super Black" or lone hero who challenged dominant culture and won (*Superfly*).

The second wave of blaxploitation films are very different. They are coming-of-age stories in which the characters struggle to define themselves in relationship to the environments in which they live. As a result, the principal characters are younger—generally teenage boys embroiled in intragroup conflicts (i.e., Black-on-Black crime), which is sometimes linked to racism in mainstream American society (*Boyz N the Hood*; *Menace II Society*). The protagonists exist in an environment that perpetuates criminality (*South Central*; *Juice*; *Set It Off*). Loyalty to one's peer group is more often than not central to the plot. Finally, "realism" and the desire to graphically depict that realism is a defining characteristic of the new wave of blaxploitation films.

By the mid-1990s, the wave of new blaxploitation films was, for all intents and purposes, over. The end of this period in cinematic history has been attributed to its failure to create a diversity of images, settings, and themes (Bogle 1994). This can be seen in the theatrical release of *Don't Be a Menace to South Central While Drinking Your Juice in the Hood* (1996), a parody of Hood films. However, it can also be argued that, much like the films of the first blaxploitation period, Hood films are no longer needed by Hollywood to boost box office receipts. Nevertheless, the genre continues to be the subject of debate because it illuminates the concerns of the Black urban underclass. And although the films in the genre have waned, the conditions depicted in the films focus attention on the racial and social class tensions that still exist in America but are not being adequately addressed in public discourse.

Culturally Diverse Readers

To explore the role of immediate social context in meaning making, I tape-recorded and analyzed the group discussions of college undergraduates of diverse cultural backgrounds, in a classroom setting at a major research university, in response to *Menace II Society*. *Menace II Society* was selected because it was thought to be the catalyst for violent activity at the time of its theatrical release. Twelve students were present on the day of the discussion, ten women and two men. Prior to screening the film, students completed a background questionnaire in which they self-identified their race/ethnicity. Of the two men in the group, one identified himself as Irish and Italian (Robert), and the other of mixed racial heritage that included Black, Native American, and White (Mark). Of the ten women in the class, there was one Latina (Samantha), one Caucasian woman (Cathy), and one Jewish/Caucasian woman (Tracie). One student identified herself as Asian (Soo) and another as Asian American (Mary). There were three women in the class who identified themselves as African-American (Paula, Donna, and Brenda) and another woman who considered herself both Black and Filipina (Erika). In answering a series of questions regarding household income, educational level of parents, and so on, all of the students indicated a middle-class background.

Immediately after viewing the film, students were asked to express their opinions about what they had seen. I started the discussion by asking them to tell me what the film was about. From that point on, my participation in the group was minimal—designed only to keep the conversation going. As a result, the direction of the conversation was always shaped by a member of the group. Since *Menace II Society* was the first film the participants screened in class, I was somewhat concerned that they would not feel comfortable enough to express themselves and to initiate new topics for discussion. However, that was not the case. To my surprise, the conversation flowed rather freely. In order to identify the students who played a role in shaping the discussion and therefore held some degree of power within the group, I looked at who established or changed topics. I also looked at the types of topics raised, and their frequency, in order to determine what topics were of greatest importance to the group.

Overall, there were sixteen major shifts in the focus of the conversation precipitated by nine of the twelve participants present that day. Eight major topics were discussed among group members: the film's "message," or the moral of the film; generalizations about the response of other viewers, or the "audience" for the film; the representation of criminal activity in the film, as reflected in their character analysis of O-Dog and Caine; the degree to which the film was "realistic"; their experiential connection to the film (their personal experience in either watching the film or knowing the kind of environment represented in the film); the responsibility or role of the director to his audience; the representation of non-Blacks or "others" in the film; and the reasons for Black men or women dating White men or women (and vice versa) in our society (the representation of interracial dating in the film).

The majority of the topics raised during the discussion (audience, experiential connection, interracial dating, realism, and role of director) were categorized as "outside the world of the film," in that they were only indirectly related to the specifics of the text. Generally, this seemed to suggest that *Menace II Society* was used by the participants to address societal concerns—issues that transcended the film itself.

Many of the topics raised seemed to resurface at other times throughout the discussion. Participants, however, seemed most concerned with the audience for the film, as the topic of audience resurfaced on eight occasions and was prevalent throughout much of the conversation. They also seemed to frequently return to a discussion of what they perceived to be the film's "message" and the role of the director—which seemed to be an indication of the connection they established between the effect of the message, the audience's interpretation of that message, and the director's artistic license in presenting an African-American, ghetto environment. Overall, participants seemed to take into account the responses of the other members of the group, as they addressed old topics before introducing new ones. This seemed to suggest that participants consistently thought about the issues that caught their attention during the circulation of other ideas.

Although twelve students were present on the day of the screening and discussion (ten females and two males), the conversation was primarily controlled by four women: Erika, Donna, Tracie, and Brenda. Of the participants who changed the topic on more than one occasion, Donna (some eight or nine years older than the other members in the group) appeared to be the most determined to shape the conversation into what was important to her—the response of the audience to the film. From the beginning, she articulated her views. When I asked participants to tell me what the film was about, Donna was the first person to speak. This appeared to be an indication of her strong interest in the subject. The other women who played a significant role in shaping the discussion identified themselves as at least part Black (with the exception of Tracie, who indicated that she is both Caucasian and Jewish). Two of the students, Soo (an Asian American) and Cathy (a European American), did not speak at all, and the remaining six students spoke only briefly. All of the students present who considered themselves at least part Black or African-American (a total of six) contributed to the discussion. Of the three participants who claimed European, or a racially/ethnically mixed (non-Black) background, two participated in the discussion. Of the two participants who claimed an Asian heritage, only one spoke. Since all appeared to listen attentively, by making eye contact with each speaker, the silence of those who did not speak was not attributed to a lack of interest, since participants were part of a self-selected group who voluntarily enrolled in a course on Black cinema.

Clearly, the women of African descent controlled the flow of the discussion, with talk that focused on the world outside of the film. Thus, they seemed to hold the power within the group. While the gender and ethnic/racial makeup of the class influenced the topics under discussion, the discussion also seemed to be greatly influenced by Donna, whose primary concern seemed to be teaching nonpresent and present "others" what ghetto life is really about. Overall, Donna's remarks were more political than those of the rest of the group, who generally discussed the topics raised from a sociological perspective.

Five overriding themes, derived from the content of the topics discussed earlier, emerged from the group: meaning making as acquired knowledge, interpretation as inference, interpretation as the responsibility of the viewer, realism as a reflection of life experience and belief, and vested interest in response.

Meaning Making As Acquired Knowledge

Throughout the discussion, participants seemed particularly interested in the film's message as it related to the audience's interpretation of the film. Although most thought that the message was clear—everything you do comes back to you in the end—they were concerned that Black teenagers and White audiences would not see the film the way that they did. For instance, Brenda agreed with Donna about the reaction of some Black viewers. She added that the film might present a glorified image to the "uneducated viewer." Essentially, they were preoccupied with discussing how others saw the film, rather than their own feelings about the text. This approach seemed to allow participants to treat the film abstractly, since they were unfamiliar with one another, and perhaps unwilling to expose a part of themselves that might reveal their own insecurities and prejudices. A couple of participants mentioned that they were "different," so they would not see the film in the same way that others did. Others distanced themselves from their comments by prefacing their statements with: "I'm not saying what I think . . ." and "Other people might think. . . ." Both instances suggested that participants were reluctant to directly express their points of view in front of their classmates. In purporting to know the mind-set of other viewers, and setting themselves apart from the general audience for the film, participants seemed to reveal their own stereotypes about particular groups. Further, their responses suggested a level of superiority that gave them knowledge about a particular subject unknown to others—how to interpret film. This distancing behavior occurred in comments made by both men and women of various ethnic groups.

Interpretation As Inference

Most of the students seemed to be particularly interested in O-Dog's character. They discussed how he symbolized hope and hopelessness in the community, a theme that surfaced several times during the conversation. Generally, they thought that O-Dog was a product of his environment because he didn't have a family. Several students discussed whether he was capable of changing his behavior. Far less time was devoted to a discussion of Caine's character, which was significant because the story was told through his point of view through voice-over.

It appeared that Caine's life was presented so completely and straightforwardly that participants understood him to the point that he became the background for other activity (i.e., the actions of O-Dog); that is, Caine's character left less room for interpretation. In the film, Caine's life is traced from beginning to end. Generally, participants seemed to understand why he made the decisions that he made. Through voice-overs, they could hear in Caine's own words the impact that each individual had on his life. In contrast, they were intrigued by O-Dog because of what they did not see or hear about his life. There is less information available about O-Dog than Caine, which appears to have left more room for interpretation. Viewers are never allowed to visit O-Dog's family or the place where he lives. The only reference made to his family is in the opening scene in which the shop-keeper tells O-Dog: "I feel sorry for your mother." O-Dog replies: "What did you say about my mother?" and shoots the clerk to death. Participants were probably attracted to O-Dog because he is the most sensational character in the film. He is the character who perpetrates the most heinous crimes with no remorse. Participants discussed why he behaves in the way he does. They subsequently attributed his actions to environmental factors such as the in-flux of drugs into the community by those outside of the community. More narrowly, they cited a lack of family support that the drugs helped create. On the surface, O-Dog appears less than "human" in the film because he seems to be one-dimensional and disconnected from mainstream values. In narration, Caine describes O-Dog as "America's worst nightmare: young, black, and don't give a damn." However, participants saw him as a tragic character with few choices. Brenda articulated it best when she said that she believed "there were times when O-Dog crashed and actually thought about what was going on." It appeared that Brenda could forgive O-Dog his crimes because she perceived him as not totally detached from his human-ity and therefore a multidimensional character. Although he never showed remorse for his crimes, she was able to infer from his emotional display after the death of his friends that he could possibly have other feelings as well. As a result, she believed that he had the ability to change. In general, O-Dog's actions were interpreted as less psychotic than they appeared on the surface because participants were able to attribute his behavior to a larger social ill, a racist society. In doing so, they implicitly accepted the di-rectors' sociological view of the problems that contributed to the condi-tions in that community.

Interpretation As the Responsibility of the Viewer

Although camera technique, quality of acting, and so on, were briefly men-tioned in the discussion, they were clearly not the main foci of the conversation. It seemed that participants had been drawn into the narrative because they were able to accept the aesthetic construction of the film. However, there was a very brief discussion on the responsibility of directors to make realistic films. Essentially, Donna argued that directors who produce films with minority themes should do so as accurately or as "realistically" as possible: "Whenever they [the directors] showed where Caine lived with his grandparents, I mean every fifty feet you saw somebody standing out there drinking, standing around smoking pot. You know for people here who have never been. . . . And everyone's watching the realism . . . to me that wasn't very realistic." She went on to say that Black filmmakers had a responsibility to the community to be realistic because there were so many negative images of minorities in the media, which had a negative impact on how minorities were perceived in American society. Her comment seemed to suggest that minority filmmakers should be held to a higher standard than their mainstream counterparts in order to counteract the negative images in the news media. Donna appeared to be concerned with the way in which negative stereotypes affect social position. In general, her responses were far more overtly political than other members'. The majority of participants believed that the director had the right to express him- or herself artistically. In support of that argument, Tracie cited films in other genres that did not accurately represent the environment they depicted, such as *Malcolm X* and *Immortal Beloved.*

This discussion reinforced the group's position on the importance of the audience's interpretive knowledge. In effect, participants placed responsibility for interpretation on the viewer, rather than the director, in the filmmaker/viewer relationship. Group members suggested that it was the audience's responsibility to know what was going on in the film and to draw "correct" conclusions themselves.

Ironically, however, participants did not always reach the "correct" conclusions. While discussing the impact of the "message" on the audience, Erika, Donna, and Mary seemed to think that O-Dog is the only character to survive the drive-by shooting and thus the Hood. In fact, Stacy also survives. Although he is not outside during the incident, he saves Ronnie as gunfire is sprayed into the house. As stated earlier, survival and escaping one's environment are common themes in Hood films. Stacy—a college-bound athlete—is the only one in the group who is not dead or in jail by the end of the film. Since no one in the group noticed this, the misperception seems to indicate that incorrect information can go unchallenged in a group setting—even among those who believe themselves to be more knowledgeable about the film and the genre's conventions than the general audience.

Realism As a Reflection of Life Experience

Only a few participants made direct reference to the film's realism. With the exception of Donna, participants thought that *Menace II Society* was very realistic. The majority of the participants who articulated their views based their assessment on their personal experiences. For example, Erika and Donna assessed the film's realistic qualities by comparing it to their personal contact with the kind of environment represented in the film. Erika said: "It was very realistic to me. . . . I know people who live in it." Donna disagreed: "I've been in projects from California to the East Coast, and I have yet to see . . . every fifty feet you saw somebody standing out there drinking, standing around smoking pot. You know for people in here who've never been. To me that wasn't very realistic." In response to these comments, Tracie (the Caucasian/Jewish participant) seemed to feel the need to qualify or defend her knowledge of the ghetto environment: "I don't think it's so much a glorified message. It's just the reality. I think you have to do what you have to do to survive. . . . As a White person, I might not live in it, but I am aware." While she did not have any personal contact with the environment, it seemed that she had knowledge of it through secondhand information, most likely through the media or friends—which suggested a high degree of trust in institutions and in those with whom she shared something in common.

In this case, race was a factor in the manner in which filmic realism was assessed. While the two African-American female participants expressed knowledge as cultural insiders, the Caucasian/Jewish female expressed "outsider" knowledge. But, although Donna and Erika used their personal contact with the environment represented in the film as support for their respective arguments, they did not agree on a "reality"—thus suggesting that reality was subjective even among people who share similar experiences. The viewers' judgment of the realism of the film seemed to be based on many complex factors, such as culture, socioeconomic class, gender, and the time and nature of personal contact with the environment depicted.

Vested Interest in Response

During the course of the discussion, several students raised issues related to their gender and/or racial background. Samantha talked about the representation of Latinos in the film. However, her response was not commented upon by the other members of the group. Immediately thereafter, Tracie spoke about the representation of White women in the film, which sparked a heated debate. It was more than a little surprising that no one in the group commented on the film's horrific opening sequence in which O-Dog shoots and kills the Korean shopkeepers, except to state that the shopkeeper's reference to O-Dog's mother is the only instance in the film where familial connections are made. Nor did the Black women in the class comment upon the representation of Black women in the film.

Based on their responses to various aspects of the film and the lack of responses concerning the opening scene, it can be surmised that while participants in the class spoke freely about some controversial issues, generally they did not feel comfortable enough to introduce into the discussion talk about an ethnic group other than their own. Since the opening sequence is the only scene in the film that depicts violence by a Black person against a non-Black person, it might be concluded that interracial violence created more tension in a multicultural setting than the scenes of Black-on-Black crime. In a sense, it was a topic that was "too hot to touch." Moreover, the desire to raise such a controversial topic may have been diminished because there was no one with a vested interest in the discussion, since there were no Korean participants in the group. In fact, it may have been counterproductive for Black students in the group to address such an issue because the act may have appeared indefensible and would therefore not serve in the best interest of the Black students in the group. This suggested that avoidance of controversial issues was an important response strategy.

Further, the decision of participants in the group not to discuss the role of Black women in the film seemed to demonstrate the impact of a multicultural group on responses. If we consider that the majority of participants in the group were women and that the group (as a whole) relied heavily on their experiential connection to the film, it would seem that the representation of Black women in the film would have merited some discussion. However, it appeared that the women in the group were more concerned with issues relating to race in the context of the culturally diverse classroom.

Points of Conflict: The Representation of Others
Generally, participants in the group were cordial in expressing their opinions about the film until their discussion of the representation of others.

After discussing the audience's response to the film, Samantha (the only Hispanic member in the group) talked specifically about the "Latin issue" in the film. She commented that you rarely see Latinos portrayed "responsibly" in film. In essence, Samantha seemed to say that it was good to see positive images of Latinos in film. She explained that although they (the group) were talking about the reaction of Blacks and Whites to *Menace II Society*, "it is important to look at the relationship between Blacks and Latinos in the film." In effect, she was stating that Latinos should be included in the discussion because they were also affected by the representation of themselves in ghettocentric films. Significantly, no one in the class responded directly to her comment. This lack of response appeared to be the type of apathy to which Samantha was referring, concerning issues that did not present themselves in "Black and White"—reflecting much of the discussion on race relations in American society. The nonresponse of group members seemed to be an acknowledgment of her opinion, because the subject matter was not directly relevant to the interests of the largely non-Hispanic group. In effect, the topic died out because Samantha did not find support for her argument. While it was possible that the members of the group considered her concerns valid, it seemed as though they did not find them relevant to their experience at that particular point in time.

Nevertheless, Samantha's comment appeared to serve as a catalyst for Tracie to voice her opinion about the representation of White women in the film. It was her comment that sparked a long debate that moved the conversation from the film into a discussion on interracial dating. Tracie commented: "I noticed when Mr. Butler was talking to Sharif [he said that] bringing home a White woman would be bringing home the devil. My boyfriend is Black and I took personal offense to that. . . . But that exists out there. . . . My boyfriend's not Jewish and I'm Jewish. That's a big problem with my family. But, it goes both ways." Clearly, Tracie's interpretation of the scene was tinged by her experience as a White woman dating a Black man. It appeared that due to her close connection to the subject, she could not separate the film from her own reality. The film, therefore, forced Tracie to confront her own sense of "Whiteness" in relation to a film in which she was characterized as "other." In response to Tracie's statement, Brenda, who attempted to bring the conversation back to the film by explaining what Mr. Butler meant, caused some concern and confusion among the women of African-American descent in the class: "I understand the devil part offending you in every way. Completely. I sympathize with you about that. But I think more that his point was, so many Black men get educated and find Allah and you know, educate themselves. And Black women haven't . . . all Black women haven't reached that pinnacle of knowledge yet. And, they turn to the White woman because you have—almost." After Brenda acknowledged Tracie's feelings, she tried to bring the conversation back to an analysis of the scene. However, Tracie seemed to have sensed that the group was disturbed by Brenda's remark—in that she nodded in approval after Brenda's comment, but seemed to retreat from the discussion in an attempt to avoid a confrontation. Erika responded: "As a Black woman, I take offense that you say Black women haven't reached the knowledge that White women have." The response to Brenda's statement shifted the focus of the conversation from White women to Black women. In clearly defining herself as a Black woman, Erika seemed to want Brenda to know that she had the right to be upset by her remarks. Erika had chosen to identify squarely with Black women, although in her background questionnaire she stated that she was both Filipina and Black. It appeared that as the conversation became more personal, it heated up, causing Erika to assert that part of her identity that was offended. The conversation continued as Brenda tried to defend herself: "Not all Black women. What I'm saying is that, a lot of times before Black men decide they want to take their chances with another Black woman that might know . . ." Erika dismissed this: "I don't think that's the reason why."

By cutting Brenda off in midsentence, it appeared that Erika had become agitated by Brenda's remarks and therefore chose to dismiss her attempts at further explanation. The perceived attack on her race and gender had increased her emotional stake in the discussion. As a result, she appeared to shut down opinions that did not reinforce her own ideas. Subsequently, others, who appeared much calmer, attempted to provide a satisfactory explanation of why Black men date White women. Donna and Paula (other African-American female participants) provided some sociological and political reasons for the phenomenon. Paula offered that she thought "it's because some think it's like a trophy." Erika concurred: "Exactly. Exactly. It has nothing to do with Black women not being intelligent enough." Donna suggested: "It's not a trophy. It's the whole issue of domination and control."

Paula's remark appeared to demonstrate her awareness of women and "Whiteness" in American society as they relate to beauty, achievement, and value. Donna's comment, on the other hand, seemed to suggest her understanding of the distribution of power within interracial, heterosexual relationships, stemming from sociohistorical constructions of Black women and White women in American society. In a sense, Donna seemed to be suggesting that Black men date White women in an attempt at racial equity. From Erika's comments, it seemed that she was willing to agree with any explanation that supported Black women, in an attempt to make herself feel better. As the conversation continued, it revolved around Brenda's attempt to clarify her position to the group because she felt that she was being misunderstood. Mark, in exasperation, attempted to give closure to the topic by bringing the conversation back to a discussion of the film: "There's no Black women in Kansas. That's all she said."

It appeared that Mark interpreted Brenda's initial remarks to mean that in certain parts of the country (where Sharif and Stacy plan to move) there were more affluent Black men than there were Black women. Brenda, however, did not acknowledge Mark's support. Therefore, it appeared that she herself did not fully agree with his statement. It seemed as though Brenda had been unwittingly drawn into the debate on interracial dating in the society at large, which consequently forced her to defend herself. Mark's subsequent attempt at closure was ineffective because the conversation continued and his statement was not acknowledged by any other member of the group. Since the topic under discussion involved race and gender issues, it appeared that Mark's comment was not deemed valid because he had no personal stake in the discussion. As a man of mixed racial heritage, Mark was presumably perceived as a nonexpert in that area. Finally, Brenda gave up after several more attempts at explaining her position, although no real common ground was found. It appeared that the topic became so "hot" that it could not be resolved because emotions were too high.

In examining the conversations about the representation of "others," it became apparent that issues pertaining to race and gender were introduced by a person who identified him- or herself as a member of the same ethnic group (and sometimes gender) as the character(s) discussed in the film. Moreover, it appeared that as the discussion about a controversial issue concerning a particular ethnic and/or gender group "heated up," a person from a different ethnic and/or gender group who was in the minority withdrew from the conversation in an attempt to avoid confrontation. Further, none of the participants taking part in the conversation demonstrated a shift in opinion. In fact, as the conversation developed, they became even more entrenched in their views. This seemed to indicate that the controversial topic was extremely "hot," in that the debate was personalized and therefore elicited extreme emotional responses. The discussion of race in a multicultural setting led participants to assert themselves in relation to the social space that they occupy within the larger society—thus illuminating the racial tensions between Blacks and Whites in American society. Donna, in particular, saw herself as both a defender and teacher of those who did not share her cultural view, and, subsequently, her knowledge about matters concerning the Black community. As a result, the opinions of others who were not in agreement with a participant's particular views were dismissed or not heard at all.

The Role of the Text in Shaping Response

Generally, participants focused their attention on the social world outside of the film during the discussion of *Menace II Society*. Their generalizations about how "others" viewed the film appeared to be the most important topic because it was introduced and reintroduced into the discussion on nine occasions, more than any other topic. *Menace II Society* is one of the most graphic of the Hood films in terms of language and imagery. The violence in the film is cold and spontaneous in that it occurs at any time to anyone. The most striking example is the opening sequence of the film, in which O-Dog shoots and kills the Korean shopkeeper and his wife. Due to the graphic nature of that scene and several others, it may have been difficult for participants to directly relate to the characters and their situations. In a sense, they were shocked, yet intrigued by the film's "realism." Therefore, they discussed the film from a distanced perspective by talking about the response, or potential response, of "others."

Based on the content of the discussion, it appeared that group members generally examined the film from a sociological perspective. The features of the text that best account for the critical orientation of the group concern the representation of mainstream American society. In *Menace II Society*, after the opening sequence in the convenience store, the scene shifts to dramatic black-and-white footage of the race riots in Watts, California. Through voice-over, Caine states that after the riots, the drugs came. The next scene is a party at Caine's childhood home, where his mother is high on drugs and his father shoots a man to death who owes him money. In effect, the filmmakers are suggesting that mainstream society is to blame for the conditions that exist in the hood. In this way, they provide a sociological reason for Caine's behavior.

The Role of the Reader in Shaping Response

The narrative construction of the film, which focused on the lives of young African-American males in an urban environment, seemed to encourage participants to use their own experiences and backgrounds to make meaning. Not surprisingly, many of the students discussed the films in terms of their own ethnic and/or racial group identification, social class, and to a lesser extent, gender. Some participants raised topics that reflected their own backgrounds, particularly when assessing "realism." Samantha, for example, was concerned with the representation of Latinos in the film. Several participants also talked about their life experiences as a means to support their statements. Most notably, Tracie mentioned that even though she is White and middle-class, she understands that racism exists because she has a Black boyfriend.

Similarly, the critical orientation of the group's members was greatly influenced by their socioeconomic class. Many of the participants felt the need to educationally and economically distance themselves from the target audience for the films. Brenda routinely mentioned how she would not interpret a film the same as nonpresent "others" because of the educational level that she had attained. In a sense, participants believed that they had acquired knowledge that allowed them to interpret the films in a particular way. None of the students directly identified with the characters on the screen.

Memories of past viewing experiences also played a small role in shaping participants' critical orientation. Clearly, participants held specific expectations for the film because they compared and contrasted it to other films, both inside and outside of the genre. One of the reasons that *Menace II Society* was analyzed from a sociological perspective was because it was perceived to be "realistic."

Each participant's aesthetic distance from the text was significantly influenced by his or her personal characteristics and experiences. For example, some participants made reference to their ethnic group, as a means to define themselves for the other members, to defend a position, or to justify the way that they felt. In most instances, the discussions that surrounded the comments were "warm." For instance, while talking about *Menace II Society*, Erika stated that as a Black woman she was offended by a statement that Brenda made about Black men dating White women. Brenda's remark sparked a very heated debate on interracial dating. It appeared that the ability (or inability) to experientially connect to the characters in the films made participants more (or less) involved in the narrative content of the film. In effect, their experiential experiences seemed to increase or decrease the emotional tone of their response. It seemed that personal life experiences and statements of identity elicit strong feelings because they reveal a part of a participant's character. In this way, the characteristics/experiences of the reader played a major role in determining a participant's aesthetic distance from the texts.

The Role of the Immediate Social Context in Shaping Response

During the discussion of *Menace II Society*, the first person to raise a topic helped to determine where participants focused their attention. For example, Donna was the first person to respond. During her comment she began to talk about the audience for the film. In raising the topic of the audience, she helped to direct participants' attention to the world outside of the film. Generally, topics were maintained throughout a discussion because participants incorporated the previous comment into their own response before introducing a new subject. When a participant raised a topic that was ignored or not supported by another member of the group, the topic died out. Generally, that participant did not raise the topic again. For example, Samantha's comment on the representation of Latinos in *Menace II Society* did not receive a verbal response from her non-Hispanic classmates. As a result, the issue was not debated. This strongly suggests that the interaction of culturally diverse others had a significant effect on the direction in which participants focused their attention.

When a participant raised a topic that led to a dispute, he or she either intensified or modified his or her talk, accepted the other participants' statements, or withdrew from the conversation. Generally, as participants discussed the film they intensified their responses in the face of actual or anticipated rebuttal. The critical orientation of the group was decided early on in the discussions. The first few comments set the path for the participants to follow. While other forms of analysis surfaced throughout the course of each discussion, the critical orientation remained relatively consistent. Participants' responses to one another contributed to the original position. However, as mentioned earlier, the critical orientation was best accounted for by the features of the texts, because participants essentially followed the path set by the directors of the film.

Generally, participants' responses to one another had somewhat of an impact on their aesthetic distance from the texts. Although it appeared that supporting statements by others did not intensify the emotional tone of the conversation, conflicting statements almost always increased the emotional tone of the response, because participants often relied on their personal experiences to make their points.

Conclusion

Based on my analysis of the group discussion, the text, the personal characteristics and life experiences of the reader, and the immediate social context all played an important role in shaping participants' meaning-making responses. The direction in which participants focused their attention was most significantly shaped by the features of the text. The representation of violence in *Menace II Society* and the participants' interactions with "others" shaped the topics that were discussed. Similarly, the critical orientation of group members was also best accounted for by the features of the text. An analysis of the representation of mainstream American society in the film seemed to suggest that participants followed the critical orientation of the filmmaker. Finally, a participant's aesthetic distance from the text was most significantly shaped by the personal characteristics and life experiences of the reader and the immediate social context. Participants made reference to their race, gender, socioeconomic status, and life experiences as a means to position themselves in relationship to the text. Clearly, certain cultural positions held by participants within the larger society led to certain positions of power (or perceived power) within the group. The African-American women in the group, particularly Donna, saw their ethnic identities in articulation with the film's African-American focus as a vehicle through which they could exert control over the discussion. In Donna's case, although she could not directly identify with the characters on the screen, she seemed to feel some responsibility to direct the manner in which they were constructed within the context of the multicultural environment.

Earlier it was suggested that the theatrical showing of 'hood films could have had an impact on the violent outbreaks that accompanied some of the screenings in theaters across the country. Although the responses of college students in a classroom setting do not replicate the social context of a theater, the findings suggest that a film in the genre can elicit "warm" responses from viewers. Clearly, images of African-American males when constructed as ghettocentric and thereby embodying the negative features of the 'hood, elicit strong responses. Participants expressed deep emotional and experiential connections to the themes addressed in the film. The images seemed to tap into the cultural fears, anger, and hopelessness of its audience. Hence, it could be suggested that the social context of meaning making—specifically, an interactive, intercultural dialogue, such as the one discussed here—is a significant moment in this process. This is just as, if not more, important than the physical context (a darkened theater). As this study supports, meaning is not constructed in a vacuum of isolation but through the interplay of individuals and their cultural contexts.

References

Bogle, D. (1994). *Toms, coons, mullattoes, mammies, and bucks: An interpretive history of Blacks in American films.* 3d ed. New York: Continuum.

Diawara, M., ed. (1993). *Black American cinema.* New York: Routledge.

George, N. (1998). *Hip hop America.* New York: Penguin Putnum.

Guerrero, E. (1993). *Framing Blackness: The African American image in film.* Philadelphia: Temple University Press.

Jones, J. (1991). The new ghetto aesthetic. *Wide Angle* 13: 32–43.

Landis, D., and S. Stewart. (1991). Violence doesn't hurt "Boyz" gate. *USA Today*, July 15, p. A1.

11

The *Menace II Society* Copycat Murder Case and Thug Life

A Reception Study with a Convicted Criminal

Robin R. Means Coleman

In 1994, Appellant, Caryon Johnson, then fourteen years old, pled guilty to facilitation to murder, facilitation to robbery in the first degree, facilitation to kidnapping, and complicity to attempted theft over $300.00. . . . This case involves what eventually came to be known as the "Menace II Society" shootings, the name of a violent movie which Appellant and his friends viewed immediately before embarking on a crime spree.
—Johnson v. Commonwealth of Kentucky

I don't want to talk about it [the possibility that their film might provoke violence]. What about the White kids coming out with baseball bats after "Lethal Weapon"? . . . You don't hear about that. But anytime that violence happens, everybody goes and pushes it off on some rap song or some movie.
—Allen Hughes, director, *Menace II Society*

On May 18, 1993, twenty-one-year-old twin siblings and film director/producer duo Allen and Albert Hughes (the Hughes brothers) made their cinematic debut when their hyperviolent, urban drama *Menace II Society* premiered at the Cannes Film Festival, and a few days later opened in movie theaters across the United States. The film, a coming-of-age tale, chronicles a summer in the life of Caine, an African-American teen male and recent high school graduate. The film's focus is on Caine's attempt to move into manhood by making some tough choices about how he plans to map his (potentially bleak) future. His growth is hampered at nearly every turn as Caine is forced, often violently, to negotiate the mean streets of South Central Los Angeles. Caine has little going for him. He is an orphan left behind by a heroin addicted mother who dies of an overdose, and a trigger-happy father who is gunned down during the course of the film. Caine's surrogate father figure, Pernell, is in prison for life. Caine himself is facing fatherhood as a result of a sexual relationship with a young woman he cares little about. Most notable, however, is Caine's penchant for violence. Caine is a cold and violent criminal who pistol-whips an acquaintance, beats and stomps a relative of the young woman he impregnated, commits an armed carjacking, is an accessory to a convenience store robbery that ends in a double homicide, and commits double murder as he seeks revenge for the carjacking/murder of his cousin Harold.

Menace II Society garnered accolades from numerous film critics who found the film's depiction of Black ghetto tribulations, including the frequent and gruesome violence, as particularly realistic. The Hughes brothers, reared in an upper-middle-class home far from the ghetto, were hailed for possessing great acumen. Noted film critic Roger Ebert of the *Chicago Sun-Times* and the movie review television program *Siskel and Ebert at the Movies* awarded the film a perfect four stars in his column and a "thumbs up" on the show. Ebert (1993) wrote: "*Menace II Society* is as well-directed a film as you'll see from America this year, an unsentimental and yet completely involving story of a young man who cannot see a way around his fate. . . . If *Menace II Society* shows things the way they often are—and I believe it does—then the film is not negative for depicting them truthfully." Other arbiters agreed on the film's quality as, in 1994, *Menace II Society* was nominated for the Independent Spirit Award's Best First Feature and Best Male Lead awards. It won the Independent Spirit Award for Best Cinematographer and MTV Movie Award for Best Movie.

Menace II Society moved from the lauded into the infamous, however, when it took center stage in an eerily similar, real-life urban drama of murder, robbery, and carjacking involving five, also coming-of-age, African-American male teens.

This chapter presents a reception study with Caryon Johnson, one of the five youths who was ultimately convicted of copycat crimes in the case that came to be known in the media as the "*Menace II Society* Murder Case." The purpose of this case study of Caryon's reception practices is to lay bare the relationship Caryon had with the film specifically, and with mass media in general. Here, I detail Caryon's emergent constructions, or interpretations, in response to media's presentation of the urban, ghetto-centric narratives, as well as media's representation of young, often criminal, African-American men. This study seeks to understand his identification with the characters, behaviors, lifestyles, and messages in such presentations. More, it seeks to account for how Caryon views the symbolic world as it informs and merges with his own African-American, urban, male teen identity. I introduce three themes—masculinity, viewing style, and desired representations—that emanated from Caryon's constructions and typify the manner in which he engages with media and identifies (or not) with its representation of a distinct social world. I conclude by discussing the implications of Caryon's socialization as a media consumer and how his familiarity with very specific media symbolic systems plays a significant role in his life. Echoing JoEllen Fisherkeller (chapter 7 in this book), I maintain that it is important to extend our insights in meaning making and media consumption by examining the role media play in youths' everyday life, and how media have the potential to converge with their identities.

Interviewing an incarcerated individual who was part of a high-profile case proved to be quite challenging.[1] A major hurdle was access. Not only is Caryon confined in the maximum-security Kentucky State Penitentiary, but it is an institution that is very restrictive regarding access to inmates (only immediate family or legal counsel), inmate privileges (only select materials that arrive by mail are given to inmates), and other freedoms (no incoming calls, limited outgoing calls, and restrictions on postage stamps and envelopes). A second difficulty was securing the trust of a young man who took part in a crime that attracted national media attention. Caryon believed that reporters were seeking to exploit him and sensationalize the crime for ratings. Trust was established and reestablished through a number of methods, which included securing the endorsement of a defense attorney involved in the case, sending educational materials that evidenced the kind of work scholars engage in, explaining that the purpose of this research is educative, not profit-motivated, and member checks—providing the participant with a chance to elaborate on the researcher's interpretations of the participant's constructions. Given Caryon's confinement (in-

Menace II Society. *Courtesy of Photofest.*

cluding over two hundred days that he spent in solitary confinement during this study), the individual, in-depth interviews that I desired to engage in had to be conducted via letters. I sent Caryon interview questions, he wrote back, and I responded with questions that prompted him to expound upon his answers, and new questions. While the interview process was not ideally hermeneutical and dialogic, I worked diligently to maintain the spirit of such an engagement.

This chapter is based largely on letters Caryon wrote to me from December 1999 to January 2001 that contain data specifically regarding his meaning making of *Menace II Society* and his relationship with media that inform his identity. Though Caryon is the focus, this study is supplemented by interview data collected from one other young man involved in the murder case, Sylvester Berry. Kunta Sims is also a research participant; however, for this chapter I have relied on his constructions for background information, and therefore do not present his constructions. I have also utilized media reports, attorney interviews, family interviews, and court documents collected since 1994. Because the five did not go to trial, but entered plea agreements to avoid the death penalty, official testimony on the night's events from the teens, their families and friends, or their victims was never entered into record. This study focuses on Caryon, as his constructions are some of the most compelling in their ability to contribute to a knowledge base about youths' relationship with media. My research with Caryon,

Sylvester, and Kunta continues today. The other two young men involved in the murder case declined to participate.

The *Menace II Society* Murder Case

On the evening of January 23, 1994, in Paducah, Kentucky, four youths— Caryon Johnson, thirteen; Steven Johnson, sixteen (Caryon's cousin); Calvin "Kevin" Smith, sixteen (Kunta's close friend); and Kunta Sims, seventeen—viewed the film *Menace II Society* on videotape. Later that evening, they would find themselves the perpetrators of a crime spree and murder they would link to the film. The teens had all viewed the R-rated film on video and in the theater many, many times before. Each viewing exposed them to particularly violent and bloody scenes. In one scene that would later prove key in the boys' lives, the film's main character, Caine, and his cousin Harold are carjacked at gunpoint by a group of African-American men. Harold resists, and is shown getting blown away, at close range, by a shotgun. Caine is seriously wounded by the carjackers. As Caine lies bleeding profusely on the street near his cousin's body, the carjackers drive off in Harold's car, now awash in blood. After viewing the movie on that January evening, the four Kentucky adolescents devised a plan: steal cars and shoot people "until their bullets were gone" (Groves Hayes 1994, 8A).

Late in the evening of January 23, the four came upon James "Shane" Pearson, a high school sophomore and star athlete, as he was driving home from his part-time restaurant job at a steakhouse. They carjacked Pearson at gunpoint, kidnapped him, and took his vehicle. After riding Pearson around for some time, Kunta, described by prosecutors as the ringleader and by defense attorneys and family as having a low IQ and being easily influenced by others, repeatedly shot Pearson. His body was later discovered dumped on the lawn of a home not far from the shooting.

Soon after the murder of Pearson, the four picked up their friend Sylvester Berry (sixteen), filled him in on their plan, and offered to take him joyriding in Pearson's car. Berry, too, had repeatedly viewed *Menace II Society*. While driving around, the five came upon nineteen-year-old Matthew Fiorentini and his passenger Melissa Hall. The pair's car was stuck in a snowbank on the side of a road and they were working to free it. Fiorentini and Hall were confronted by Steven. Sylvester, who was sitting in Pearson's car, exited the car with a concealed gun that he surreptitiously passed to Steven. Steven shot Fiorentini twice and believed he had killed him. Fiorentini was seriously wounded, but survived. There was some discussion among the five about abducting or shooting Melissa Hall. Eventually the five fled the scene without Hall. A day later, most of the five were taken into custody or arranging for their surrenders. During police questioning, the five youths offered that they were motivated by the film *Menace II Society*. Indeed, their crimes, especially the carjacking and shooting of Pearson, closely paralleled the fate that Caine's cousin Harold faced in the film. The survival of Fiorentini, though eerily similar to Caine's survival of the carjacking in the film, was certainly serendipitous.

Masculinity and the Thug Life

> I see myself in some of the characters. I identify with whoever is playing a *thug life part* [emphasis mine], like Ice Cube in *Boyz in the Hood*, or Chris Tucker in the movie *Friday*. Because I always had to struggle to reach the top, and I still haven't made it yet.

> The character that identify with me was Caine because he was layed back selling drugs, getting his money. That's my style right there—even though I wouldn't do it now. He done a little shooting and fighting too, but very, very little. So he's similar to me.

And so it began. These were Caryon's responses to what was supposed to be a generally benign warm-up question asking him to discuss any of his favorite media presentations. From the very first letter, Caryon revealed a pattern of admiration for and identification with a single character type—the African-American male criminal; and a specific type of media text—the ghettocentric, violent drama. Admittedly, Caryon was keenly aware that he was contacted to be a study participant because of this potential affinity for such imagery. However, it would become clear that he was not simply conforming to the interests of the researcher. At every turn he would work to *disassociate* himself from the film that made him infamous, and at every turn, his interpretations of his world, life, and relationship with media led him right back to it.

Living the Thug Life

It is not surprising that Caryon states he identifies with portrayals that present a "thug life part." Indeed, Caryon has led, and according to prison officials in the state of Kentucky, continues to lead the thug life. In April of 2000, while housed in the medium-security facility Greenriver Correctional Center, Caryon wrote to a family member asking that the individual "bring him some stuff" because he needed some money. It was risky to make such a solicitation, as Greenriver officials randomly monitor outgoing prisoner mail. For Caryon, it turned out to be a bad move. Though written in code, Caryon had requested that a relative smuggle drugs into the prison during a visit so he could sell them.

Inmates learn a great deal about the legal system while incarcerated, and come to rely on two important tenets: (1) admit nothing; and (2) to be charged with a crime, there must be proof of wrongdoing. Regarding this drug solicitation infraction, Caryon did not deny his actions, as he wrote, "I needed some money Mrs. Coleman." He also lamented "they had no proof" that he was asking for drugs. Though not charged with a crime, much to the chagrin of Caryon he received a category 4-5 write-up for attempting to smuggle drugs into the prison, and was sentenced to one month in solitary confinement, or "the hole." He also "lost visits for six months and sixty days of my good time." While in the hole, it was believed by prison officials that Caryon, a Gangster Disciples gang member since the age of twelve, committed a category 5-10 for gang activity by instigating a gang fight. Upon this second charge, Caryon was transferred to the maximum-security facility Kentucky State Penitentiary and immediately placed in their hole. Later Caryon was cleared of this infraction, but the transfer stayed. While in the hole in his new prison home, Caryon tried to make contact with fellow inmates who were friends from his hometown. This communication attempt earned Caryon another 5-10 charge of being a gang leader and attempting to organize a gang. This Caryon vehemently denied, writing, "I used to be a gang member. But that was on the streets in my past. Not now." Sylvester Berry expressed a similar concern when he wrote to me for help: "Was you able to find out anything about helping me with the 'gang' stereotype in here?" In the end, between April 2000 and January 2001, Caryon spent over two hundred days in the hole.

Caryon is no stranger to trouble. Sadly, much of his very short life before going to prison was defined by violence and dysfunction. At the age of four, while enrolled in a Head Start program, he was expulsed for disciplinary problems. Every year thereafter, until his imprisonment during his eight-grade school year, Caryon was expelled from school. Though from kindergarten to eighth grade he never completed a full school year, he was never once denied promotion to the next grade. Nor was he or his family counseled about his problems. In fact, his mother claims that school officials often failed to contact her when Caryon was absent from school or expelled. Once a teacher questioned whether Caryon might have been suffering from a mental illness, given that one of his siblings had been diagnosed with paranoid schizophrenia. However, this inquiry did not go well as the teacher asked Caryon's mother (with Caryon present) if he was ill. Caryon reacted angrily to the accusation, proclaiming he was not sick. Because the two adults left it up to the then nine year old to indicate that he needed help from mental health professionals, there was never any further discussion about his psychological well-being.

Today, most who know him best—family and friends—believe that what Caryon really needed was a stable home life. Caryon's father was not part of the household. Though Caryon lived with his mother in her housing project apartment, she was often physically, emotionally, and morally absent. She engaged in criminal activities (including selling drugs to supplement her public assistance, theft, and illegally possessing a firearm). His mother served three years in prison prior to Caryon's own incarceration.

Young, emotionally underdeveloped, minimally educated, and impoverished, Caryon was largely left to his own devices and reared himself (though for brief periods of time he stayed with various relatives and friends, including his father and stepmother, older sister, cousin, and two different girlfriends). Beginning in the second grade, Caryon began running the streets and committing small crimes with other young boys. He wrote of these escapades:

> On the south side of town in Elmwood Court Projects my friends were King, Preston, Charles, and Tucker.[2] We all came up fighting the whole neighborhood. Breaking out people's windows, playing knock knock run, where you would knock on a person's door at nighttime and run while they're coming to answer the door. We had to sneak out of the house at night every night to do the things we were doing. We would bust out streetlights, car windows that drove by. We flattened people's car tires. Cut out their screen doors. Anything you could name we done it.

With each year, Caryon and his friends became more rebellious and their crimes began to escalate in seriousness. Caryon talked about his criminal activities around the ages of six and seven: "In Dudley Court [Projects] we clowned out there too. [My friends and I] started breakin' into houses out around there." And around ages eight and nine: "In the Forest Hills Projects my friends were C-Note, Tall Jack, Luke, Chaney, Shaggy, Nevin, and two of my cousins. We didn't do nothing [because] those dudes was scared except for my friend C-Note. We done alot of bad stuff including smoking marijuana. We call that stuff 'trees.'"

By ten, wholly unsupervised, Caryon turned to those young people who were similarly socioeconomically situated for friendship and support. However, the composition of his group of friends changed often. Some moved away, others became part of the penal system. Without a family unit, around age twelve Caryon sought out, and was accepted by, a notorious street gang, the Gangster Disciples. He wrote:

> I was about 12 years old now. They used to have shoot-outs in T.J. [Thomas Jefferson Projects]. Yeah, T.J. was the hot spot with gangs and stuff. . . . My cousin Jessie, Jr. was in a gang called G.D. which is the Gangster Disciples.[3] He put me [and a friend] in the gang by Jessie and some gang members beating us up. We wanted to be in though. We wasn't forced at all.

As street gang culture goes, Caryon had hit the big time:

> This is where I got my first gun, and drugs to sell. I loved T.J. It's on North 13th and North 14th, then the sides is Martin Luther King, Jr. Drive, and the other side is Madison Street. It's two liquor stores right across the street from that project. I had to quit going home. I had this girlfriend named Toya that I lived with. I was going to school, but I was skipping school also. They would call my mom's and she would come to my girl's house to see what was up. I was going to 21 and up clubs every night. Smoking big trees—I'm talking about ounces with my partners. We were driving dope fiends' cars. We would give them cocaine to drive their cars for a certain amount of hours. We would wreak [*sic*] the cars. The dope fiend would report it stolen, so we would leave the cars in ditches, alleys, people's back yards. Just anywhere. . . . We mainly used those cars to go out of town in. I've been to places like Carbondale, Ill., Houston, Texas, Union City, TN, Mayfield, KY, Clarksville, TN, Memphis, TN, Chicago, Ill., Gary, IN, and many more other places. My family didn't even know I was out of town.

Caryon, the gang's youngest member, took on a nickname, "Bambino," and worked hard to prove his worth to the older (teen and adult male) gang members. He, indeed, earned bragging rights:

> We kept hotel rooms payed for mostly on the weekends, so that we could take girls up there and have sex with them any time we wanted to. That was all fun stuff. I was known all over the whole Paducah, Kentucky and I'm still known to this day. I was the youngest dude down there selling

drugs, stealing, staying with grown women, robbin', and all of that. I even kept different kinds of guns. I had already turned 13 by then. I never needed money because I kept my own at all times. I would never be broke.

And then that fateful January night was upon him.

All of my friends were always older than me, and they would look out for me if I ever needed it. . . . I started hanging with these guys. I liked two of them which was Sylvester Berry, and my first cousin Steven Johnson. The other two I didn't like very well [Kunta Sims and Calvin Smith]. Plus Kunta wasn't in my gang. He was in another gang that was against mines. . . . My real true partnaz from T.J. Projects told me not to leave with them guys that night our case happened, but I didn't listen. We were chillin', smoking some trees and my case partners [Sims, Smith, and Johnson] came to pick me up to go out of town with them to mess with some girls and to go to the clubs. My real partnaz said "man forget them, they on some stupid stuff," but I was hard-headed and didn't listen. So here I am today. Locked up in prison with a 20 year sentence. There you go.

The Process of Thug Life Identification

Caryon's self-worth continues to be situated within the so-called thug life. In his world, he is richly rewarded for it through respect and admiration from his cohort: "I'm known world wide." An extremely powerful symbol of bravado and the macho male myth, the thug life identity position is male gender masculinity marked by an overt desire for dominance and power. In this, the thug life, men (even twelve-year-old boys) must be powerful. Here power is displayed through dominance and control. In Caryon's world this means controlling the streets (other youths, criminals, and the drug trade), frightening neighbors (and thereby keeping them from contacting police),[4] abusing drug addicts who are at his mercy (e.g., taking their cars), possessing women (heterosexuality is key in this world), and keeping enemies at bay by any means necessary. It means being a member of a notorious gang, and, if prison officials are correct, being a leader of a notorious gang in prison.

The thug life is a practice of identity that also includes displaying strength, often through (physical) aggression. For Caryon, this was defined by his participation in community sports (football and basketball) and robbing and warring with rival gang members. More, the mere practice is not enough. In the thug life, great competence in the areas of dominance, power, and strength is requisite to the persona, and, frankly, to survival. One cannot simply control the street, but he must have a *thriving* drug trade. He must be in *irrefutable* control over neighbors and drug users, and maintains this through random acts of terror (violence and harassment). This role of the thug is hailed through an antihero worship where the more notorious are prized. Likewise, those who perish (be it by death or imprisonment), if courageously (e.g., by defending the gang, continuing gang activity and adopting the thug persona capably inside prison), are exalted. It is a "live by the sword, die by the sword" masculine heroism.

However, Caryon's fate may not have been sealed by his identification and participation in this hyperbravado. Caryon believes, and I concur, that it would have been very likely that he would have ended up in prison, but not for an unusual murder that may be connected to a film. He wrote: "If I did get locked up, it would of been a drug or robbery case, not no murder case."

Through his emergent constructions it became clear that media was really the only other socializing institution in his life, outside of his gang, and one he spent a significant amount of time with. For this study, I probed Caryon on a variety of issues to gain some sense of his social world. Though media questions did not take center stage for weeks at a time, Caryon kept media at the center of his discourse. I learned that, be it in lived experience or in media, Caryon encountered no messages against the conditions of his thug masculinity and his violent world. What he did encounter was a Black manhood framed by and (re)produced through media spectacle (e.g., celebrities and Hollywood films) that reaffirmed an identity position marked by power—sexual conquests, aggression/violence, and wealth.

Caryon saw real-life celebrities blurring the lines between thug life fact and media-created fiction. He saw rapper Tupac Shakur, with "thug life" tattooed prominently across his midsection, whisked off to jail for his involvement in a shooting and in a sexual assault against a young woman, and finally shot to death. Caryon noted the street credit Tupac earned, the records he sold, and the media attention he garnered as the rapper moved closer and closer to thug life authenticity. He saw rapper Notorious B.I.G. lead the same lifestyle and garner the same kind of media spotlight. And Caryon purchased their records, for they were heralded for living the kind of life Caryon was leading in Kentucky. Caryon wrote: "[One of my] favorite music artists is 2 Pac [Tupac] because he's a real thug that had knowledge." Caryon listened to the music and watched the music videos of these rappers, and others, such as DMX, Ruff Ryders, Master P, and the Hot Boys, who rhymed of women, violence, and material wealth. He noticed when gangsta rapper MC Eiht moved from narrating his thug life on CDs to portraying that life in *Menace II Society*. MC Eiht played A-Wax, a thug described in the film as "always doing dirt."

It was also obvious to Caryon that the athletes who wrapped themselves in displays of excess such as wealth (gold, diamonds, fancy cars, drugs), who were boldly sexual (frequenting prostitutes, in the company of a lot of beautiful women), who were defiant in their narcissism (from fights with opponents to victory dances to bragging) were the ones who received the hero worship that was so valuable to ghetto/street life. Toward this end, prior to his incarceration, Caryon took up playing football and basketball.

Caryon also noted that media cannot help but focus on the thug, even as it castigates him. As often as the thug lifestyle is hailed in the spectacle of celebrity, it is also featured in news magazine programs, documentaries, and print exposés (e.g., all those "crisis of the urban Black family, of the Black male, or of Black youth" front page features and television specials). The thug life is profitable for more people than just the thug. Such positive reinforcement proves to be confounding for Caryon who, ironically, wants to secure a film deal that will chronicle the violence in his life, to include the crimes he committed that in some ways were informed by other violent films. Caryon does not see the irony in this proposition. Nor, at times, does Caryon see it necessary to end the thug life cycle. On this point, Caryon opined: "Yes, the thug life should be looked up to, because it's just a lower part of living which is surrounded by hard times, sometimes violence, and just struggling in general. There are no reasons it shouldn't be looked up to." Sylvester, too, seemed to adopt a strange logic about his participation in the thug life. He wrote: "I get to take part in this study and help people because of what I did."

And then there is the genre of film that is so attractive to Caryon. Some call it ghettocentric (as Celeste Fisher does in chapter 10 in this book), others, "neo-blaxploitation" (Guerrero 1995). Both terms define a popular culture form rooted in rap and hip-hop iconography that features a Black, urban-based "street style cool" persona (George 1992). The film genre frequently taken on by young, African-American filmmakers such as the Hughes brothers, John Singleton (*Boyz N the Hood*), and Ernest Dickerson (*Juice*) relies upon a narrative that often focuses on Black-on-Black violence, street/thug life, and the hurdles encountered as young, African-

American men attempt to improve their lot and/or escape the ghetto. Nelson George, in his book *Blackface: Reflections on African Americans and the Movies* (1994), describes these films as marked by an urban imagery and fast pace that can be thought of as hip-hop moviemaking. For example, one of the early offerings from this new genre was the 1991 *New Jack City*, directed by Mario Van Peebles. Focusing on the rise of a drug dealer, it was ghettocentric, full of Black-on-Black violence, and moved at a fast and rhythmic pace, keeping up with the tempo of its rap soundtrack. It came along to "reclaim and deconstruct" the Willie Horton, threatening Black male, recasting him as young, tough, glamorous, wealthy, attractive to women, and savvy (Means Coleman 2000). Popular culture critics such as Guerrero (1995), however, do not sing the praises of these films' Black hypermasculinity and their counterhegemonic potential, finding them troubling thanks to the "wave of neo-blaxploitative, violently toxic, ghetto-action flicks, which too often package and sell the extermination of black men as entertainment while profiteering filmmakers offer up shallow alibis about only depicting 'what is real'" (396).

Indeed, in recent years these ghettocentric, new-jack stylized, Hood based, thug life films have become inescapable. *Juice* starred Tupac Shakur as a ruthless, teenaged villain of the ghetto streets. *New Jersey Drive* featured Black, male, teenaged carjackers. *Clockers* turned the Black male drug-dealing youth into a sympathetic hero. *Above the Rim* cast Tupac Shakur in yet another thug role as it focused on ghetto hoodlums who shot guns as often as they shot basketball hoops. *Original Gangstas* pitted Black, aging, former rulers of the hood against a new, younger wave of thugs. Every one of these films featured a hip-hop or gangsta rap soundtrack that, in many cases, equaled or exceeded the popularity of these films thereby extending the popularity and profitability of the thug icon.

Thus far, I have been detailing and working to make sense of Caryon's process of "identification" with the symbolic. A central concept from psychoanalysis and Freud's theorization that a child's understanding of itself is as a (sexed) subject during the Oedipal stage, identification is defined by the psychological process whereby an individual, such as Caryon (the subject), takes on or assimilates (not to be confused with copying or imitation) "an aspect, property or attribute of the other and is transformed, wholly or partly, after the model the other provides" (Madan 1996, 30). Hence, it is through identification(s)—gang street culture, symbols of power and wealth, media spectacles and fantasies of celebrity, and so on—that identity (here, the thug life) is realized. My starting point is *not* the primordial, but a more developed self who negotiates the self and the other—in this case, people or the symbolic—by identifying similarities and/or differences. Caryon was able to identify similarities between the self and stars' depiction of the thug lifestyle, or the thug lifestyle that some stars came to live. His close reading of stars/thug life helped Caryon to recognize differences, such as evolving masculine identities and desires (power and dominance) yet to be fulfilled. The relationship between media consumer/spectator (Caryon) and the mode of address (symbols of thug life), according to Stacey (1994, 126–75), permits identity to be transformed and affirmed by attending to symbolic representations such as media images/music, through a variety of ways and a range of connections. These include: (1) enjoyment in viewing and recognizing the familiar and everyday life; (2) looking to media fantasies for cues for something better and qualities already possessed; and (3) imagining oneself in the position/situation depicted and deciding on a course of action based on the pretense that one is actually in that position. These three moments of identification emerge in the constructions offered by Caryon.

Recognizing the Familiar

The films that make up the ghettocentric genre, like *Menace II Society*, are attractive to Caryon because they acknowledge his social/subject position. Again and again, he talks about how his favorite media are those that closely depict his life experiences. He likes these films, which he calls action movies, because he can identify with the situations based on his own practice. He wrote: "I can relate to action movies because I've always been a hyper person. Some of the things I can relate to is fighting, robbing, and driving vehicles very wild and unsafe." Of the ghettocentric film *Boyz N the Hood* he makes clear that he prefers the film because of its perceived realism, which is defined by how closely a media presentation parallels his own life. Caryon explained: "*Boyz N the Hood* is one of my favorite movies because it's real. What makes it real is when they show the runned down parts of California neighborhoods. And the shoot-outs, liquor drinking, attempted robberies, the fights, the custody disputes of [the character] Trey being with his mother or father. These things were all similar to my life."

In one letter, I prompted Caryon to clarify statements he made that seemed to indicate that he only liked thug life media representations and rejected characters that did not take up that lifestyle. He indicated that he could not identify with what he called "good guy" representations because they did not measure up to his definition of verisimilitude. Although media consumers engaged in the process of identification often turn to media representation for cues on how to behave in situations, good characters (non-thugs) do not provide Caryon with an alternate identity, as they are too dissimilar from his lived experiences. Caryon explained:

> Yes, I identify with the thug life. And no I don't identify with Black characters who are good because they made it to a up-to-date type living. [This is] unlike myself. Even though they may have struggled, they climbed up the mountain dodging big rocks that came tumbling down toward them. That's how they made it to the top. But as I climbed a little bit up that mountain, the big rocks that came tumbling down always hit me, and would knock me back to the bottom every time. They [the good characters] also seen opportunities. But I was blind to opportunities and couldn't see far enough.

I encouraged Caryon to talk freely about what he identified as his two favorite movies, *Boyz N the Hood* and *Menace II Society*. Most often, he turned his attention to *Menace II Society*. In this final example, Caryon's talk about the film is one of the best indicators of his connection to its symbolism specifically. He wrote:

> The Black people in *Menace II Society* are most definitely like real people because most Black people that live in project housing, and neighborhoods that are ruff like that movie. Poverty is poverty, and it was there. . . . The Black people in the movie found theirselves in poverty situations. That's why they robbed, sold drugs, and shot stuff up alot through that movie. It was called survival to me. . . . What makes this movie one of my favorites is that it's a action movie, and that I could relate to it. I feel their pain when they do illegal stuff to *survive*. I've been there, done that. I can comprehend to it.

Sylvester shared the same insights about his identification with the film and its depiction of ghetto street life:

> You asked me what made this [*Menace II Society*] my favorite movie. The fact that I could relate to this movie completely is one reason. Another reason is because I felt Caine's pain wholeheartedly. I felt that I was going through all the things that he was going through. I wanted to pack up and get away from the streets, but ended up in the pen. He [Caine] wanted to do the same, but he ended up dead.

Cues for Fantasies and Identifying Qualities Already Possessed

Much of this study has been about how Caryon relied upon *Menace II Society* and other ghettocentric media representations to reinforce his fantasies about the thug life and hail those practices he already participated in. I have presented examples of how the self (Caryon) and media representations can be united around preexisting identities, identities that Stuart Hall (1996) reminds us are always formed within the symbolic and discursive. Hence, Caryon's desires for power, dominance, and wealth, as well as his thug life participation, do not presuppose media consumption, but are formed within a media culture. It is within this culture that media representation, consumption, and production work through identity. In both setting a standard for Caryon's identity fantasies and confirming his participation in the lifestyle that is part of that identity, media help create a social world that Caryon reaps rewards for and is fulfilled by keeping in line with the lifestyle. Pierre Bourdieu (1994) with his notion of "realized myth" is useful here. Bourdieu, talking of members of an Algerian community, observes that groups within a community may act in accordance with mythical structures (in this study it is spectacles of the thug life) and that collective practice emerges as realized myth. He writes: "Moreover, when the conditions of existence of which the members of a group are the product are very little differentiated, the dispositions which each of them exercised in his practice are confirmed and hence reinforced both by the practice of the other members of the group . . . and also by institutions which constitute collective thought as much as they express it, such as language, myth, and art" (162).

Caryon, as an individual, and as a member of variously constituted groups such as the Gangster Disciples, or as one of five who had a role in the murder case, saw his myths realized when his thug life beliefs and fantasies found reinforcement through practice (he earned respect from his fellow gang members) and symbolic discourses (those who led a similar life were prominently featured in media). It may be this realization that permitted the self (Caryon) to not only engage in identification (assimilation of parts of the other), but to work to resemble, in the physical, the fantasies of the other. It was not that Caryon was imitating thug life crimes, but that, constrained by frequent ghetto/thug presentations, he saw that certain mythic behaviors were reinforced by various institutions (gangs, the media). Therefore, Caryon saw no reason *not to* work to see the myth fully realized in the physical by participating in crimes.

Course of Action Based on Images

The realized myth with its reinforcement of the thug life practice and of fantasies of penultimate thug life desires such as gross accumulation of material wealth, beautiful women, and dominance (as often seen in rap music videos), confirms and opens the door for a range of possible thug life behaviors. Caryon maintains that he was not engaged in some sort of play-acting or mimicry (though with real guns). That is, immediately after viewing the film, he did not seek the promise of attaining pleasure from the performance of thug life crimes he'd just seen. Rather, Caryon saw ghetto-centric media (in mythic proportions) and real life conflate to create a series of acceptable courses of action for him to choose from in a given situation.

Time and again, Caryon has weighed the feasibility of possible behaviors and courses of action seen in media as exemplars of how to handle real life situations. In one letter, Caryon wrote of how the film *A Time to Kill* showed how African Americans are forced, unfortunately, into "do or die situations" when they lose their power and control. The film depicts a Black father exacting deadly revenge on two White men who raped his young daughter. For Caryon, this is one possible reaction to a situation of injustice. Caryon proposed a second course of action, based on the images, but more suitable to his current view (in part, based on personal experience) of punishment. He wrote:

> I like the movie *A Time to Kill* because justice was served in the end. Justice was served because Samuel L. Jackson killed those two White guys that raped his little Black daughter. And he walked free at the end he walked free because he killed with a good cause even though killing is wrong. If I wrote the end of the movie about me, I would of had myself torturing those two White guys, just like they tortured my little baby girl. I probably would've let them live also. Only if they were sent to jail for life, after I tortured them.

With seven years between him and the realized myths he encountered as a twelve year old, Caryon saw *Menace II Society* as being more useful (clearly, with hindsight, more useful to him) if it presented a different course of action for at least one thug character. He created a revised *Menace II Society* narrative that included a second chance at life for a young man who led a thug life:

> I would have the characters to do just what they did, but I would have

one of them go to prison for a short period of time. Then I would let him back out. And have him leaving the criminal game and doing positive things like going to college, or having a very top-notch job. I would make it like that so people watching it would have a choice between good and bad.

This revision of the outcome of the movie reveals how Caryon once turned to media as a barometer of an ideal outcome for living a thug life. It also reveals (certainly toward a self-serving end) how today he wishes that message of the ideal end game to a thug's life had been different. In one letter, Caryon said he recently talked with another inmate about the limited number of options African Americans are depicted as having. He explained: "I talk about the Blacks in film that's going through coming up from childhood to now. I always seem to come to the conclusion that [there are] 2 choices, either penitentiary or death."

Finally, Sylvester was more pointed in his discussion of media's potential to inform his life choices. Sylvester "dialogued" with me about media he turns to to help him make sense of his experiences. During this exchange he provided two examples of how media presentations help him determine the path he will take. First, he recounted how the film *Freedom Song* (a civil rights film about African Americans securing their right to vote) with its lessons of goodwill helped him to conclude that he should manage his temper and to not commit any other crimes. In a unique dialogic moment, Sylvester decided to pen the outline for a new film in an attempt to explain how he regrets the decisions he has made in his life, and how film can help youth make wiser choices. Sylvester contributed this version of *Scrooge*:

> I'd like to see a situation in a Black film, where a young Black male, maybe played by Jaleel White, anyway, the guy makes a mistake that has him on his way to prison. While he is on the bus, his life flashes before him, and all of the wrong he has done is now going through his mind. I think the movie about Scrooge comes to mind. Anyway, a guardian angel played by a very serious Eddie Murphy takes this person through every mistake he ever made, and tells him what choice he should have made during those situations.
>
> This is the majority of the movie, but in the end, he wakes up in his own bed, not on the bus going to prison. He vows to make a change in his decision making.
>
> As soon as he goes outside his house to go to the bus stop for school, some of his friends pull up in a stolen car, and tell him to get in,

because they are going to skip school today. The young man says, "nah, I think that I will go to school today." Faced with his first test, he passes with honors in decisions. As his bus pulls up, he looks behind him, and he thinks that he sees his guardian angel smiling at him.

I know this is unrealistic, but I believe it is a type of movie that would open alot of youngsters' eyes.

Viewing Styles and Media Consumption

Caryon's media diet has not been a steady stream of thug life representations, though that is his favorite body of media fare. Caryon does not have a television in his cell (Sylvester does), therefore, Caryon watches television in a semiprivate viewing area, "so that I won't be disturbed and that way I can get the full understanding of what I'm watching," he wrote. The television is on at all hours, giving Caryon unfettered access to the medium: "[I watch] late at night, all through the week, mainly alot on weekends and holidays. I listen to my own music. But we can't watch video tapes. I watch TV, and listen to music 7 days a week. If I don't watch or listen, I'm probably busy at those times."

His passion for the kind of media fare that is said to have landed him in prison continues to be met. He detailed: "I watch drama TV shows, mainly things with a lot of action in it like fighting, killing, etc. Like *Scream*. I watch action movies the most, because I've related to it in the past, at least some of it. Like *Boyz N the Hood* 'cause it was real." Of the media he has attended to most recently (1999–2000), Caryon offered that *Scream*, *Boyz N the Hood*, and *A Time to Kill* were his most favorite because of his penchant for the scary and horror (*Scream*), for "what was real" (*Boyz N the Hood*), and for a film where "justice was served at the end" (*A Time to Kill*).

Interestingly, Caryon revealed to me that he had seen *Menace II Society* numerous times since his incarceration, but also offered that inmates are not afforded access to videotapes. Sylvester, though confined in the same prison as Caryon, had seen the film only a few times since 1994, but reported viewing other movies on video, such as *A Time to Kill* and *Freedom Song*. The truth came in a review of prison practices. Caryon continues to have an opportunity to view the film *Menace II Society* often, though he has no access to videotapes, because twice a week the prison guards show a film over prison monitors. Caryon views *Menace II Society* (as with most movies shown) via this opportunity. More, the prison is equipped with cable television, and the prisoners have access to some cable networks. Sylvester, who works the night shift in the prison, often works during movie time and sleeps during the day. He has fewer opportunities to view films, and maintains that he would choose to not watch *Menace II Society* if it were shown.

When he moves out of the action genre, Caryon turns to comedies like *The Jamie Foxx Show*, "because his shows are so comical," and to the syndicated comedy *Thea*, "because she does a good job on discipline when it comes to her three children." Here again, with Thea, Caryon shows that he is seeking out media that most closely resembles his life experiences. *Thea* is a single mother with three children. She is stern and feisty (much like the character Roseanne) in her approach, but, unlike Caryon's mother, she was physically, morally, and emotionally present for her children. He wrote: "She did good as a single mother, and the show is similar to my life experience because my mother had three of us, and none of our fathers lived in our household." It is this quest to "see himself and his life" that also draws him to the weekly talk show for African-American youth, *Teen Summit* on BET. An issues-oriented program, *Teen Summit* addresses topics that directly affect the lives of Black youth. Caryon likes it as he is able to attend to discussions about the dilemmas that are faced in his world: teen pregnancy, employment, and education. He shared: "I like *Teen Summit*. It's Black history. Black history is more than just in the month of February. Because it is very important that young people grow up with integrity and dignity about theirselves. It shows teen pregnancy—hard times on teen mothers due to the fact that they have to get their schooling, jobs, baby sitters. Jobs would be another issue tied in with education, because a large percentage of Black teens have low education rates, which could determine what kind of job they're qualified to get."

Narrative-Based Viewing and Image-Based Viewing

Thus far, this discussion has focused on the role media play in everyday life and on identity-centered meaning making of specific texts. What has not been accounted for here, and what needs to be attended to as we explore the relationship between media and an audience member, is the overlapping considerations of viewing culture and viewing practices. That is, simply, the manner in which media consumers may engage media's discourses. Lembo (1997) in his audience analysis takes us "beyond the text" to offer a typology of media audience viewing practices as he attends to the varied complexities of audience involvement and identification. Focusing on television viewing activities, Lembo argues that people can enter into two viewing moments—narrative-based viewing and image-based viewing. The first moment, narrative-based viewing, describes the manner in which people, when watching television, work to gauge the plausibility of the discourse. In an effort to make this judgment, viewers look for what seems believable, probable, or "the real," based on their individual lived experiences. Even as plausibility is uncovered—and narrative-based viewing (involvement with the story and characters) entered into—critical viewing stances may still emerge. When critical viewing occurs, which is often, the viewer distances him- or herself from the narrative and may question the plausibility of depictions of specific social actions, identify broader implausibilities/critique more general depictions, or recognize the commercial basis of programming. In sum, people will question what they see, consider television's ability to represent social realities, and work to create meanings around those depicted realities. As viewers assess the quality of the narratives and reconstruct the discourses based on their social worldview, Lembo argues, viewers engage in two more specific viewing practices within narrative-based viewing: viewing at the *representational* level of social action and viewing at the *real* level of social action.

Viewing at the representational level is defined by an audience member's attention to media's form and text construction, including production techniques and aesthetic qualities such as writing, plot development, directing, dialogue, and camera work. At this level, viewers are clear in their understanding that media texts are constructed, and look at how those constructions work to create the plausible. Lembo (1997, 240–41) describes this viewing practice as one where *how* things are represented are noted as the viewer becomes emotionally involved in the narratives; yet, it is a more distant viewing position. Viewing at the real level of social action moves the audience away from form ("ignor[ing] or fail[ing] to notice the 'construct-edness'") and to a direct involvement with the stories, the characters's lives and motives, and to anticipating and speculating about coming actions and potential consequences. Lembo reminds us that requisite to the depth of this engagement is plausibility—similarities to real life—so that the viewers can act out the story, recreate it in their minds, and place themselves in the narrative.

Caryon's experiences with (thug life) narratives tend to recombine and blur media technologies. For example, his listening to rap music is accompanied by viewing music videos on cable television. His preferred cinematic presentations are viewed outside of a darkened theater and on network or cable television, complete with commercial breaks. Given this state of symbolic and technological merger, I believe Lembo's television audience study can be extended to a more general framework of media discourses consumption to identify viewing practices.

Caryon has provided compelling insight into his, by definition, narrative-based viewing practices. His responses have revealed what I believe to be a unique engagement style with media. This knowledge is based on more implicit constructions Caryon provided over the course of this study to date. I work hard to present moments to illustrate his viewing style. Narrative-based viewing is about the viewer looking for the "real." As already detailed throughout much of this study, Caryon's principle criterion for even attending to a media text is its plausibility. If a text passes critical viewing muster, such as the presence of plausible actions, then the viewer becomes emotionally involved. Caryon has already established here that ghettocentric narratives are the real. Science fiction, however, fails his plausibility test in the arenas of specific depicted actions and broader patterns of representation. On science fiction, Caryon wrote: "I never watch TV shows like Star Trek, Sci Fi Channel, or any space type stuff. I hate that with a passion. What I don't like about it is that they're hardly ever on earth. That's fake to me. I never watch movies with aliens in it like *Independence Day* with Will Smith. That stuff is wack. It's also fake. That's why I hate it."

Over time I came to understand that Caryon adopted very literal readings of plausibility. Humans, with the exception of astronauts, spend their time on earth, not in space. Space aliens do not exist, and if they do, the creatures do not pay earth a visit toting destructive laser zap guns. Hence, for Caryon it is fake or implausible, and he will not attend to such texts.

As I sought further exposition on this rejection based on this cynical reading of implausibility, Caryon explained that he once saw a documentary that claimed that a UFO had been found in New Mexico. The documentary format gave credibility to the UFO tale, thereby the narrative approached plausibility. His religion, the Egyptian Order (which is detailed later in this chapter), is based on the arrival of extraterrestrial superhumans. Given these two experiences, Caryon offered: "I find myself curious to find out about these different galaxies that surround us in the *real world* today [emphasis mine]." He noted reading about the discovery of water on Mars: "To me, if there's water, then there some life also." Yet, space aliens have not really bombed earth or needed to "phone home." Nor have we been "trekking," "voyaging," or moving through "deep space" with Klingons

or Borgs. Caryon possesses what Potter (1999, 114) describes as a "low tolerance for ambiguity": "During exposure to media violence, people with a
low tolerance for ambiguity are likely to encounter the messages on the surface and latch onto easily accessible schemas. . . . If the message does not
meet the easily accessible schema, it is ignored." Thus Caryon ignores or rejects the fantasy text: "I still wouldn't watch sci-fi." However, should aliens
make themselves known, then, he explained, "[I'd watch] the news." Also
quite interesting is that this low tolerance for ambiguity and rejection based
on implausibility seems to be present among Caryon's peers. Sylvester offered a purely emergent, similar critique of science fiction. He wrote, "I
never watch any science fiction, unless *The Matrix* is considered science-fiction. Other than that, sci-fi movies are very boring movies that I really find
it hard to relate to."

In the coming Emerging Tastes and Desired Representations section, I
talk about Caryon's increased critical viewing savvy that I believe has improved dramatically, in part as a result of participating in this study. This
savvy is evidenced through a third critical viewing practice—recognizing
the commercial basis of media. In the last letter he wrote to me that informs
this chapter, he displayed a level of insight into the profit-driven nature of
media industry not previously seen. He observed: "I don't knock that
[stereotyping of African Americans] because that type of stuff will always
sell and make plenty of money, just like sex sell, violence sell, as well as
criminal activities, so get your money."

Lembo also describes how viewers focus on production qualities in
narrative-based viewing, as well as place themselves in the text as they get
directly involved with a media narrative. Caryon has shown little engagement with the text at the level of the "how" or the production level. He has
intimated repeatedly that he understands that though the discourses presented seem quite real, he knows that it is offered by actors: "The Blacks are
like real people, but they're acting . . . real life situations. They had to learn
a role that they have to play." I believe that what makes Caryon's engagement with media unique is that he believes media narratives are closer to
the real than most would assume. He seems to indicate that the actors are
simply learning how to act out real life incidents, as they would if, as he so
desperately desires, his life story were to become a Hollywood movie. When
I worked to explore this separation between the real and the text, he wrote:
"This stuff really happens to people . . . but they're acting, and off the show,
they got a lot of legal money to survive with." What is clearer is how Caryon

places himself inside the narratives, becoming directly involved in the social action and even, as we have already learned, makes choices for his life based on that involvement. In one letter, Caryon revealed his envy for the characters in *Menace II Society* as they never spent lengthy periods of time in prison for crimes that were similar to those he committed: "They got small prison time. Probably even probation, but me, I got slammed and had to cop out and I'm doing flat time. No probation or nothing."

According to Lembo, in addition to the complex narrative-based viewing practice, there is a second possible viewing encounter—image-based viewing. In image-based viewing the media audience member is wholly familiar with the conventions of programs. He or she comes to see images as "movable" or interchangeable across programs and channels because the stories offered in media are similar because so few stories are told. For example, in viewing daytime television, there may be only two narratives being presented—the tabloid talk show narrative (*Jerry Springer* or *Maury Povich*), and the personal courtroom drama (*Judge Judy* or *Divorce Court*). Because of the great familiarity with these shows and their formulas, image-based viewers do not attend to these texts deeply or emotionally, as in narrative-based viewing. Rather, they pick up bits and pieces of the story, but rarely focus on the unfolding narratives. Lembo argues that these viewers' engagement is decentered on the narratives, as they instead take part in activities such as channel switching. Channel switching/simultaneous viewing can sometimes result in an ironically funny game where, given programs' segmented nature, they can be pieced together across stations, ultimately resulting in a new, grand narrative that is little different than if a single narrative had been followed through to its completion. In image-based viewing, the self is not as well established as in narrative-based viewing. At times, viewers may engage in a mythic moment where they see themselves as the star of a program, but not with any great emotional depth, as when young boys see themselves as Rocky Balboa and momentarily shadowbox with the screen. Image-based viewing is also characterized by a state of "vegging out." Here a program is used for more than background noise, but its narrative is minimally attended to. Instead, a viewer may play with the colors, form, or contours of the production, for example, when older teens marveled at the stark, surreal richness of the coloring of the *Teletubbies* world.

In my interviews with Caryon, he did not indicate that he disengaged with media by "vegging out." Nor did he indicate that he physically engaged in channel switching. I believe that, in fact, he cannot channel switch given that he views television on prison monitors; hence, he is not allowed to control the programming. This does not mean he is not engaging in a form of channel switching and simultaneous viewing in his mind. Caryon's responses indicate that he is aware that the narratives of ghettocentric films are quite similar in content, style, and formula (e.g., *Boyz N the Hood*; *Menace II Society*), thus, he creates a bricolage of thug life narratives. Most obvious is Caryon's engagement with media at the mythic level. He has indicated that he sees himself, his life and experiences, in the narratives. More, he has talked about viewing the celebrity and heroic status of thug life as worthy of emulation. It is this viewing practice of seeing himself like the stars, at the mythic level, that is important here as it augments his more emotional, narrative-based engagement. These two moments, channel switching/simultaneous viewing and the mythic viewing level are evidenced by him placing himself in the role of the main character in both *Menace II Society* and *A Time to Kill*, and in each case doling out punishment in what he sees as heroic proportions. Lembo argues that such image-based viewing is cultivated in those who regularly attend to media, and Caryon certainly does. However, Caryon's critique of science fiction may give us a clue that rich visual imagery is not enough to even minimally pull him in; rather, narratives that address the real are far more important. What is important to take away from this insight into Caryon's viewing practice is how viewing is an extension of the self—how the meanings around social action, offered through storytelling, are "elaborated" as Lembo calls it, in viewers' minds. Lembo believes that because this meaning making takes place in a televisual world, the self during media viewing becomes different than the self outside of viewing and when interacting with other people. However, in Caryon's case, his is a world fully intermingled with media narratives, hence his becoming an active participant with a narrative is not so different from his real-world self.

Emerging Tastes and Desired Representations

Thus far, I have introduced Caryon's preference for thug life depictions, his identification with these representations, the notion that the mythic was "realized" in this life, his continued consumption of thug life depictions, and his continued quest for media messages that speak directly to his lived experiences and his unique media engagement style. All of these give us some insight into Caryon's relationship with media, and how he came to be involved in the *Menace II Society* murder case. Still, the leap from attending to, and prizing, a certain type of media presentation, to participating in a carjacking, kidnapping, murder, robbery, attempted murder, and attempted kidnapping that is similar to those crimes depicted is confounding.

Violence

Morley's (1980) reminder that social class is an important mediating factor is well taken. Caryon comes from an environment of poverty and where school, religion/the spiritual, and family were unavailable as role models. The media, however, were present. Also present was his gang cohort, who consumed media, with their thug presentations, as much as, and in the same ways as, Caryon. In this media culture, life and the mediated are hardly separable. Potter (1999) in *On Media Violence* places media in the same position of culpability for dysfunction as the breakdown of the family or poverty. He writes: "They [media] manufacture a steady stream of fictional messages that convey to all of us in this culture what life is about. Media stories tell us how we should deal with conflict, how we should treat other people, what is risky, and what it means to be powerful. The media need to share the blame for this serious public health problem" (2). As presented here, Caryon chose to attend to media stories rooted in what he called "action"—violence, killing, and robbery. It was these media stories that, beginning when he was in elementary school, schooled him on how he should deal with conflict, how to treat other people, what actions and behaviors were risky, and what it means to be in power. Indeed, the constructions presented thus far have indicated that the more he identified with portrayals of a thug character/lifestyle, the more he used those texts as a basis to construct meanings and make sense of his world, and the more reinforcement he received to behave aggressively.

Copious attention has been paid to the consumption of violent media. Media watchdog groups, government, scholars from virtually every field, the press, educators, politicians, and parents have all weighed in on the media violence debate. Generally, all have come to the conclusion that media violence alone does not move an individual to engage in violence, but that there are a variety of other factors (psychological, social, behavioral) at play that move a person to engage in such actions. Turning our attention to Caryon's preference for media violence and how he encountered violent texts, we get an even clearer picture of his relationship with media.

First, Caryon had no parental monitoring of his media consumption.

There was no supervision over his media choices. It seems no one in his world attended to the ratings of movies or the parental warning labels on his music. Hence, he was able to seek out media that should have been off limits to an under-seventeen audience member. When I inquired if his access to media was ever restricted (e.g., denied access to an R-rated movie, not able to purchase music marked "explicit"), he indicated that such restrictions were "discipline" or punishment, and that his mother did not mete out punishments in this way. He wrote: "I wasn't disciplined as a child around my mother too much. Restricting TV show or music is most definitely discipline. . . . I like to have freedom of choice where I wouldn't have to sneak over a friend's house to listen to explicit lyrics or hard core movies."

Second, as we have already learned about Caryon, portrayals offered in a realistic manner are most attractive to him (recall his shunning of science fiction such as *Star Trek*). Gerbner et al. (1980) in their "cultivation" research found that the consumption of large quantities of violent media create a worldview in an audience member that sees the world as "mean" and hostile. In the video documentary *The Killing Screens* (Jhally 1994), Gerbner provides examples from films such as *Robocop* and *The Terminator* (films attractive to and/or marketed to youth), with their depictions of "body counts" that number into two or three dozen, to illustrate the quantity of violence. However, it is the genre, setting, and quality of the (violent) presentation that are prized by Caryon. He repeatedly talks about preferring media that are close to real life. He chooses most often those presentations that possess production techniques that closely resemble possible lived experiences. If *Menace II Society* were an apocalyptic tale set in the future (think *Road Warrior*), he may not have attended to it. This film's strengths, for Caryon, were that it was housed in the action/ghettocentric genre, a genre whose pace and activity presented a life's tempo that Caryon worked to emulate. It was set in a housing project community and featured a thug lifestyle that was similar to his own. And then there was the quantity and quality of violence. *Menace II Society* had a body count of seven, a plausible amount of killing that a gang member could encounter in a summer. However, the killings were graphic and brutal—they represented the hyperviolence that complemented the hypermasculinity and bravado also depicted. More, unlike films like *The Terminator* or *Robocop*, death did not come at the hands of a robot, nor was it presented couched with humor ("I'll be back") and futuristic fantasy. *Menace II Society* showed the weaponry that Caryon was accustomed to seeing in his life. It was also a no-holds-barred depiction of the impact of violence on a community. It is this characteristic of realism that brought *Menace II Society* so much praise from film critics (recall one film critic proclaiming he believed it "told the truth" about what happens in the ghetto). It became "good" action/drama, not only for Caryon, but, given its MTV Best Film Award, for many American viewers. Further, extending the work of Nelson George (1994), an additional, important production technique in the media Caryon prizes is the music, the "new jack swing" pace and the symbiotic rap lyrics and their message. The music, coupled with the realism, works to prompt visceral feelings of identification (Potter 1999).

There is little normalcy left in Caryon's life. Access to his family, educational opportunities, role models, the potential to see alternate lifestyles are now all gone. He is fully immersed in a sort of ultra-thug life in prison, and if the state of Kentucky has its way, he will remain in this state for at least the next thirteen years. What is changing is that Caryon is growing older. This brings us to the third and final observation about his tastes. Caryon is seeking out more mature social discourses. His attention to BET's *Teen Summit* may be seen as one example. His joining a religious movement called the Egyptian Order is another. The Egyptian Order is a religious sect that teaches that the center of the universe was, thousands of years ago, a planet inhabited by an advanced civilization of people of color. According to the religion's literature, the planet faced an environmental crisis, so its inhabitants came to earth, landed in Egypt, and built the pyramids. The leader of these people, who for (earth) members of the religion is thought of as God, is several millennia old and resides on a compound in Atlanta, Georgia. The Egyptian Order is largely comprised of Afrocentric, Black nationalists who have taken up Marcus Garvey's mantra to return to Africa—the land of diasporic Black peoples. The return to Africa has not yet taken place. In the meantime, followers of the Egyptian Order (many of whom are African-American men who are, or who have been, incarcerated) take a pilgrimage to Atlanta where their God has built an enormous pyramid that is said to be in-line with specific star systems. The religion has, of late, received considerable media attention because of the pyramid, and also because its membership is said to be surpassing that of the Nation of Islam, rising into the tens of thousands.

Caryon's attraction to this religion is expected given his lifestyle thus far. He has sought out a religious icon as role model that is masculine—

powerful, dominant, displaying power prominently, and, importantly, Black. His God, then, fits in neatly with those already in his life that embody hypermasculinity or display it through spectacle, including the rap artists, sports stars, and gang leaders Caryon admires. For Caryon, all of their bravado is praiseworthy.[5]

Identifying Another Lack

Through the process of identification, Caryon filled a lack in the self by turning to the other—the symbolism of the thug life. His consumption practices indicate that representations of the thug life are preferred and he fully surrounds himself with it. Indeed, he seeks this content out, especially since it speaks to his life experiences. However, in the world of African-American media representations, and given his preference for the genres of drama and action, he may have had few options outside of the ghettocentric. In fifty-three years of television there has been only one Black family drama, *Under One Roof*. Instead, on network television, African Americans remain largely relegated to the comedic, specifically Black situation comedies—from *Amos 'n' Andy* in the 1950s to *Good Times* in the 1970s to *Martin* in the 1980s and *The Parkers* today—Black life and culture have been offered up as sources of entertainment. Taken at its worst, these images have been rich fodder for the ridicule and demeaning of Blackness. *Under One Roof*, the critically acclaimed drama series, did not last half a season. The Black condition in media has been so dismal that even the civil rights organization the NAACP has recently (1999–2000) placed media industry diversity at the top of its agenda, alongside gun and election reforms. Hollywood has continued to disappoint with their filmic offerings as the "brutal buck" (the African-American male who menaces and is to be feared) often takes center stage. African-American film producer Warrington Hudlin (*Houseparty, Boomerang*) intimates that "the Black experience in America has had two incarnations on TV and film . . . one is the comic performer, who usually has a buffoonish, demeaning persona. The other is the pathological victim in so-called 'hood movies. Both images do very little to promote the notion of black equality in American life" (Fine 1995, 3D). This "modern racism," as Entman (1990) labels it, on the part of media exhibits a hostility and ignorance toward Black culture.

It is within this media culture that Caryon was reared. It is one that lacks representations of African-American men that could speak to the needs, concerns, and desires of youths such as Caryon (and the other four involved in the case, and who were similarly situated). The real and fictional representations provided by Bernard Shaw, Colin Powell, Eriq LaSalle, Bill Cosby, Denzel Washington, Danny Glover, and Will Smith act as a sort of "anti-interpellation," failing to hail Caryon. They tend to not embody the kind of masculine, economic, educational, and street respect dilemmas that are part of Caryon's world. Over the course of our correspondence, Caryon indicated that he wished he could communicate with members of the media industry about representations he would like to see. I strongly encouraged him to draft a letter. He chose the Hughes brothers, makers of *Menace II Society,* to write to. The letter was poignant, and demonstrated a newly displayed savvy about how media industries work, and a critical eye. It also made clear the kind of representations and situations (overcoming thug life) that were absent from media that he desperately wants to see. He wrote, in part:

Dear Hughes Brothers,

. . . I don't know if you remember back in 1994 around January some kids in Paducah, Kentucky went out and car-jacked one car killing the driver, and then tried to car-jack another one that same night. But the second shooting was not a killing. But it was said that those kids attempt to kill that driver also. It was 5 kids under 18 years of age on that case. And one kid claimed that all of those kids watched your movie and decided to go out and car-jack some cars. Do you remember this case? It was all over the world in January 1994. . . . I'm one of the guys that was on that case. Me myself. I didn't do what I did over no movie. I do not act off of what I have seen or heard, some people, but not me. . . . In movies as your own, Black people are always represented kind of bad. And put down. Which I don't knock that because that type of stuff will always sell, so get your money. I got a question, when will Black drama films start out with violence and criminal activities and end with the Black people on top. From violence to running they're own positive business. Where they won't have to resort in violence, drug sells, and robberies. Basically when will Blacks go from rags to riches in movies without getting locked in jail or killed?

Guerrero (1995) describes this lack that Caryon has identified as "empty space in representation." This notion recognizes the polar opposite African-American male portrayals that are represented by a Healthcliff Huxtable (in *The Cosby Show*) and a Caine. It cites Hollywood for its "flat, binary construction of black manhood" and recommends the inclusion of "intellectual, cultural, and political depth and humanity of black men." Guerrero (1995, 396) takes on the representational lack that media consumers like Caryon may face, writing: "To say this is not to argue simplistically for a wave of insipid, compensatory positive images of successful doctors and attorneys or happy, 'buppie' fathers. Hollywood has given us enough 'noble Negroes,' de-sexed comedian buppies, and upwardly mobile, black 'exceptions' to fuel several film waves to come." Then the author proposes a solution, much like the one Caryon offered to the Hughes brothers: "We must now proceed to fill the empty space in representation with movies about the deeply complicated and brilliant black men that populate the African American narrative tradition." Today, Caryon understands the profit-driven nature of media, and he understands that images of gross consumption, sex, and violence are popular, money-making fare. He, and Guerrero, are simply asking that within those images of hypermasculinity the African-American male become more complex by moving out of the mire of the brutal buck, savage stereotypes. Contrary to media myth, hypermasculinity is not an essentialist trait for the urban African-American male. Without this change, society is provided with few narratives that work to counter the traditional Black-male stereotypes.

Ontological Authenticity

According to Lincoln and Guba (1989), a criterion for "good" qualitative, constructivist research (such as that presented here) is that of "ontological authenticity." Ontological authenticity describes an elevating of consciousness—the moment when a participant has, according to the authors, "improved, matured, expanded . . . it is literally improvement in the individual's (or group's) conscious experiencing of the world" (248). Such growth is beginning to manifest itself in Caryon. For example, in recent letters Caryon has started to critique and criticize the ghettocentric presentations he values so much. He does not like that African Americans' lives are not valued in media, "they're presented and portrayed very poorly because they always end up getting killed in the movies I watch." He is realizing that there is a class bias in the films that he attends to, "plus they're barely ever high class, and they're always the foolish ones . . . I see high class White people like doctors, lawyers, senators, presidents, FBI agents, etc. You never see Black characters like doctors, lawyers, or someone that holds a high position; on the top basically. . . . I would like to see more characters with higher qualifications instead of being pawns." And he understands how images may inform how African Americans are viewed by those outside the racial group:

"I would like to see situations where Blacks get to shine for a change and be looked up on instead of down. I would like to see that so that Blacks . . . wouldn't feel like we're outcasted from the world or from other races." Finally, he offers an adept critique of how racial depictions are tied to race relations in the real: "When I see this, I'll know that things are becoming equal between Blacks and Whites." As a researcher, I am most pleased with this level of engagement on the part of Caryon. I agree with Lincoln and Guba's charge that researchers are not simply working with subjects who are data sources, but that through interactions, people grow and change. Teaching Caryon, raising his awareness, and thereby achieving ontological authenticity has been one of the greatest rewards.

Conclusion

To be clear, the argument here has not been that *Menace II Society* had a direct effect on Caryon's behavior that January 1994 night. I make no claim that after Caryon viewed the film there was an immediate attitude change that prompted him to engage in mimicry of the violence seen in the film. Caryon vehemently denies that the film, or media like it, made him commit a crime. And I agree with him. Predictably, Caryon feels the need to deny such a relationship because to admit such a correlation would mean, in his mind, that he is a dupe and "follower" of media, a condition that *other people* (especially children) may have, but certainly not him. This reaction is expected. Like limited-effects theorists would argue, I believe that *Menace II Society* did not serve as the single catalyst for the night's violence; rather, it was part of a number of socializing institutions, people in his life, and lived experiences in his neighborhood that made Caryon perceive violence (thug life) as a reasonable social response, and that some media images contribute to that repertoire of potential actions. This study does not work to make excuses for his behavior, making the claim that something or someone forced him into these social actions. Caryon himself admits that he would have probably ended up on the wrong side of the law eventually, just not for murder, or murder under these unique circumstances. What this study has revealed is that, in cases like Caryon's, media have the potential to be a principal socializing institution, particularly when family, religion/church, school, positive role models, and normalized values around law and order are all absent. It reveals the symbolic language that is prized by youths socially situated like Caryon. It details how the symbolic and the real come together and lend credence to certain values, behaviors, and choices.

What are we to take away from this learning experience that Caryon has provided? We know that as agents of change we must work together. Social workers could have assisted Caryon when he was repeatedly kicked out of school, government agencies could have been alerted when it was realized that mental illness, poverty, and dysfunction were crippling this family, and media educators could have helped this youth to learn how to consume media, particularly to engage in media with greater critical savvy, balancing narrative- and image-based viewing, and with a higher tolerance for ambiguity. For media researchers and educators in particular, Caryon has helped us to see that change must come from within the contexts that, in this case, youth operate. It would serve us well to understand Caryon's and other (Black) youths' identification process with a system of symbols that frequently present African Americans and Black culture as ghettocentered and violence prizing. We too should come to understand how behaviors, gender identity (masculinity), and social world are all in articulation. Caryon makes clear, given his social situation, that he is going to continue to attend to these kinds of media presentations; hence it would serve us well to take up his wise recommendation to start from within the genre he prizes—"When will Black drama movies start out with violence and criminal activities and end up with Black people on top?"

Epilogue

Neither Caryon nor Sylvester communicate with Calvin "Kevin" Smith. Among the five, Calvin was the only one who was reared in a traditional, nuclear family. He is especially close to his father, who prayed with him and counseled him during the trial. Calvin's father also advised him not to talk to the press or any others soliciting information (which would include me as a researcher). He also warned Calvin to stay away from those that landed him in trouble—particularly, Caryon, Sylvester, and Steven. Calvin and Kunta had been friends before the shootings. Calvin is currently incarcerated in the Northpoint Treatment Center serving a twenty-year sentence.

Steven Johnson declined my invitation to participate in this study, despite a letter from his attorney supporting this research effort. He does, however, closely monitor my research inquiries, thanks to Sylvester who maintains a close relationship with Steven. On occasion, Sylvester will share insights offered by Steven. Steven is confined in the Eastern Kentucky Correctional Center. It is unclear how Sylvester and Steven communicate to each other beyond sending messages through prisoners who are transferring between the prison where Sylvester is held, Kentucky State Penitentiary, and Steven's Eastern Kentucky Correctional. Steven escaped the death penalty when his plea agreement of two life terms plus 110 years was accepted.

Kunta Sims took a hiatus from this study for a period of several months while he pursued an appeal in the hopes of getting a sentence reduction. He worried that writing to me about the shootings may jeopardize his appeal. On November 27, 2000, Kunta wrote to me announcing that he successfully had parts of his case overturned. He is facing retrial, and a court date has not yet been set. He remains in Kentucky State Penitentiary.

Sylvester Berry continues to write me often about his relationship with media and about prison life. As a result of our correspondence, and my desire to send him textbooks and literary works, Sylvester successfully appealed to his warden at Kentucky State Penitentiary to provide inmates with access to reading materials beyond popular magazines such as *Jet*, *Source*, and *Playboy*. Sylvester completed two college-level courses (English and sociology), however his education halted prematurely when the state of Kentucky ended a program that offered inmates college courses. Sylvester hopes to resume his studies in sociology so that he may become a youthful offender counselor and social worker. Sylvester is currently serving a twenty-year sentence.

Caryon Johnson continues to be the most eager participant, writing lengthy letters during his spare time. He hopes that his life story will ultimately become a feature film and/or the subject of a best-selling novel (much like *The Hurricane*). He maintains a journal, which I sent him, that he uses to write his life story and to pen raps about his life. While spending over two hundred days in solitary confinement in 2000 for drug and gang activity, Caryon found religion in the Egyptian Order. Upon release from prison, he hopes to move to the religion's headquarters in Atlanta. He is pondering moving his two sisters, two nieces, and his mother to Georgia as well. Because inmates cannot receive visits from convicted felons, Caryon's mother had been unable to visit her son. In late 2000 an exception was made on her behalf. She has not yet gone (as of early 2001) to pay him a visit. Caryon is serving a twenty-year sentence, but is up for parole in April 2001.

One Final Note

In December 1997 Paducah, Kentucky, was sent reeling yet again when a fourteen-year-old boy shot and killed three classmates as they conducted a prayer meeting. The young teen told police investigators that he had always wanted to break down a classroom door and shoot people, just as he had seen in the film *The Basketball Diaries*.

Notes

1. See Means Coleman (2001) for a detailed methodological account of interviewing the incarcerated.

2. I have replaced his friends' real names with pseudonyms to protect their identities.

3. On October 2, 2000, Jessie Jr. was murdered, execution-style, in his home while his family was held at gunpoint and forced to watch. His murder, at the time of this writing, is unsolved.

4. For example, on eleven occasions before the *Menace II Society* murder Steven Johnson was arrested. Three of those were felony allegations, including shooting at a neighborhood youth. However, nine of those charges were dismissed when witnesses failed to appear.

5. I credit Herman Gray and his essay "Black Masculinity and Visual Culture," with helping me to make sense of Caryon's triumvirate interest in rap, ghettocentric films, and thug life.

References

Bourdieu, P. (1994). Structures, habitus, power: Basis for a theory of symbolic power. In N. Dirks, G. Eley, and S. Ortner, eds., *Culture, power, history* (pp. 155–99). Princeton, N.J.: Princeton University Press.

Ebert, R. (1993). *Menace II Society. Chicago Sun-Times*, May 26 [online]: http://www.suntimes.com/ebert/ebert_reviews/1993/05/859437.html.

Entman, R. (1990). Modern racism and the images of blacks in local television news. *Critical Studies in Mass Communication* 7: 332–45.

Fine, M. (1995). Drama's color block. 'Under One Roof' bucks the odds against blacks. *USA Today*, March 14, p. 3D.

George, N. (1992). *Buppies, b-boys, baps, and bohos: Notes on post-soul black culture.* New York: HarperCollins.

———. (1994). *Blackface: Reflections on African Americans and the movies.* New York: HarperCollins.

Gerbner, G., L. Gross, M. Morgan, and N. Signorielli. (1980). The "mainstreaming" of America: Violence profile no. 11. *Journal of Communication* 30: 10–29.

Groves Hayes, D. (1994). 2 carjackers face 20 years. *The Paducah Sun*, August 16, pp. 1A, 8A.

Guerrero, E. (1995). The Black man on our screens and the empty space in representation. *Callaloo* 18: 395–400.

Hall, S. (1996). Introduction: Who needs identity? In S. Hall and P. DuGay, eds., *Questions of cultural identity* (pp. 1–17). London: Sage.

Jhally, S. (Producer) (1994). *Killing Screens* [film]. Northampton, Mass.: Media Education Foundation.

Johnson v. Commonwealth of Kentucky, 97-SC-354-MR (S. C. Kentucky 1998).

Lembo, R. (1997). Beyond the text: The sociality of image-based viewing practices. *Cultural Studies: A Research Volume* 2: 237–64.

Lincoln, Y., and E. Guba. (1989). Ethics: The failure of positivist science. *Review of Higher Education* 12: 221–41.

Madan, S. (1996). *Identity, culture and the postmodern world*. Athens: University of Georgia Press.

Means Coleman, R. (2000). *African American viewers and the Black situation comedy: Situating racial humor*. New York: Garland.

———. (2001). Maintaining perspective during troubling research interviews: A reception study with three convicted murderers. Manuscript submitted for publication.

Morley, D. (1980). *The "Nationwide" audience: Structure and decoding*. London: British Film Institute.

Potter, W. (1999). *On media violence*. Thousand Oaks, Calif.: Sage.

Stacey, J. (1994). *Star gazing: Hollywood cinema and female spectatorship*. New York: Routledge.

Waxman, S. (1993). *Menace II Society*. Washington Post, May 19 [online]: http://www.washingtonpost.com/wpsrv/style/longterm/movies/video s/menaceiisocietyrwaxman_a09e60.htm.

Contributors

Jacqueline Bobo (Ph.D., University of Oregon) is chair of the women's studies program at the University of California, Santa Barbara. Her research interests include film/television, cultural studies, race, and cultural production. She has published in *Jump Cut*, *Callaloo*, *Camera Obscura*, *Wide Angle*, and *Screen*, and with Routledge, Bay Press, and Ballantine Books.

Leda Cooks (Ph.D., Ohio University) is an associate professor in the Department of Communication at the University of Massachusetts, Amherst. Her research interests include the communication of identity, power, and culture. She has published in the *Howard Journal of Communication*, *Women's Studies in Communication*, *Discourse and Society*, *Rhetoric and Public Affairs*, *Mediation Quarterly*, *World Communication Journal*, *Negotiation Journal*, *Western Journal of Communication*, and *Communication Theory*.

Nancy C. Cornwell (Ph.D., University of Colorado, Boulder) is an assistant professor of communication and women's studies at Western Michigan University. Her current research, which includes developing a feminist philosophical approach to hate speech and critical analyses of media products, has been published in the *Journal of Intergroup Relations*, *International*

Journal of Listening, and *International and Intercultural Communication Annual.*

Joe R. Feagin (Ph.D., Harvard University) is a graduate research professor in the Department of Sociology at the University of Florida. His research on racial and ethnic relations, racism, gender relations, and urban political economy has been published in *American Sociological Review* and *American Journal of Sociology,* and by Beacon Press, Routledge, Prentice-Hall, and Rowman and Littlefield.

Celeste A. Fisher (Ph.D., New York University) is an assistant professor in the Department of Communication Arts at Marymount Manhattan College.

JoEllen Fisherkeller (Ph.D., University of California at Berkeley) is an assistant professor in the Department of Culture and Communication at New York University. Her research interests include young people's identity development and cultural learning, popular media audiences, media education and social change, and interpretive/ethnographic methodologies. She has published in *Anthropology and Education Quarterly, Communication Review,* and *Journal of Adult and Adolescent Literacy.* She has a book forthcoming from Temple University Press.

Herman Gray (Ph.D., University of California, Santa Cruz) is an associate professor in the Department of Sociology at the University of California, Santa Cruz. His research interests include cultural studies, popular culture, mass communication, and minority discourse. He has published in the *Quarterly Review of Film and Video* and *Popular Music and Society,* and with Temple University Press, Guilford Press, and Aldine de Gruyter.

Leslie B. Inniss (Ph.D., University of Texas at Austin) is an assistant professor in the Department of Sociology, Anthropology, and Criminal Justice at Florida A and M University. Her research interests are race and minority group relations and sociology of education. She has published several articles to include in the *Journal of Black Studies* and *Social Justice.*

Robin R. Means Coleman (Ph.D., Bowling Green State University) is an assistant professor in the Department of Culture and Communication at

New York University. Her research interests include representations of race in mass media, identity, and audiences. She has published in the *Howard Journal of Communication, Journal of Black Studies, Encore,* and with Garland publishers.

Mark P. Orbe (Ph.D., Ohio University) is associate professor of communication and diversity at Western Michigan University, where he holds a joint appointment in the Department of Communication and the Center for Women's Studies. His research, which examines the inextricable relationship between culture and communication in a variety of contexts, has been published in *Communication Quarterly, Communication Studies, Management Communication Quarterly, Howard Journal of Communications, Communication Theory, Women's Studies in Communication, Southern Communication Journal, Western Journal of Communication, International Journal of Intercultural Relations, Health Communication, International Journal of Listening, International and Intercultural Communication Annual,* and *Journal of Intergroup Relations* (of which he currently serves as editor).

Debbie A. Owens (Ph.D., University of Florida) is an assistant professor of communications in the Performing and Fine Arts Department at Fayetteville State University in North Carolina. Her research interests include media dependency theory, mass media and social construction, race, ethnicity and culture in media, and gender and aging role portrayals. Her research has been published in the *Howard Journal of Communications, Journal of Communication and Minority Issues,* and *Journal of College Student Development.* Professionally, she has worked at the *Charlotte Observer,* the *Chicago Tribune* and *New York Amsterdam News,* the Department of Defense American Forces Press and Publications Service (AFPPS), as well as Voice of America, Radio News Division (Washington, D.C.), and WCIA-TV and WPGU-FM (Champaign, Illinois).

Corey Rinehart (Master's Candidate, University of Massachusetts-Amherst) is in the Department of Education.

Catherine Squires (Ph.D., Northwestern University) is an assistant professor in the Department of Communication Studies and the Center for Afroamerican and African Studies. Her research focuses on how marginalized groups use indigenous media resources to bolster social movement efforts and debate identity issues. She has published in the *Harvard International Journal of Press and Politics*. Dr. Squires is currently finishing a manuscript on the impact of Black-owned media on the Black public sphere.

Chyng F. Sun (Doctoral Candidate, University of Massachusetts-Amherst) is in the Department of Communication. She has won several international awards for her children's books.

Stacy A. S. Williams (Doctoral Candidate, University of Massachusetts-Amherst) is in the Department of Education. She is the recipient of several fellowships, including most recently the John Woodruff Simpson Fellowship. She has published with Lawrence Erlbaum Associates.

Jennifer F. Wood (Ph.D., Bowling Green State University) is an assistant professor in the Mass Communication and Communications Studies Department at Towson University. Her research interests include interracial communication, organizational communication, and African Americans in the mass media.

Index